The Healing Chambers

Love beyond Life

Thea Terlouw

1st edition

September 2022

Obelisk Books

1st edition, September 2022

ISBN/EAN: 9-789-49307-12-85; NUR 720
Original in Dutch, Copyright Obelisk © 2017:
'De Heelkamers'

Key words: spirituality, philosophy, religion, near-death experience, NDE, dying, death counseling, suicide, reincarnation, extra-terrestrials, Atlantis, Pleiades, Arcturus, Sirius, Adromeda, spiritual guides, guides, dimensions, spheres, light spheres, city of light, coma, euthanasia.

Content

Foreword

Readers of my earlier books let me know that they were deeply touched by the subjects I addressed. Instinctive knowledge and recognition were terms most used. In the letters I received many asked if I had new insights and how my own process was developing.

As we are all in the process of growth through life, so did my own growth and awakening continued. This resulted in new insights and more in-depth knowledge. I received gentle hints that gradually pushed me towards creating a new book. When Kumeka asked me to continue my work it felt as all the confirmation I needed. Together with my spirit guides Leviahnarah, Hadoh and Aïcheh, we decided that the subject of the new book would be about the 'Healing Chambers' of humanity: places where humans can heal from the difficult and challenging lives they had in a multitude of incarnations on Earth. In this way we especially respond to the questions people have about suicide in relation to their previous incarnations, not an easy subject to tackle. After my earlier book 'The Cycle of Life and Death' I am giving a more complete picture of what happens when we leave our physical body behind.

The people who are 'awake', are more than ever conscious of the horrible state in which our beautiful planet Earth is now. Together we create these beautiful fields of Light-Consciousness which we drape over the negative aspects of Earth's societies. Most of us already know what we want to change and, just as important, how to make that change happen. The souls residing in the Light Worlds can see and measure the ongoing changes. Together we work towards the shift or the transition to a loving society, a consciousness of win-win, instead of an I-win-you-loose consciousness, the latter being embedded in our society for such a long time. We are going toward a world that cannot and should not uphold the Culture of Greed. Many can now see such a culture is present in every aspect of life, something that is simply not sustainable. Everything not based on the Energy of Love is coming to the surface; the Cosmic Light that flows to Earth is making the unseen visible. This means we can see the things that no longer serve us, as loving beings, and that we can leave all the negativity that is holding us back behind.

Thea Terlouw, January 2020

1. Leviahnarah

This book cannot possibly give a complete picture of the spheres. The spheres form an area many times larger than the Earth and who can describe the Earth in the scope of one book? I can only describe a few aspects. Fortunately, there have been many people who, from an inner source, have described the spheres in detail.

Nevertheless, for the sake of clarity and a better positioning of the spheres discussed in this book, I would like to give some more insight into the different layers and levels.

Usually seven lower astral and seven higher Light spheres are taken as a starting point. And between each sphere of Light there are areas of transition. Between the seven lower and seven higher layers there are three twilight spheres, each with their own transition areas to the next sphere.

In the last decades of the twentieth century a lot has changed. Accelerations are happening, entirely in the spirit of the great transformations. The Earth is moving to a higher dimension and for a certain group of people the dimensions are already intertwined. They can perceive other levels and are, therefore, ahead of most people. However, their knowledge in this area filters through into everyday life and thus flows into the light grid of humanity. Everywhere the accelerated awareness of people brings about change. To the great frustration of many, this is not always visible, but it is there.

A lot has also changed in the spheres themselves. As part of the great purification on Earth during this period of transition, the souls who stayed in the lower levels of the dark spheres all incarnated on Earth. This process was guided from the Light Worlds. They were often souls who had already been trapped there for ages and had ended up in this place as a result of their own life choices. As part of Thea's awakening and education I already took her to all spheres, including the deep, dark sphere, years ago. I encapsulated her in a light cocoon; otherwise you can't stay there. What she saw there was an impenetrable darkness where souls stayed in a state of total unconsciousness of the light. Such a visit makes a deep impression on a human being, a sight that is impossible to forget. This sphere is now dissolved. This was completed in the nineties. At the start of the new millennium, the sixth lower sphere had also been dissolved, gone, no longer necessary.

For the souls who stayed in those spheres there were basically two options: reincarnate on Earth or continue to a galactic healing chamber. No soul is ever lost. From the Realms of Light, this work was completed. The souls who incarnated on Earth came to places where they could undergo rapid learning processes and these souls made progress toward the Light. Some did so relatively quickly, at a time on Earth that was optimally suited for that purpose. Every astral sphere that is above that seventh layer is a bit lighter, but there is still a certain amount of darkness.

There are souls who choose a galactic healing chamber when they return to the spiritual world from the lower layers, after their incarnation, after their physical life. Many from the dark spheres have gone through a life of purification and have been helped by beings from the Realms of Light. These can be angelic beings, or souls who once lived on Earth and could grow to a higher state of being through their own incarnations on Earth and who now no longer need to incarnate. All of these masters are a great help on the path of the souls who incarnated from the dark spheres on Earth. After all, they usually know from their own experience what a human being can experience.

When people speak of 'damned souls' within certain religions on Earth, this is done out of ignorance. As said, no soul, which is originally a spark of the Great Light, is ever lost. However, the road can be longer and more difficult for one person than for another and that has all to do with one's own free choices, made on Earth during one's journey along the Golden Thread of Incarnations. But that has nothing to do with 'damnation'.

The major shifts that are now taking place are made possible by the Laws of Transition. One of the most important aspects of those changed laws is that every soul now arriving in the spiritual world *must* read his or her book of life. In the times before that, people had the choice whether or not to do that. Thus, it could be that, on this planet of free will, people refused to evaluate their past lives, life after life. They accumulated karma on karma. Refusing to look at yourself and your actions is a certain state of consciousness. This allowed many people to create, as it were, immense barriers and blockages in the flow of their lives. Eventually things will get completely stuck and nothing will be able to flow through. By the end of the eighties and the beginning of the nineties - Earth time - these new spiritual laws came into effect. From that moment on every human being is obliged to read his or her book of life. By this we do not mean to look at the 'film' that every soul sees during its transition, but to consciously study the book of life and see what was and what all human experiences have led to. To look at causes and consequences of one's own life stream.

Without judgment - See what Is.

We must keep coming back to the phrase: 'See what Is, without judgment'. In the 'evaluation' every human being gets the best possible help, regardless of the past. We see countless people now cautiously becoming aware of the principle of cause and effect. One gains insight into this when the events of their lives are shown very clearly to them on holographic screens in the spheres. In this way large groups of people begin to gain insights into the context of the events in their lives. Lives indeed, not only their own various lives but also the lives of the people in their group. This is a group process and working in groups in the spheres shows positive results with regard to enhancing understanding. Together they see how that wheel of karma - the wheel of cause and effect - kept turning. One sees how over and over again old beliefs and negative ideas continued to win from the positive impulses given by guides, among others, throughout all time.

It is now a time in which old dogmas are being abandoned. This happens on Earth, but also in the spheres, exactly because one reads the collective books of life and contemplates them with each other. How difficult it is to let go of old dogmas is clearly visible in today's world. The time in which we find ourselves now, however, will energetically encourage reflection, detachment and transformation of old beliefs that no longer serve mankind. Beliefs that contain no food for growth and awareness of mankind. But at the same time, precisely at this time when incentives are being given from the spheres to let go of old dogmas, a large number of people will resist this positive energy coming to Earth. People will continue to cling to old things and even vigorously try to revive them. They will fight hard against the new, perhaps condemning it with strong words, like they have been doing for many incarnations. This reactionary power can become very strong and leave many people in doubt about the innovative path they have taken themselves. But that reactionary movement will reach a critical point, only to merge with the new stream in which humanity is led. As if it has never been any other way.

For the sake of clarity, people who live on Earth in a material body also read their books of life when they are out of their physical bodies at night. So everyone - above and below - is doing the same great work of purification. Every human being on Earth. This happens under the inspiring guidance and light of Lord Kumeka, Chohan of the Eighth Ray of Purification. Partly because of this you see enormous waves of consciousness going over the Earth with enormous influence on local and global social life.

At the beginning of 2000 an immense process of accelerated awareness started. However, these waves are getting bigger and bigger and continue their way all over the globe. This is not always visible as much happens in a layer that is not directly apparent to most of mankind. But the observant individual 'Sees what Is' and notices the changes.

Because each individual has now started to read their own book of life and begins to recognize the results of certain (free) choices in the field and the periphery of their own lives, changes will manifest themselves more quickly. Many people discover with a shock that they have lived in a collective mindset for centuries and have allowed themselves only to be carried away by the expectations of the group. People will start to choose more consciously; will say clearly 'yes' or 'no' and show what they want. And that no longer needs to be what a group expects them to do. The same goes for those who have always remained neutral, live after life. Those who joined in on what others had set in motion: did everyone go to the right, then they would also go to the right, was everyone go to the left, then they went to the left, without an opinion of their own or a clear choice of their own. That will now definitely change.

From the angelic worlds a lot of help is given in these great processes. For many will be overwhelmed by feelings of guilt when they look back on their many lives in which they acted in a certain way, or where they refused acting. Lives of letting things happen and watching them happen. If it weren't for that intense help from above, the Earth would be overwhelmed by waves of such guilt. In the hours of the night we work hard to transform those feelings of guilt that are released as a result of an awareness of what has happened in all those lives. Especially in groups this has already brought much to solution and to light. In the last decades of the twentieth century the lower spheres were able to flow empty. In those lowest spheres souls resided who had created such heavy karma that they remained in a permanent self-created darkness. The Councils of Karma, with all the assistance of the Light Worlds, helped to guide these processes.

People have incarnated on Earth from higher areas of Light to assist these souls on their way back to their own light. These are acts of love, for it is certainly not easy to assist souls who incarnate with an attunement to the lowest spheres. In the mean time the lowest spheres have been dissolved by these acts of love. Fortunately, all those Light Beings who dedicated themselves to this were able to see significant results of their efforts.

Thus, the 'sphere of hatred' was a preferred hiding place for many, and every conceivable help was deployed for resolving this as well. This was completed some time ago. A group of souls, who had once been stuck in that sphere for a long time, devoted themselves with all their being to reaching the people trapped in the darkness. They were experienced experts themselves, who knew very well how difficult it is to get rid of feelings of hatred. Precisely they were ideally suited to help transform old stuck beliefs. People who, in the present time, transition with deep hatred, are now going directly to a Galactic Healing Chambers, of which there are many. They can no longer return to the sphere of hate, where there was a strong concentration of souls with the same spiritual low attunement. In the various Galactic Healing Centres their dark layers are being removed, layer-by-layer, until they reach their encapsulated God Core. In such places in the various dimensions Light Beings are active, who from their profound knowledge, at the end of this 26,000-year cycle, can help to transform old hatred.

The same goes for those enormous amounts of people on Earth who, for a very long time, have been caught in some kind of addiction. That can be addiction in literally every imaginable form: alcohol, sex, drugs, power, medication, compulsive behaviour, violence, money, you name it. With addiction we mean *absolutely not being able to do without*, total dependence and often with a repetition of that pattern in different incarnations one after the other. We do not mean enjoying a glass of wine with a meal, or a beer with friends, or using recreational products in general without being mentally and physically dependent on them. Actually, many people are already engaged in change without being aware of it. It happens unconsciously, therefore, because these changes are not spectacular but part of the simple everyday life and simply occur in the circle of family and friends or within the professional environment. Here too we see how countless people, from the spheres as well as on Earth, are busy helping each other. Here too, experienced experts, assisted by the Angelic Realms and the Light Beings, are doing a lot of work.

Some people are 'waiting' for a real task within that great transformation, but we are all already working on it together. So many invisible processes are going on already. We have a deep respect for all those silent workers - for you - who, wherever they are on their path, make choices with their hearts to the best of their conscience. Head and heart are capable of beautiful things together.

Spheres and frequencies

Each subsequent sphere or intermediate sphere contains a higher frequency of light. The soul that rises in the light - in its light - can endure more and more of it. Therefore, collectively a lot of goodness is released in this time; goodness that has been pinched off for too long. This positive energy can now multiply rapidly. Small individual lights can multiply very fast and become whole waves of light. However, this also leads to an increase in polarity. Increasing distance between people who anxiously cling to old dogmas and people who choose to let go of it and purify.

It takes confidence to follow your heart in a world where people think they have to do the opposite. Therefore, pay close attention to the inspirations you get, often very short and concentrated, just as they present themselves. These can be feelings as well as thoughts, dreams and visions, the form in which they reach you is not important. It helps you later to interpret these telegrams of the light. They can be valuable signposts on your way. Trust is a very important aspect of it. Trust in intuition is for many people like dancing on a rope. As you increasingly dare to listen to your feelings, you develop trust and see the wholeness that lies behind this process. Then you increasingly dare to trust your own wisdom. It makes the way you need to go easier. Asking for help from the spiritual world is one of the important aspects. Ask and you will be given. Put a sweet angel on your shoulder every day and know that you don't have to go the way all by yourself.

New Age Children

All over the world children are now being born who are already highly familiar with the different dimensions. There is now, much more than in the past, a real future for such children, because a great number of pioneers have quietly prepared the Earth for them. In a world that was not yet ready, they ploughed the fields for the innovations of our time. As a result, the seeds that have been sown for some time now can actually germinate.

However, many pioneers are still waiting to know what their task on Earth is to become. In their meditations and prayers, we are asked the question: 'When will my task become clear within the great plan of the transformation of the Earth?' Many wonder when that big sign will finally come. The answer is simple: most of the time they already do what they came for. And that is: being your own 'light' wherever life brings you; tackling the things that are offered to you. To be! Fortunately, this is beginning to become more and more clear to these pioneers, and they discover that for themselves in their meditations and prayers. Everybody contributes and that this doesn't always have to be spectacular and is often invisible on the outside also becomes clear to most of them now. That it's good as it is. There are also many silent masters on Earth - simple, inconspicuous people, everywhere in the world - who together have carried this process for some time now. The Earth is now ready for change, and step-by-step it will go through its birthing process.

The children who incarnate from higher areas of Light do so out of love for Mother Earth and humanity. A selfless act that can hardly be comprehended on Earth. These children of the New Age are in danger of being put on a pedestal by well-meaning people and that is the last thing they themselves want. Their soul wisdom is great.

It is also true that the average school system on Earth is no longer suitable for these children. It no longer works; schools have become sluggish, inefficient institutions. But that's also a sign for conscious people that all human systems are out-dated. This applies to education in general, but also to other areas of society, such as health care, the legal system, governance structures, the money system and so on. Unfortunately, many of these children of the New Age have become bogged down in the old systems. They became entangled in what is normal these days, namely to 'label' these children with a syndrome and often drug them with medication from a very young age. Those who want to hold on to the old system try to encapsulate the incarnating high frequency New Age Children. Clairvoyants see how these children are being caged in low frequencies, unable to do what they came to do. The number of suicides among these incarnated souls is unimaginable. Fortunately they are lovingly welcomed and cared for after their self-chosen departure, but it will be clear that this premature end of life was not their intention.

Since about eighty Earth years these old souls are incarnating. Many of them were and will be system breakers. Already incarnated or still to be incarnated in this day and age, people who are able to actually bring about positive changes. These incarnating Light Souls carry with them a great 'we'-consciousness. They are aware of their responsibility for the whole and they show this; many of them already as children. They have transcended their ego and have all come a long way through many incarnations to get this far. Many of them were in the higher Spheres of Light and taught people the Love of Life and Creation and, therefore, the care for each other. These souls are not ruled by the fears that cause so much misery on Earth. Fear of shortage; fear that another person will get a better job; fear of death, all those negative aspects that are the most important motives for many people. They form a growing wave of souls, which began with a few drops after the Second World War, and they contribute more and more to the growing Light in this time by doing their work in silence and from the peace and quiet that reigns in them. They live their light and anchor it deep in Mother Earth. All over the world they form a human grid, an energetic supporting field in which they feed each other and their environment. Thus the early pioneers carry each other and the New Age Children, and from our spiritual world we enjoy the beautiful spectacle that the growth of this human light network offers us.

2. Beyond fear

Thea: After the publication of the book 'The Cycle of Life and Death', I went to Portugal for a few weeks. I stayed in the Estrella Mountains, in a place where the veil is thin. During that stay I had an experience that completely changed my life, something I could not have imagined in my wildest dreams.

While walking with our group we arrived at a special place with a beautiful view. While I lingered there the group I was in had already walked on. Later Anna, who was with the group, told me that she had looked back for me, to see where I was. I had disappeared. Anna said to me later: "One moment you were leaning against that big stone and the next you were gone." She couldn't see the two big dogs that had stayed with me either. Leviahnarah would later confirm that.

When I was 'gone' I met Altea from Altair. He told me about bridge builders and showed me where and how all kinds of bridges are built between 'there' and 'here'. This book, for example, is such a bridge, but there are bridges and bridge builders of many shapes and sizes. This in short, because in my book 'The End of the Circle' I elaborate on this.

The events in Portugal left a deep impression on me. They changed my life, nothing was the same after that. I needed time to process these far-reaching experiences into my life. It was a strange time anyway, these months after September 11th 2001. The fear in the world was stirred up globally and individually to extraordinary levels. Because of my experiences in the spheres, I deliberately did not want to connect to it. Nor could I, as a period of lecturing began for which I had to prepare. Fortunately, in between the lectures I had time to rest, which was necessary for the integration of the intense experiences in Portugal. I slept a lot at that time and took memories of it back with me to my waking consciousness. My world opened up quickly to other realities in other dimensions. I started writing and couldn't stop any more.

At that time I had already written about other dimensions in 'The Cycle of Life and Death', the earthly spheres of light and dark around the Earth, and the great changes that were taking place there. I went to each of these places with Leviahnarah in my light body, which allowed me to portray the experience from within. The book 'The cycle of Life and Death' also provided a lot of work at that moment. Requests for help came in and took a lot of time to process. Death counselling is heavy and intensive work. Once again I became imbued with the deep, mostly collective fears in people. In my case I mainly came into contact with the fear of illness and death. At a certain point I was able to divide those fears into three categories:

- fear of suffering before death, through illness for example,
- fear of being judged right after death,
- fear of eternal hell and damnation.

I felt that people who had turned their backs on the Roman Catholic Church at an early age to seek their own truth, came into a deep crisis especially at the time of their dying process. They had discovered other truths during their lifetime, but as their lives were coming to an end, the programs of their youth began to reappear. I discovered the same with people who came from Protestant churches. No matter how free and inquisitive they had been during their lives, now that they were sick and dying, the old program began to operate again. Deeply ingrained tracks.

I discovered with joy how family members and close friends from similar backgrounds, who understood what these people were struggling with, helped these people. Especially the help of people who had experienced similar upbringings and who had also chosen to seek their own truth during their lives proved valuable.

During death counselling I was shocked by some of the ideas that people have. Inner beliefs of hell and purgatory. Actually, I didn't expect that anymore in this day and age. However, the outside looks completely different from the inside; people's inner world of thinking and feeling. If you go a long way with someone, as I did several times, you will discover deeply seated destructive thought forms and beliefs. I am aware that this has been in the collective field of mankind for a long, long time. Influences, imprints and beliefs coming from those who had power and control over many; the influence of the dark energetic web that lay around the Earth. These were not acts of the Light, although the secular or ecclesiastical rulers wanted to give you that impression. We are now leaving behind the worlds of lies and appearances.

Fear is the means of control par excellence. As long as mankind lives in fear, whatever fear, it can be controlled. Exercising power in a negative sense is very addictive. Now that so much is being written by people, often from their own transformational experiences but also through beautifully transmitted material from the Realms of Light, conscious people are more and more able to transform their old fears. This is no longer just reserved for small groups of people who are aware of the transition we are making from the third to the fifth dimension. Because in the earthly Light Spheres a new area is working towards all the people on Earth, they are working very hard on this necessary purification.

Lord Kumeka, Chohan of the Eighth Ray of Purification - a white-golden ray - is working on this purification with legions of angels, people in their subtle bodies and people in physical life. I bring with me clear memories from the night. Knowing of this great purification, it is easier for me to accept the consequences of these processes on Earth: the chaos we see around us in the world has everything to do with the great purification that we as humanity are going through. Aware of the karmic interaction between people, I tackled my own processes. When you have balanced your earthly energy, there comes a short period of rest. Everything can then be anchored in the material, physical reality, before a new phase presents itself. Thus a period in my life began in which memories I always carried in me about extraterrestrial realities drew closer.

Although I would very much like to write this down and share it, I find it very difficult to put into words how this process exactly went. What was important to me was that I realized that my fear was gone so that I could respond to my inner desire to share my experiences with many. After a deep and extensive cleansing process of several years, I no longer cared what people would think. From the exchange with different people I know that more and more people have similar memories. While writing I began to understand a little bit about the process. It is a multitude of old experiences that can make it tangible and visible in the material part of a human being. Dreams, visions, clear memories, inner knowing; the clairaudient contacts with my guides and teachers; the telepathic connections to which I am so accustomed in my life. I entered other dimensions and I came home. Every next step I made was full of recognition and joy. A period of intense processing began, memories of past lives in relation to extraterrestrial realities. At first they were still connected to lives on Earth and souls who, like me, were starseeds and entered into contracts with each other. A little later I saw the links to other planets. Now I had a completely different way of looking at things.

I understood people's fears, the far-reaching dreams that were told to me many times. Everything began to fall into place. I became aware that I still had one fear to conquer, and that was to talk about extra-terrestrials, their diversity, and their love. But I also had to talk about the lovelessness of some extraterrestrial races. The peoples of the universe, like us on Earth, know about light and dark - as above, so below - free will, choices that we all have here.

After my experiences in Portugal, I found myself in a vortex of events. I started to remember things and wrote them down, just for myself. I also worked together with Margaret who told me stories of different people in the Beyond. Shortly after the release of my first book she told me that she was going to leave the earthly spheres, which she did a short time later. A few years later I met her again, but this time in our light bodies, on a planet closely connected to the star Arcturus. It was the planet where Hadoh lives, one of my spiritual teachers. There, Margaret was called Mahlah, her soul name.

No matter what exactly had happened to me, it had changed my reality, broadened my consciousness. The memories of beings from elsewhere, not of this Earth, became an open and inner knowing.

3. Margaret

My contact with Margaret in Ireland

Thea: It was a moving event in that special place by the water when she first appeared to me in spirit. First I heard her deep warm voice. Everyone who knew her will remember her voice, because it was so special. After I recognized her voice, I saw her appearance before me in the spirit, with my third eye. That did not surprise me, because also when I am working on a reading, I see everything so lucid as if I am actually there. That ability was always there but since a number of years it is even more intense than before.

My whole stay in Ireland was actually a revelation, because so much happened to me. I saw myself in previous lives in that country, happy lives. A memory of a previous life is not always pleasant, but I know from years of experience that those images never come by for no reason. Old, negative aspects are purified at a high pace. It suits me; I have worked with it in many lives. I later visited the places in Ireland where I had lived before. I hadn't felt that need until now. I know of so many places where I have lived before, but these are closed parts of my being; they have served their purpose. I see the memories of them as a precious gift. They gave me a lot of insight into who I am - all my positive and negative experiences - and they have made me who I am now. It was a school that taught me a lot.

I often met people who felt the need to go back to the villages and cities where they once lived. Then, carefully, the trail can be traced back. I never felt that need, but because Ireland kept appearing in my dreams, it felt it was reason enough go there.

Going to Ireland was food for my soul. I never expected to find Margaret back here. The fact that I had no premonition about it made it so special. Tears of joy I cried. This is what I wrote about her.

Margaret: Hello, dear Thea. I'm so happy to make contact with you. I've been looking forward to this moment. It's taken a while for this to happen. A lot has happened in the period after my transition. I think it's wonderful that you found this place in Ireland. It was a journey in confidence. Puzzle pieces fell into place, which led you to this country.

The energy here is very high and pure. The period before was an important growth phase for you. I was with you when you and two men from the hostel, John and Robert, went looking for the stone circle of your dream. Coincidence does not exist; the right people were together at the right time. When the stone circle was found, you had an experience from ancient times. Before your mind's eye a different landscape unfolded, a clearing in the forest. You all realized that you knew each other for a very long time. All three of you saw Druids in the circle, images from a past life, a distant past. I was moved when I saw three people who actually only knew each other for a day, standing hand in hand inside this beautiful spectacle. Words were superfluous, even later when each of you went your own way again. Words are always inadequate for an experience like this.

Something beautiful happened: things were healed, contacts restored. The light that passed through you and that you could see, will not be forgotten. John is a connoisseur of ancient sacred sites and has often protected them in simple lives on the land. On a soul level, I know these men. I was pleasantly surprised to be able to witness this moment. I like that you're not surprised by anything: that you're like a child on a quest, in silent amazement.

When we first met up here on the green hill, I was as moved as you were. For me, it was the first time I made such a contact. It all came together at the right moment. Our deepest wish came true and it's all so simple. In the water, down from the cliffs you can see a large dolphin. I see his traces of light in the water. This dolphin is a healing presence to the people who are attracted to this place. It's not a myth that children are healed here. Dolphins belong to a species with a higher spiritual attunement; they come from a higher dimension.

I looked at you when you meditated, high on the cliffs in that piece of eroded rock. You'd forgotten about that whole dolphin, you'd forgotten about time. You sat there for hours and you were aware that something special was happening. You felt how the energy changed, was increased. You can now maintain this new frequency. When you opened your eyes you saw how the dolphin jumped up into a pure white aura. I saw it too. From this dimension I can see even more, a whole range of colours in and above the water. This being transmits pure love. I understand very well that people are attracted to dolphins and whales.

Please continue to experience things like a child, out of pure wonder. Many people meditate and expect miracles. I've studied that extensively. Once one has had a spiritual experience, many people start meditating in anticipation of a similar kind of experience. Meditating to experience that kick again. I have studied many kinds and ways of meditation and prayer, which was very fascinating. The most beautiful thing for me remains the open, silent meditation; in connection with the Great Light, or whatever name you choose for it. Being Connected with the Light and with all people who are attuned to it.

On Earth I was not aware that there is such a thing as spiritual greed. I think an even better word is 'spiritual materialism'. Your teacher and now mine, Leviahnarah, taught you that word. He also showed me what it is. In amazement I saw that in some places it has taken on great proportions under the influence of certain energies. But there is a growing amount of people who meditate from the heart, in many ways, but with the same goal in mind. These global connections in this period of transition of the Earth from the third to the fifth dimension are extremely important. They lay a solid foundation upon which the Beings of Light can build a solid house. Without all these people, that is not possible. All those sincerely meditating or praying people are creating very powerful Fields of Light. At a distance from the Earth, you can see very clearly that the Earth is getting lighter and lighter. Gates that were closed for many thousands of years by dark, dominant forces are now opened one by one. There has been a major breakthrough in that area. Big changes became visible.

I, along with Ohan and Leviahnarah, have been able to look at these developments through the holographic screens. The fall of the Berlin Wall was a very clear turning point that could be achieved by the change of energy on Earth; an increasing flow of light and a changed, higher collective consciousness. The foundation that is being laid is growing and now shows a solid foundation on which the Forces of Light can continue to build. I hope to be able to explain more about this in this book.

The changes are happening so fast. With the increasing light, everything that is still hidden in the world now becomes visible. This applies to the as yet unexposed history of mankind as well as to all aspects of current society on Earth. Nothing can remain hidden any longer. You can see that we are growing towards a light consciousness and whoever wishes to fully flow into this consciousness is busy with his or her purification processes. Sometimes these are very old vibrations from previous lives. That purification covers an entire cycle of 26,000 years. People who choose not to go along and still need the energy of the third dimension - living in duality - will go to a world where that is still possible. "My father's house has many dwellings," master Jesus said. There are still people who need the feeling of power and so many other lower desires. People who have not yet sufficiently worked that out and still want to experience it will incarnate in other places in the universe, until they are ready to grow into a higher dimension.

The process of purification is hard for many people; I know that from my own cancer process. But no matter how hard the road was, I succeeded completely. Everywhere on Earth these kinds of processes are now taking place. Many people experience chaos in their inner world and are confused. The incoming light reveals those unprocessed aspects that our Higher Self feels should now be purified. All parts of our soul being, with their unique experiences on Earth, are searching for wholeness in order to be able to go forward. A God Spark is present in all people and when, touched by the light, the sometimes many layers of concealment start to disappear, people begin to search for answers to many different questions. The journey home starts, to wholeness, inner peace, abundance and spiritual riches. Every human being longs for this in the depths of his being. After all, we all come from the same Source of Light.

After I had made my way through the spheres and reached my place of spiritual attunement, I followed a lengthy training in the Hall of Wisdom: among other things to pass on the material to you in the right way. It was in fact refresher training, because I now know that I have worked in this way with people on Earth many times in other incarnations. The whole process was like opening up old shutters. I now know that I've also done this work with you before: I passed it on and you were the telepathic receiver. We were then able to review the material and discuss it. Everything was always first prepared in the spiritual world, just as it was in this life with the cooperation with Leviahnarah in passing on life readings to your clients. It was wonderful to be in the Hall of Wisdom again, a feeling of coming home. Like a sponge I absorbed it all.

You will probably know that after I died on Earth, I did not immediately go to the Hall of Wisdom. That went only very gradual, but I had already done a lot of work on Earth, which made it easier and quicker for me to proceed here, in the spheres. I was already aware of so many things. Dear child, you have prepared me so incredibly well for my death and my new life here. Your absolute certainty and knowing about life after death is a great support for someone who is very sick, as I was. When you hear that your life is over, all sorts of things happen to you. From this dimension I talk about my process and what other people I spoke to here went through. I came to the conclusion that there are as many different ways of dying as gradations of conscious-ness. Now that I am no longer in earthly life, I only fully realize how important it is to live consciously. To heal and transform old fears, just as you taught me in all these years. Years of intensive reading of esoteric books preceded this. But I now also realize that spiritual healing is a natural process that can take many lives, because people are lazy by nature. Unfinished business, negative vibrations from previous lives, cleaning everything up completely, that takes effort and pain. Many people prefer to avoid that pain.

My study in the Hall of Wisdom taught me that an increasing number of people are consciously trying to break out of the wheel of karma. You and I belong to that group and fortunately we both know a lot of people who share the same interest. I can now assure you that this search for truth and wholeness is very much worthwhile. What I love most of all is the experience of the Light and Love in which I am allowed to live. I am so intensely enjoying the redemption of my old, sick body. It has served me as the temple of my soul. I was allowed to work a lot with it, but now it is so wonderful that I no longer have to live in that heavy, pain-filled body. A few times you told me that you felt my time had come to leave. Now I know you were right. Twice there was an opportunity to go; both times it was in my sleep at night. It was my mother who came to get me, but I was so busy and refused to go. I thought I still had to help certain people on Earth, pray for them, and ask for physical and spiritual healing for them. Again and again I found a reason not to go away. Twice I asked you for a reading and twice I was told that in the advanced stage of my illness I had to think only of myself, in order to die in wholeness and peace. Sometimes you apparently have to turn eighty-three to go on like this with blinkers on, as your body is slowly giving up. I now know that if you are attuned to the Light, you can sometimes do a lot more for others on this side of the veil, much more than I thought I could do in the last months of my life.

I have to say that I had so many wonderful people around me during the years of my illness. That was a great gift. In the last period in the hospital there was a growing awareness with my daughters, a growing light. Then I could see how different we were and yet had so much in common.

We grew closer to each other. With my granddaughter I always felt this seamless connection where words are unnecessary. Three women I can proudly and lovingly admire. Once you are here and read in your book of life, you discover the meaning of your incarnation and the specific family ties, at least with those people who are also related to your growth process. Issues to which I bore certain guilt were from a previous existence, something I was now allowed to solve completely. If you read your book of life so consciously, it is the hour of truth. You see every aspect as it is. And what a liberation to be freed from old karmic issues that are often carried along life after life. Because I, too, was lazy and left a lot of possibilities untouched in the life immediately before I was Margaret. Together with others, I could have solved karma. Due to the fact that I left so much untouched in that previous life, there was now a possibility in my life as Margaret to work out a number of aspects at an accelerated pace.

I am grateful to my old, material body for the opportunities offered to work out all the remaining karma. It's like a fire that burns you clean, a purification process. I read my book of life through, as you predicted, holographic images. In this way I can look at every aspect of the previous life and also the lives before that, at my own pace. Nobody says I must. It is a possibility that is lovingly offered to you and then it is up to you to do something with it in complete freedom.

There are people who, life after life, obstinately refused to look at their book of life. But I gratefully made use of it after my last life. I process things in peace and quiet and sometimes, when I feel the need, I go to the healing chamber for a while, for a day or afternoon in earthly time, where I choose the light that suits me at that moment.

The last weeks of my life I was in hospital. For a long time I managed to live in my own home with the loving domestic help I had. These people work so hard. Most of them are extremely loving and work from the heart. I would like to thank them all for their good care, but they are not able to hear me like you do. Maybe they'll read this book again and remember me. When you are so sick and helpless, specific care is very important. That care is crumbling dramatically and rapidly, due to cutbacks, but also because some jobs in health care are so poorly paid. It's work that a lot of people look down on and that's not right. This work should be better rewarded, you realize that when you are seriously ill and can do almost nothing yourself. These loving people are priceless.

The wish and intention to pass on to you how it is here, was in my head. You are a medium and your readings are like cascades of events from past lives, down to the finest details. As you write you see the images pass you by holographically as in a film; very vividly and in colour. It's a bit like reading a book of life. You are, when you describe past lives, in the middle of its holographic image.

Ohan took me to a place in the Himalayas, where you received your nocturnal lessons from Master Lau-Me. You told me about it once. Now I was taken to a place where people who work like you receive their lessons. It was a beautiful place. Now that I pass this on to you, I feel that you will be happy when you think of that place, of Lau-Me and of the big hall built high in the mountains, with on one side only glass and on the other side a huge holographic screen. This space is built in another dimension and at night Ohan, one of your spiritual teachers, takes you there. The material you are going to pass on to people will be discussed and worked on there. It is responsible work to pass on parts of someone's book of life.

One time I was allowed to go there, together with Ohan. That was when Leviahnarah prepared a major reading with you; one for a psychologist. People ask special questions to the spiritual world, some of them very profound. Of course it provides a lot of insight into the consciousness of the applicant. Leviahnarah taught me that each reading is adapted to the consciousness of its applicant. That's why sometimes it seems so simple to you and other times so comprehensive and complicated. Everything is designed to prevent damage to the applicant. I know you are always aware of that. The readings are made with the personal guides of the applicant. An applicant who, in this case was stuck in the rational field of regular medicine and psychology. Applicants like this are subsequently inspired by their spiritual guides to explore a different path. They can then come into contact with people like you who can see beyond the veils of the third dimension. Fortunately, there are more and more of them in this day and age and I think they are desperately needed. It has helped me enormously to understand things that remained hidden in my own field of vision. Ohan taught me how every reading contains certain keys. An open and free story about a previous incarnation sometimes contains more than one key, which releases something in people's subconscious. Old issues can be brought to life, as it were, and be understood and processed in the here and now. The insight you were allowed to give me in my previous lives brought me to process and transform certain matters. It speeded up my personal process enormously and that turned out to be necessary, because I only had so little time left on Earth.

My days in the hospital gave me a great inner peace, necessary to come to the realization that it was really time to go. I enjoyed the complete care. Of course, nursing never has a whole lot of time for the patient, but it was good that way. The lack of the enormous stress that is so connected with being sick at home was so wonderful. In the hospital I felt less alone, because there is always activity around you. It had a reassuring and relaxing effect on me. No matter how wonderful it was, to be at home surrounded by my own belongings, the long hours of being alone in a state of need weighed heavily on me. If you can do something as simple as changing your bed, doing the laundry, bathing and going to the toilet, that is an enormous wealth. You will only realise this when you can no longer do it yourself. You become obsessed with clean things when there is no help available. I have found it very difficult to be bedbound and perhaps even more difficult to accept than the fact that my body had cancer.

I could talk to you about that at length if I had a hard time accepting it again. The fact that I was going to mentally decline seemed really terrible to me. I learned to accept my physical decay little by little. You have no option of course, as life would become unbearable. You stimulated me to certain thought processes that were completely in line with my own interests. One day you told me about Elize, my personal spiritual guide. You described her. Do you remember how I had to cry then? I always loved to play *Für Elise* on the piano. How beautifully things interlock. As my situation progressed, I gained more and more insight into these amazing processes. You comforted me when I expressed my fear of the hospital to you, or - what seemed even worse to me - a nursing home. In the end, the hospital turned out to be my liberation. There I could surrender to what had to be done. I finally had the time and inner peace to think about my approaching death. It felt as if the suitcases had been packed for the journey and I only had to wait for the train to take me to my new destination. There was no fear, only a deep desire to go. A complete surrender descended upon me and I decided that I would come along when my mother would appear to me again. I now know that I had no choice, that third time, but to go with her.

My daughters went through their own processes at a rapid pace, also with regard to their relationship with me. Most people think that if your body is lying there, so sick in bed, you're also dying mentally. Some people, also in nursing, talk to you in a way as if you were immature, childlike or even stupid. I remember being clear-headed, that my perception was sharper than ever. While my corporeal body slowly died, everything became more beautiful every day. It is important that you are surrounded by loving people and fortunately, I was. A warm kiss, a hand caressing your hair, someone who holds your hand in peaceful silence, lovingly and truly. When you are dying, you are able to pierce through all the masks. It must be terrible to have loveless people at your bedside, as I have often heard in this dimension in countless conversations with others. It taught me a lot while gathering as much information as possible about the transition and the spiritual world that awaits us afterwards.

My experiences in the last phase of life were beautiful, like pearls on my path. Sometimes I was outside my body and then I observed the thoughts of those who love me. Apparently this is also the case with coma patients, who are able to perceive all the thoughts around their bodies. For me they were short moments, moments with a golden edge, moments without pain, without the impediments of a sick body. That is wonderful, being outside your body, especially when it is so sick and in a lot of pain, is a great blessing. At such a moment you realize that your body is not everything there is, but that you are immeasurably much more.

That gave me more and more confidence in the upcoming journey. Your words resonated in me very often in those days. Here in this place I know how important dying guidance can be. You meditated in front of my picture and you prayed for me. In those days I have experienced what it is like when people pray for you. They call upon the assistance of helpers of the Source of Light, the angels, the Beings of the Light Spheres. It was good to experience that for myself. I now know that what I did every day, from the heart, for sick and needy people was good. It doesn't matter how you pray or meditate, but always do it with your whole heart. Otherwise you'd better leave it. Habitual prayers lack any power.

In my last days I had a very beautiful experience. It was getting worse and worse and I was in great pain. It was quiet around my bed. Then I had a vision. I saw you walking along wide water; the weather was beautiful. You sat down on a big stone, half in the water. You were all alone in that place. You put your hands open in your lap and started praying for me and other people. Then I really felt what it's like when someone does that for you with his or her whole heart. At the same time, I knew that more people were doing this for me, and knowing that brought great peace to my heart. Now that I am completely in my new life here, I know that you have really been there. Thank you for that and I also thank all those sweet people who did this for me out of selfless love. To experience that with the people around you is a true Gift of God.

Now I am about to describe the hour of my death, it is important to know that such an experience is different for everyone, and depends on everyone's own spiritual attunement. I am merely describing my personal experience that is connected to my own spiritual attunement. My fear had gone and that is very important. This is what I wish for every person when he or she passes on.

A few days before I passed away I saw two women appear: a small blond woman in a soft blue tunic and a somewhat darker woman in a purple blue tunic. In the beginning it was only for short moments that they were there, before leaving again. But now I know that for the last three days before my journey, they waited together for the hour of my transition. One woman was my mother; she was the one I recognized first. You had told me that people in the Spheres of Light looked younger, like in the best years of their lives. My mother looked like forty, and so did the other woman. She turned out to be my grandmother from my last incarnation. On my deathbed I was taken care of by them. Every now and then they stood very close to me and both held one of my hands. That was so wonderful. I was probably lying there with a blissful smile. How wonderful when they are there for you. Mother would put a hand on my head every now and then, at which point it seemed like I was floating away on the clouds. I felt like a child being lovingly cared for. How precious these moments were. The spiritual was becoming more important; the physical body began to lose my interest. I had surrendered to the birth process to the spiritual world. My two sweet, light mothers beside me were my midwives, together with my guide Elize. When the hour of my death had come, I saw you appear. You stood at the end of my bed and just smiled. You saw me coming out of my body and watched a spiritual doctor break the silver cord. You radiated, my child, I will never forget that image.

It was an unforgettable experience for you too, I know now. What followed is something you have seen many times in your work, showing the shining path to people who, after their death are still earthbound. But you never get used to it. My dear mothers and Elize took me to the shining path that appeared. I experienced everything consciously, that was also my deepest wish. I looked back once more at my material body and thanked it from the bottom of my heart, for all the years it served me well. We crossed a crystal bridge. A whole range of beautiful colours passed me by. I was led to a large gate where a few people were waiting for me. There was a dear friend there who had died of the disease ALS some time before. She looked young and radiant. Next to her stood a man. He stretched his hands out to me and touched me for a moment. There was recognition and joy. Later I saw everybody again, when I was more aware of what was happening and conscious about who else was present. The man turned out to be my husband - he had passed away a long time ago - and it was a warm reunion. I was lovingly welcomed and taken to the healing chamber.

A woman in a light tunic with long trousers took me in. I remember the modern style of her clothes. She had a sweet face. I was lying in the healing chamber for a few weeks, counted in earthly time; a very special experience. The bed on which I was lying had no legs. It floated a little above the ground. At first I found myself lying in a golden-blue-green energy. I surrendered to it and let myself float away in that wonderful light. When I woke up Elize was there. I just had to think of her and she would be there again. The power of thought sets everything in motion here. I was so happy with her loving presence. That support is so important.

My cancer process was fully worked out on Earth. All I needed was that recovery period, in total peace of mind. Dying is hard work, just like a baby has to work hard to be born. Loving help in such a process makes it easier. I am deeply grateful to my family and friends for their loving help. When I woke up for a moment, I looked at my hands and feet with amazement at how slim and without wrinkles or spots they were. It was a game, getting used to that new life, that young, subtle body. At those moments I didn't think about Earth anymore, that only came later.

One time I woke up and saw an enormous alabaster vase on the ground, creamy white, containing beautiful white roses. I looked at it full of admiration. Between the roses were little blue flowers. Then all of a sudden I had to think very strongly of you. You always said: "Margaret, when you're in the Beyond, I'll send you a big bunch of white roses for a new beginning." And as always, we used to make jokes about these things. And then I'd say to you, "Add some blue flowers to it, so that I know they are sent by you, for the book we're going to write." After all, we both had no idea whether our wish to write this book would actually come true.

When Elize came, she said the flowers were yours. I know you teach this to many people, it's wonderful to get such a floral greeting. Spiritual flowers don't wilt. Later, when I left the healing chambers for my own home that had been prepared; I took the flowers with me. They are now in the corner by the large window and reach all the way to the ground. A few months later (in Earth time) there came a beautiful red rose of yours; it's still there too.

At that time we hadn't made contact yet and didn't know if that would happen. You waited until the right moment. A few other people sent me spiritual flowers too and I cherish these sweet gifts. It is a wonderful opportunity for contact without expectations: a kind of acceptance of one's passing, without expecting anything in return. Nobody on Earth pulls at me and that's a very rich feeling, because by now I have often seen that with others, who are not let go by those who are left behind. That's a big hindrance to your progress in the spiritual world. And of course also for those you left behind on Earth.

Sometimes I went out of the healing chamber to walk with Elize. Once in a while there was a man who visited me, admired my roses and later also went for a walk with me. He became my guide to teach me and show me all those new things. Elize introduced me to the power of thought, to telepathy and teleportation, and it wasn't all that difficult. It was a surprise to be able to perceive her completely now. On Earth I was aware of her presence as a spiritual guide and sometimes I saw a glimpse of her, a lovely light appearance. Now we were sitting there in full glory, under a huge tree, on a green bench. We were just radiating towards each other. Elize taught me to visualize a cup and then a drink. I chose grape juice. At first I couldn't hold the thought, so the juice fell to the ground. It took me a while to master it. We don't eat here as we are used to with our earthly bodies, but we absorb the essence of the fruit. The other day I was offered a drink, a kind of spiced honey drink that on Earth I thought was called mead. It was delicious. With Elize I walked through the gardens, in an undulating landscape in which I immediately felt at home. She told me about the new life. We walked past gardens with lavender. The colour was deeper, more intense than I had ever seen on Earth; the smell was delightful. In the vicinity of all those healing chambers that are everywhere here, you can always find gardens with lavender. Essential oils from lavender have a healing effect and that's why there is lavender in the places where people make a new beginning. I now know that many people have a certain fear at first, but only because they have absolutely no idea that such a beautiful and loving thing exists.

We walked through the rose gardens. I saw roses, three times the size of a peony, in colours so delicate and so perfect in shape that I kept looking at them for a long time. Roses represent a very high vibration of love. I cherished the moments in that beautiful energy. Sometimes such a walk was so overwhelming to me that I went back into the healing chamber for a while. I would take the spiritual rest that I felt I needed. Refreshed and full of energy I then continued later on.

I also saw others, accompanied by their guides. Most of them radiated bliss, relieved of the physical pain of their heavy material body on Earth. The wing of the healing chamber where I stayed was especially for people who suffered from cancer on Earth. Some people have to stay in the healing chamber for a long time to complete their process. Elize told me that there are many assistants present who were oncologists or nurses in oncology on Earth. Many spend this time in different light chambers in the frequency needed for their total recovery. Time doesn't exist on this side.

It's nice to lie in the colours that are attuned to your being. There is always gold in the healing chambers for cancer. That gold is like an all-pervading fog, which is put in a blue-green space. I became part of those colours myself; I was absorbed by it. What a blessing to be there.

After my transition I arrived in the third Sphere of Light, but my spiritual attunement was above that. It takes time to transform and to be able to go a step further. A human being would not be able to endure that much light all at once. The Third Sphere was already such a revelation to me, the beauty of nature, the beautiful flowers I saw there, the variety of birds and butterflies, the scents and colours. The green colour of the heart chakra pervades everything. It has a calming and healing effect. My final destination turned out to be in the Sixth Light Sphere. You don't have a clue about something like that on Earth, and maybe that's for the best, then you can work without prejudice to purify body and mind and there will be no predetermined limits.

Elize escorted me to my home. Remember when you told me about the houses you had seen during your visits to the Beyond and their enormous diversity? Everyone creates what suits him or her. You once sent me a beautiful picture of a small white stone house, overgrown with beautiful roses: Joanne's cottage, with the big chestnut tree. How many times have I looked at that picture and drew strength from it on my sick bed? Yet my house looks very different. On a soul level you already create what suits you, before you arrive. My new life here is first and foremost focused on the healing of my being. The house is beautiful, very spacious and with a beautiful view. Seen from above, it is somewhat dome-shaped. On one side completely closed and on the front side completely open. I can, if I feel the need, shield the space from the outside world and darken it. I enjoy the pure simplicity of its design, the space inside and around it, the tranquillity. In my house there is a comfortable sleeping area where I can retreat if I feel the need to relax. By the way, there is no rhythm of day and night here. The sleeping area is in soft colours, a bit peachy, very pleasant to lie down in. In the large living room you'll find those colours too, but here and there I choose to apply some bright colours.

I have a beautifully shaped chair that floats a little above the floor and can be put in any position you want, even stretched out. This way I can look outside and enjoy the landscape. There are flowers everywhere. I felt such a need for them after all those years of being sick and locked up in my earthly home. I missed the beauty of nature so much. Around my house is a field of small white flowers. On the edge are white and pink roses; those very large ones again, bigger than peonies. I cannot describe the beauty of this place with earthly words; there are simply no words. I am enjoying it and I can't get enough of it. Around the house there are huge white chairs, that's where I usually receive my visitors. There are beautiful long blue flowers in large bunches and before that small low growing flowers of different colours.

It's a beautiful place. Over the sloping landscape hangs a silver haze that penetrates everything. The spiritual attunement you have chosen as your goal when you die. My transmutation from the Third Sphere of Light to this place was a miraculous and happy process. We can go to all the spheres below, but not necessarily to higher spheres. I know that this is only possible in a special protective cocoon and that it is reserved only for special occasions. People like you, who pass things on to the people on Earth, are transported in such a cocoon to learn about the spheres.

I now read my book of life, slowly, at my own pace, and first with Elize and later in the Hall of Wisdom, I have focused on what I had intended to do on a soul level during my illness on Earth. And that is to pass on to you what it is like on this side, hoping that it will help the living. And above all: to overcome the fear of death. Death doesn't exist; we're like butterflies crawling out of a cocoon to ascend brilliantly.

With regard to your books, I have met many people and discovered that everything happens according to a plan, a kind of agreement between you and me and many others who all had the desire to eliminate the fear of death and dying. When I started my studies in the Hall of Wisdom and was trained to get in touch with you in the right way, bits of old knowledge presented themselves: windows to old knowing. Little by little I came into contact with all facets of my life before I incarnated as Margaret. While searching I discovered our old connections, the times of cooperation from the spirit, friendships on Earth.

I discovered that in a life in the seventeenth century I could play the violin beautifully. I also had a beautiful singing voice. In a life after that I played the piano and you were my piano teacher. That took place in Vienna. We were dear friends. Until your early death at the age of forty-two, we were inseparable and I was allowed to do for you what you have done for me now. You died of tuberculosis. Your mother couldn't bear to be with her dying daughter. Together with your father and your twin sister, we took care of you. High up in the mountains, where your twin sister and her husband, who was a doctor, founded a sanatorium. It was a special time, full of emotion together, but that last year was wonderful. I played the piano in front of the open doors while you and other guests were outside on the terrace. They were very special moments. Leviahnarah, one of your spiritual teachers and who passes you the readings, was then your father. Your twin sister is your granddaughter Eva of today. How beautiful everything is. You can see these things through the thousands of life readings you've passed on. You've seen, and you know from your own experience, how beautiful things fit together. Fortunately, more and more people in this day and age gain insight into these kinds of processes, of themselves and others.

In the Hall of Wisdom I met people who were in a choir. We started talking and that's how I joined their choir. I really enjoy singing together. What a wonderful thing to do. I also get piano lessons in a building where they practice the fine arts. Many community buildings here look like ancient Greek buildings; simply beautiful. I am especially interested in the music of Chopin and Mozart. I go to concerts with friends. The music cannot be compared to the music on Earth. Almost indescribable, so beautiful, so pure, it touches me in my deepest being. I now know that I have been involved with music in different lives. All those pieces of knowledge I thread together like beads and each time my reality is expanded a little bit. An enormous richness. Not everyone, like me, is occupied with incarnations other than the last one. It depends on the extent to which they have processed their issues from their last life. That's why I'm so happy now that in my last life I tackled and worked on my unfinished business. Processing old issues and acquiring consciousness goes deeper when you do that during your life on Earth. Now I also understand why so many different therapies have been brought to Earth. For everyone there is a possible way to come clean.

In the Hall of Wisdom I got to know your teachers and guides very well: Ohan, Leviahnarah, Eduard and about four others. You had told me about their sense of humour. I have experienced that now and their humour is indeed heart-warming. I needed that at a time like this. While window-by-window was being opened, at a pace that suited me, I began to gain insight into my past lives and could now also see how our connections were and how old they were. We worked together many times. Like in the life you know as Anne Mary's, in Berlin around 1650. Leviahnarah was your brother then. Together you worked on pamphlets, small writings for a gnostic society. I passed you a book in those years from the spiritual world. A collaboration between a human being in the spiritual world and a human being living in the material world. This book was then distributed under a masculine pseudonym all over Europe. You travelled a lot with your husband, who attended conferences as a neurologist and gave guest lectures in other places. Even though the Inquisition was officially over, persecution of dissent took place on a large scale and this still had a great influence on society. The Gnostic Societies, scattered throughout Europe, were very important in preserving messages of Light, until the time was right for them to come out again. During your travels with your husband, the copied writings were transported in a secret space in your carriage.

It is miraculous when you start to open the records of past lives, because with the necessary amazement you start stringing the beads, and little by little you gain insight into the size of your being and what you have done. At this point I also understood where my inner feeling of certainty that we could accomplish this together came from, after all, we had done it before. Is that why it's so easy? It's as simple as making a phone call. You can ask me things, and we communicate.

When I read my book of life, I see so many beautiful things, but also my stumbles. I think it's so important to mention that there is no judging and condemnation here, except perhaps by yourself. If you have hurt or offended other people, you feel and experience that in yourself when you look back on it. You would like to change it, balance it. Sometimes it's nice to see how you hurt or offended people terribly in a life, and how you resolve that in the same life. Actually, we are always trying to balance the scales. I think that's good news to pass on. Between fathers, mothers and children you see that happen very often. As long as we pay attention to it, you can see that these possibilities are always being offered. We are so often unconscious of these things and do not see the possibilities that are offered to us. More and more people are very consciously cleaning up and tidying up their lives. They create new fields of light with their larger and higher light consciousness. Through their conscious growth they take many people with them into something we can call the formation of a morphogenetic field. It is also called the hundredth-monkey effect: when enough monkeys (people) have learned something, it flows naturally into the field to all the other monkeys (people).

In the Hall of Wisdom I was shown how the growth processes of many people, both in groups and individually, are progressing at a rapid pace. They in turn take many people into that new, lighter consciousness, and that is very beautiful to see. I myself learned to develop my previously acquired talents. My first contact with you went smoothly and naturally, as if I was talking to you on the phone. Your talent as a channel has of course been in full use for years and it is constantly developing.

In Ireland where you write these words, many people still live with fear of hell and purgatory. Yesterday I was with you when you were meditating in that beautiful old church. There I discovered such thoughts of fear in a few people who were praying there. People still go to confession with fear in their bodies. A lot of dogmas still exist in

Ireland, but an increasing number of people, like all over the world, are outgrowing these things. A young generation is searching for the truth, wants to be free and disengages itself from the imposed precepts of the church. Gently we are moving in the right direction. The way I see it here, this awareness and the choice to be free may be going faster than many people think.

The truth has many layers; you discovered that yourself and we often talked about it during our intensive conversations during my final year. It was concentrated food for thought in those days. I have to say in all honesty that I had no idea that so many people, mostly invisible to the outside world, are searching and are growing, sometimes slowly, sometimes at a fast pace.

My new life on 'the other side' is a great pleasure after my long illness, after all those years of cancer, pain and sorrow. A lifetime of health was not my strongest point. I know now that you have to respect your body - the temple of your soul - and take very good care of it. I have to admit in all honesty that I didn't always do that very well. I see a lot of people here who need to acknowledge this. People who have already healed on Earth have learned to say 'no' more often and take better care of themselves. The more people learn to listen to their feelings, the better they are doing. Contact with your soul makes it possible to take the only right course and to bring you where you want to go in life on a soul level. If more people would learn to listen to their feelings better, more things would be solved during life and in a shorter time. Fortunately, more and more people are learning to listen to their feelings. That is the way they have to go. It's not always nice what you attract on your way through life, but it's the thing you need in order to heal the unhealed parts in yourself. Then you can often quickly clean up and heal old aspects and old, unhealed parts. In this way you can reach a certain degree of wholeness, making life calmer, obtaining a more visible and tangible harmony, with increasing light. Not everyone is open to this and such people unconsciously leave many chances for healing unused. I am now looking at my own path, my own choices, to transform my old karmic issues at an accelerated pace.

4. The Healing Chambers

The Reversal

Thea: Never has there been a period in human history such as this: an end time of multiple cosmic cycles. Liberation from the darkness that has nested in this solar system like a parasite for aeons. In this period of growth and of awakening, people who were kept in a low frequency for centuries in every conceivable way, we see how more and more people are consciously attuning themselves vertically to the Light. We now see a clear hundredth-monkey effect with regard to the becoming aware of the slavery in all its forms on Earth.

The specialized healing chambers are large centres in the spheres - the dimensions where people go after their transition. Healing chambers have also been created for people who still live on Earth in a material body. During their sleeping hours, massive use is made of these possibilities to heal very specific traumas in each person's subtle and consequently material bodies. This is part of the end time process. There are very many people on Earth who have deep traumas from past lives, but also from this life. There are traumas that are related to occult rituals in all its forms, from ritual pedophilia to satanic human sacrifices. In this period of 'reversal' and an increasing Light on Earth, many of these things come to light. That which was hidden for so long becomes visible in all its essence.

Throughout time, in the last Earth cycle of 26,000 years alone, billions of souls were damage. People serving the darkness have caused immeasurable damage through theft, imprisonment, murder, torture, sexual violence, slavery, wars, genocide, etc.

By the carefully constructed soul theft of the Light Beings, the darkness could feed itself for millennia, as well as all those people who, because of their choice to serve the darkness, had lost their connection to their Source of Light also. It has all become so habitual: the far-reaching manipulation of religions, the wars, the created epidemics... It was harvest time for the darkness for centuries, always robbing people of their light. All attempts to establish world domination, the so-called New World Order, are opposed by amongst others the mass awakening and growing awareness of the people of the Earth.

Years ago, there were stories circulating in the New Age world that we would be saved by extraterrestrials; messages that seemed to suggest that we could sit back and wait. Yes, we are helped from the Realms of Light by Peoples of Light - by those in the Beyond alongside those of other civilizations - but we also do it ourselves, and we are obliged do it ourselves: conscious people, working and collaborating.

In my book 'The End of the Circle', I describe our Selves, being split off from our own originally Divine Spark, who have all entered different areas. Many have now healed different aspects together with their Selves from other areas and are working closely with them on a spiritual level; consciously but mostly unconsciously as well. Cooperation based on cosmic laws.

The dark grid around the Earth is disappearing, fading visibly. Truths are coming to light; lies of centuries are becoming crystal clear, which does not mean that everyone wants to see it. The traumas of this Earth cycle of over 26,000 years, relating to the hidden crimes, are healed in specially created healing chambers. At the same time, with the help of other liberated peoples in the universe, many stolen souls were found. Indeed, in the Realms of Light, people work closely together to retrieve everything that has been stolen and take it back to the higher Selves of Earthlings, through specialized areas in the dimensions. After their transition, many scientists, doctors and healers are working with many others on these processes of global healing. For soul fragments of babies and children, there is a specialized healing centre of a size unimaginable to us.

In a City of Light, Lord Kumeka showed us how people's Higher Selves were weakened by the traumas and soul theft that took place in the process. Once a life is so traumatized and split up, people remain very vulnerable in subsequent incarnations. Their old wounds, of whatever nature, are ethereally visible and can act as a hook-in point for the darkness. People's God Sparks weakened with time, also because of a low vibration. This comes on top of all the other technologies that are meant to keep human energy low these days - radiation, telecommunication, food, drugs, medication, violence, pollution, etc. All this is now being reversed, which has been going on for quite some time. Awareness of the many aspects in today's society to keep humanity at a low frequency is growing worldwide. That is what we call The Great Reversal.

Pieces of fragmented light souls were found in many places on Earth. This was done with the increasing help of the Realms of Light, through the magisterial work of the Ray of Purification and all the people who were able to participate. The souls trapped in the stolen light reservoirs found in many places on Earth have been taken to special healing centres after which, following their healing processes, they will return to their Higher Selves, purified and cleansed. Within the reversal now taking place, we see people's soul sparks becoming brighter and brighter, more whole, lost strength is returning. We monitor this reversal process in the Spheres and Cities of Light and we see how many people in their current earthly incarnation are coming into their strength. This helps to heal old traumas of today's life at night.

The result of all this work towards the light souls on Earth is that those who live from low vibrations, from fear, all kinds of unloving events, are gradually becoming less able to steal energy. Here and there we see an enormous energetic famine. As the god sparks become more whole and strong, because of the return of their stolen soul fragments of many lives on Earth, they will transcend the uninvited guests, the parasitic creatures and entities. In an immense process of liberating the Earth, we see a collaborative process with our extraterrestrial families, many of whom once experienced such liberation on their own planet.

Superstition

Superstition is a meaningless,
simple word, with which coarse
ghosts are mocking the very finest
emotions, perceptions and talents
of the human soul.

Louis Couperus

5. Martin

Seeing What Was and Seeing What Is

Leviahnarah: Martin is part of our collective. The topic of the healing chambers has his full interest in the work he does in the spiritual world and his own experiences in previous incarnations.

Martin: The openness that is now possible around this subject makes it possible to work on different levels, both in the 3D material world and in the spiritual world. '*Seeing What Is.*'

So many aspects of life on Earth have long been obscured, truths hidden behind beautiful words or no words at all, 'silence' all around. Making visible and discussable what was hidden for so long makes it possible for us humans to grow, to become aware of *What Is and What Was*. My own history of incarnations shows how many people were once encapsulated in energy that was not of the Light. Leviahnarah calls it "*being drawn into the darkness*". A clear distinction is made in the spiritual world between people (souls) who consciously chose to serve the darkness and people (souls) who were drawn into it. What usually followed was an assimilation process: becoming one with the dark, gradually downward, to a lower frequency than you had before that assimilation. Reaching a point where you no longer have the faintest idea that you *are* a light-bearing soul and have ended up in lives in which the misery and dramas have almost become a self-evident part of your life on Earth. Not having the faintest idea that the dramas in which you live are the result of old karmic baggage.

Where does the assimilation come from?

There are so many ways to do that in so many eras. Lower desires can be a deep trap for a soul, and control you in many subsequent lives. I have met people on my path of incarnations who were completely focused on power, prestige, and wealth. It is an opening to the darkness that we then provide, a lure. And before you know it, you attract the energy that offers you ways to realize what you have wished for. After all, you focus in a constant stream on certain thoughts and desires, which can also be of a low frequency.

Often, I saw that people, who once had been very strong themselves, used the obtained wealth solely for the purpose of personal gain. Mind you, these were people who were thus fully in their strength and were sufficiently strong to be able to carry the wealth of such great power. People who might have been put on a pedestal by their environment but who nevertheless remained themselves, to do, from an intuitive knowing, what they had come for to do. Those who allowed themselves to be drawn into their lower desires, often created very heavy baggage through what they then received. Even though people let themselves be drawn in by the lure of the lower frequencies, dark energetic areas, it was in most cases conscious choices to achieve what they had desired. In such a life they would enjoy what they had wished for, but were not aware of what they were doing. Cause and effect was then experienced in the next incarnation.

Such causes can sometimes haunt people (souls), incarnation after incarnation, depending on the seriousness of what one had created from that lower frequency. Many layers can be discerned in this. There are people (souls) who in an immediately subsequent life solved what was unbalanced. That success resulted in harmony, with which the energy was immediately balanced. However, it can also be different. This is, let's say, the other side of the coin, that the choices in several previous incarnations were of such low frequency, that one can hardly 'bear' the consequences of that heavy luggage anymore.

The starseeds

As we will see in Jonathan's chapter below, many starseeds incarnated on Earth at the beginning of the Atlantis period. Also later, about 12,000 years ago, a lot of starseeds came to Earth out of free choice. Most of them followed a spiritual, telepathic call that was sent out on their home planets to assist the Earth and all life on it. The main task was to help neutralise the increasing darkness. They brought knowledge and beauty, such as for example in so-called 'simple' lives in craftsmanship and creative professions. People, however, who some-times had a very hard time 'being here'.

In this end time, the end of an Earth cycle in which darkness gets denser and comes to the surface, it is again a hard time for these souls. Therefore, they begin to intensely long for 'home', for balance, for both inner and outer peace, for a harmonious society. They came from, among others, the Pleiades, Andromeda, Arcturus and Tau Ceti, and many other places in the universe. Light Souls.

Great composers and artists came, painters, sculptors, builders, architects, teachers, scientists, and inventors. They brought supreme beauty and knowledge. Music and art can be enjoyed by anyone who needs it. Frequencies of high quality light that can lift people up and carry them to a higher consciousness: for some people only just for a moment, while others regain the energy they had lost on their long journey of incarnations. It is a coming home into forgotten vibrations. A long time ago they taught their Earthly soul brothers and sisters how to neutralize negative energy. In their self-created polyphony, intuitive people 'sang' dark energy away and neutralized it in this way. People sang in nature, on streets and squares, at funerals, in churches and buildings. Traditions of peoples thousands of years old. They neutralized negative energy as it arose in places where much fighting was created, such as Corsica, the Pyrenees and Armenia. Even if you don't understand their words, you can still feel the intention of traditional folk singing in the vernacular with your heart.

In the last 650 years many new starseeds came. They incarnated with the same intention: to assist their brothers and sisters on Earth in this last, dark period on their way to a higher frequency. Extremely sensitive people they are, both creatively and empathically, with a 'State of Being' that has sometimes been roughly crushed in the last centuries. Souls, however, who can see and read the energy of their environment in a very natural way; talents that they have brought with them from their various home planets - a very natural state of being, without abuse.

In these centuries of great energetic changes a battle rages. It is the battle of the darkness that does not want to lose its power. So many light souls, people who came to Earth to anchor the positive light energy that heralds the great changes, they are a great danger to those who still have power today. There are very many souls who on their own strength reached a higher frequency in the various Earthly cycles, and who now consciously chose to incarnate on Earth in this end time. Sensitive people all of them. People who, in many cases, have more than two strands of DNA. They have wonderful possibilities in terms of talents and soul power, which they will use to create changes for a society on Earth that is completely stuck; a society that is focused on consumption and exponential economic growth. A world in which attempts are being made everywhere to dehumanize society: in business, in healthcare, at schools and universities. Major cuts are being made in all areas relating to essence of human culture: social services, art, culture, honest and clean work, health and the environment. At the same time, more and more money is being spent on weapons and 'safety'. The rich are getting richer all the time. There is more conflict, poverty, inequality and hunger in the world than ever. More and more, society is being robotised and automated. There is a strong tendency to develop artificial intelligence and genetic manipulation besides other technologies that are diametrically opposed to an increasing need for human interaction. We can see this everywhere and this is done on purpose.

Nevertheless, many people try to build up an existence within their own community, or with a small business where they can continue to live their passion, their craft. They are against unhealthy comercialisation and dehumanisation. However, everything is done so they will lose their businesses, because of sky-high taxes and loans. Nevertheless, as we can see, people will succeed, although for now it is still difficult. The battle to keep the people of the light below a certain energetic ceiling of low frequencies cannot be won.

Light

Matter is Energy
Energy is Light,
We are all Light Beings

Albert Einstein

6. Joseph

Leviahnarah: Joseph has been in the spiritual world for a number of years now and chose to stay there until the great change on Earth: the jump from the third to the fifth dimension. He was a gifted visual artist and musician, a man who brought truths to light through his art, in both words and deeds.   Born in America in the late 1940s, his parents and grandparents were Quakers, non-violent empathetic people. He grew up in a family of conscious people; conscious to what was happening on Earth regarding wars, racism, religion, abuse of children in home's, boarding schools and churches. In the fifties of the twentieth century, without the technology we have today - such as the Internet, fast mail and telephone connections - that knowledge, intuitively unobtrusive, was silently shared in small circles.

His parents and grandparents saw new divide-and-rule techniques being introduced in society. Awful things also occurred in the world of art and entertainment, which could go on unnoticed for years. His maternal grandfather worked in the music industry and saw how those who wanted to reach the top had to go along with the powers behind the scenes. Drugged and then blackmailed by all kinds of photographic and video footage, people were forced to do what was expected of them. Grandfather was a 'starseed', just like everyone in his whole family group. He saw how satanic structures in the film and entertainment world of the fifties were given more and more space and what influence this had on the masses.

He told our family what he saw and experienced, how people who chose to follow those structures changed their behaviour in order to become famous. He saw and understood that many ended up completely destroyed due to their use of drugs and alcohol. This is not a 21st century phenomenon, like many people want to believe; it is essentially a development that was set in motion long before the Second World War. Joseph's mother was a jazz singer and gave singing lessons and sang in various bands. Father taught music at a high school. Mother, who in the fifties actively worked with groups of both white and coloured people, groups dealing with extreme racism, would have some awful experiences. In the world of jazz she met many coloured people who told her about their experiences of persecution by the Ku Kux Klan.

She and a small group of activists were attacked and injured by these people. She herself recovered but one man in the group did not, he would be disabled for life. Her anger was great because of what happened, both in her own environment and in many other places in the country. The persecutors, with their cowardly masks and hats, who, by hiding their faces were able to persecute people anonymously. Thus Joseph's childhood years were determined by the consciousness of waking people. In high school things were difficult for him because of his mother's past. But there were more children like him who had to bear the consequences of such things at that large school.

Joseph: There was a moment when I could see the difference between children from 'good' families and children like me. A dear friend of mine decided to immigrate to Canada. I visited him during a school vacation. He lived in a workers' home on his uncle's farm. He was a man who had decided to leave his repressive environment. His uncle bought a farm and my friend went to work there. Because the family took part in anti-racism meetings and later demonstrated against the Vietnam War, studying at universities was made difficult for their children. Everything was registered. So, also this is not new as many people now might think.

Every child is defined by its environment, which for me were the protest meetings of the sixties, in which my family participated. For example, I was with our family at Martin Luther King's famous speech in Washington in 1963. In our family at that time, we were aware of the tremendous power and energy of many individuals. My grandfather encouraged me to actively join their Quaker community at an early age. He predicted there was a war coming. Quakers do not carry weapons, so in a time of conflict, they mostly ended up in professions such as cook, nurse or doctor, etc.

My eldest brother was leaving for Vietnam, he was a nurse. On the television we could watch it all, and we saw how everyone was brainwashed by the daily news. By, for example, the continuous repetition of the footage on which body bags were unloaded from military planes. I was disgusted by that whole display of degrading events, the suffering that was caused on both sides. A good friend of my brother was killed in Vietnam. My eldest brother himself came back wounded and heavily traumatized. I was very angry, aware of what was going on there. In April 1967 Martin Luther King openly spoke against this colonial war in the Far East. In that same year, however, I was called to go to Vietnam too. My friend from Canada came to get me, together with my youngest brother. We immediately left for Canada; grandfather gave us enough money for a new beginning. Returning was not an option. There were also kept files of the descendants of the deserted, in case they might return some day. They then would have few opportunities at schools and universities. For years my friend had been actively working on the so-called 'underground railroad', an escape route for conscriptees to Canada. Together with my brother I joined them. There were many of us who did this work, with all their heart. We simply didn't want to kill other human beings for war profits.

I was part of a group of musicians and artists and was later given the opportunity to graduate as a teacher and earn my living. I also gave painting lessons at an art academy in later years. Many people were able to process their frustrations and traumas through creative expression. As a musician we brought light into the world by letting people enjoy themselves. The sadness was great with those who had left their homeland. When the Vietnam War ended, many of us started an aid organization, in which my parents were active in the United States, like we in Canada.

My eldest brother experienced how the Vietnam veterans, who had supposedly fought for their homeland, were deserted on all levels. Many who were no longer able to take part in the workforce, ended up on the streets, disabled and severely traumatized. My eldest brother, despite the loving care and presence of our mother, could no longer cope with 'normal' life. He told her that he could not get rid of the horrible images from the field hospital at the front, where he worked as a nurse. He chose to leave this life and did so using pills.

Eventually I turned sixty-two and died in my sleep. My brother came to get me, together with my grandfather. In the healing chamber, my brother was often close to me. I only had to think of him and he would be there. My grandfather was often there as well. He looked like a man of thirty-five years old, like I knew him from old photographs. We could look back together in our holographic book of life. My brother showed us how he and many former soldiers had arrived in the healing chambers, badly traumatised. Special healing chambers programs were developed, with the right energy to help these people. I was able to follow the processes of physically and mentally severely wounded people in the Light Spheres, together with grandfather and my brother.

It was at that time that my mother, after she had reached an advanced age, arrived in the spiritual world. My father had been there for some time already, as had both my grandparents. It is not always the case that one stays together in the spiritual world, which depends on your spiritual attunement and what you want to do further in your own processes. We chose to form a small collective of like-minded people who, as experts by experience, were able to welcome people after a trauma related self-chosen transition. I joined this collective and those who had been doing this spiritual work for years. This group assisted victims of the various wars created by America in many parts of the world, in their healing processes. There are several groups working here, each with its own specialization.

Throughout time, multitudes of people have been severely damaged in created wars, both physically and mentally. The purpose of the bloodshed in wars has always been to lower the Earth's frequency: it is literally a blood sacrifice ritual. The many human beings connected to the Archons serve them by helping them to create this energetic nourishment. Through the horrific wars, and basically with all human sacrifices, suffering was maintained, both spiritually and physically. There are pictures of severely mutilated young men of the First World War. These lads suffered continuously from terrible internal and external wounds. In the spiritual world we can look at all such images whenever it is relevant to the work we are allowed to do with these damaged souls. Everything is stored in the Akashic Records; you could call it the world's memory.

I decided to stay in the spiritual world partly because of the large streams of veterans that were arriving: old veterans from World War II and veterans from Korea and Vietnam. But also younger veterans from the artificial wars in the Middle East, Afghanistan and Iraq, who all came back heavily traumatized. There are many veterans who took their own lives because they couldn't go on living with what they had experienced. Because of what they themselves had done on so-called 'peace missions'; often under the influence of the drugs that were abundantly administered to them. These people were severely damaged by the constant presence of their traumas. They were brought into a low frequency, because they were constantly seeing the images of loveless acts and their consequences; a film that was unstoppable. Here in the spiritual world we see how through time, through the excessive bloodshed, enormous fields of low-frequency energy have been created with the sole aim of keeping the Earth in a low vibration. No matter what period of time such experiences took place, the traumas are always the same, and if they are not cleansed, they will stick to a specific place and constantly emit their negativity there.

The healing chambers created for these souls, are located in beautiful areas, where just being present at such a place of high frequency, has a healing effect. In the spheres we see again and again that the heavily traumatized veterans and military find it very difficult to enjoy such beauty at first. However, the surrounding gardens with certain healing flowers, such as roses and lavender among many other species, do have a certain attraction to them. Under loving guidance, often without 'verbal' communication, healing processes are initiated and successfully completed.

In the healing chamber we saw a man who was killed in Iraq. Later in he was standing the gardens close to certain species of flowers. Nobody could reach him. He had been tortured after which he could no longer speak. His trauma was so severe that he was unable to communicate. Via the flower gardens he was taken to a place we call '*the butterfly garden*'. In the butterfly gardens specialists are present, often together with a dog or with cat creatures. It was there that this man's longing for an animal companion arose. He began to think of his loving childhood and of his grandmother's dog. He got help from loved ones who often visited him and who were sometimes there without him seeing them. After the time in the butterfly garden he opened himself for those who were dear to him on Earth. At some point, a small long-haired hound came to him who remained his faithful companion until now. That helped in the end, even though it was a long process.

The Butterfly Garden

Thea: For the book 'The Cycle of Life and Death', I was allowed to visit a butterfly garden. Children with very severe traumas are brought here, for example. I was glad that my training was apparently finished to the point that I was allowed to see this.

A little boy of eight years old was brought to the butterfly garden. He had been in one of the healing chambers for a long period of time. In his last life in Africa, he was severely abused as some sort of slave. He had been taken away from his parents, brainwashed and conscripted into a children's army. However, he did not want to conform to what was desired of him; his whole being resisted his superiors. He was sexually abused and infected with the HIV virus. He only wanted one thing, to go back to his parents. Again and again he was told that his parents had been killed in the war and that he could not return because his village did not even exist anymore. He accepted that for truth, but still didn't want to kill people. Deep inside he realized that it wasn't right what was happening there. He kept resisting them in all kinds of ways and thus did not grow old. The rulers chose him as a terrifying example for the others. Their method of brainwashing had not worked sufficiently on this boy. His horrible death had to keep the other children in line.

He went over to the spiritual world, but even in the healing chamber he remained in a subconscious state for a long time. His grandparents, who had arrived much earlier, stayed close to him and would take care of the boy until he would be ready. However, the boy remained in a state of *not wanting to be there* and closed his mind completely to his surroundings: nobody could reach him.

In the healing chamber, the vibrations of processing and healing did work though, but not up to the point where they could open him sufficiently to his new surroundings. His spiritual guides decided that he would be taken to a butterfly garden for short periods of time. There are several kinds of butterfly gardens here and some are very specialized. This specific butterfly garden is part of the children's sphere to which heavily traumatized children are taken. In my experience it was a kind of magic garden, where a child that has completely closed himself off to everything in his environment, can open up again.

I was allowed to come there several times to be able to give a better report. I couldn't mingle with the children however, because such children are afraid of adults. I had to stay behind a kind of screen, which made me invisible to the child. I would be present before the children entered. I was deeply impressed by the beauty of this place. A gently sloping garden that changed into a park landscape lots of low shrubs, flowers and big trees a little further away. The sight of this place already had a calming effect on me and I could imagine that this was a place of great healing.

The little boy was brought in and put on a deckchair. He didn't react at all to this beautiful environment, at least that's how it appeared to me. He was completely introverted. A short while later a little girl with long blond hair came into the garden. The girl seemed to be about five years old. She looked at the boy for a moment and greeted him, but got no reaction. She sat down in the lawn, a short distance away from him but in such a way that he could see her. She raised her hand and, as I had seen her do with birds before, butterflies appeared, responding to her spiritual call. The butterflies were huge, considerably bigger than the child's hand. She stood up and turned around with her hands in the air. Her clothes waved along with her body. She was wearing a multi-coloured dress that seemed to be made of bands of fabric, stitched together, each with a different bright colour and fanning out at the bottom. Her long blond hair also waved as she twisted around. A whole group of small butterflies appeared above her hands. They danced, as it were, together with the girl and formed a kind of flower. On the edge of the sloping grass a Golden Retriever with long, soft hair appeared. He stood there watching the cheerful spectacle and only after a long time slowly walked towards the girl. She sat down again and the dog lay down beside her. Every action was slow, taking a long time. Together they just sat there; every now and then the girl stroked the dog over his head, nothing else. At a certain moment she lay stretched out in the grass and seemed to fall asleep.

The little boy still hadn't reacted to anything. He just lay there. Although there is no time on this side, it is clear that everything happened slowly and without haste. Every day the little boy was taken to the butterfly garden and each time the same spectacle repeated itself. He could see her playing and laughing with the butterflies and the dog.

One time he was lying in the butterfly garden, but the girl was nowhere to be seen. He started looking around, looking for the girl. There were some butterflies flying around where the girl was always sitting. They flew down on the flowers and the little boy followed them with his eyes. Then they started to play a game, right in front of him, and his eyes followed every movement. The dog appeared and lay down in the grass, in such a completely relaxed way as only dogs can. The little boy now consciously looked at the dog. Then he was taken back to the healing chamber.

Every day a few steps of long journey were made. When the girl reappeared, the little boy was visibly happy, although he remained silent. Another little boy came along, with a dark complexion, like the one he had had in his last life. Now he watched the children lay in the grass, playing with the dog. His eyes were now alert to all their movements and he began to look forward to the dance of the butterflies and the children playing.

One day little creatures of nature appeared that on Earth are called fairies. They belong to the realm of nature and used to occur in different areas on Earth when the light frequencies were still high. Stories about these natural beings are based on truth. In Ireland they were able to hold out the longest, but even there they haven't shown themselves for a long time. In the New Age, they will return and retake their rightful position on Earth.

In a butterfly garden like this, a place of healing, they fulfil an important function. The little boy watched with fascination as the two playing children raised their hands, after which the elves sat down on them. The butterflies frolicked around it. To me it looked like a picture from a fairy tale book. A few elves sat on the flowers around the two and one sat down on the dark curls of the boy. That day would be the turning point. The next time the boy was brought in, he sat down, looked out over the field and searched with his eyes for the creatures of nature. When they appeared, he got up and walked to the flowers they had sat on, the butterflies frolicking around him at a little distance. The girl came and, as usual, sat down in the grass and watched the spectacle. Then the other boy appeared with the dog and he too sat down.

From that moment on it all went fast. The boy sat down with the children, there was no talking, but together they enjoyed the play of the butterflies and the elves. Carefully he reached out his hand to the dog and stroked the soft, blond fur: a gesture without words, in complete freedom, without coercion from anyone.

Later I visited them once more, he was playing with four children on the lawn and I loved to see that they were children of different races; for such earthly characteristics remain here, until one incarnates again and possibly chooses a different race. I've seen him laughing and playing in the grass with the other children. The dog was always very close to him. Now I know how important these animals are to people. The dog had taken on this healing task on a soul level. The little boy was allowed to return to the butterfly garden as often as he wanted. In the meantime he lived with his grandparents in the children's sphere.

I have said before that here, people assume the age in which they feel best and these grandparents looked really young. They live in a spacious, beautiful, open house, made entirely of bamboo, with a large veranda around it and a roof of palm leaves. The house looks very exotic.

The little boy now plays with other children and the skin colour is of no importance at all. In the meantime his grandparents have taken in three other children, all of them child soldiers from Africa. After they had been in the healing chambers, they were accommodated in this spacious house. They all experienced the butterfly garden. The blond dog will stay with these children until they can continue on their way. They will continue their childhood in the children's sphere and then move on to the Light Sphere of their attunement or to a new incarnation. It means a long period of total tranquillity, a childhood in the familiar atmosphere of their homeland, with the people, the house and the objects that go with it. Only their parents cannot be there, they are still living in the third dimension in Africa.

I met the little girl from the butterfly garden once more after Ohan brought me to her. She actually was a young woman, a beautiful Light Being. A somewhat older version of the cute child I had seen playing in the lawn with the elves and the butterflies. Ohan told me that she has a strong connection with the Light Worlds and the natural worlds. It is her specific task to help to heal severely traumatized children. Like her, there are Light Beings who work with other forms of trauma, also with adults who arrive here. These places are located elsewhere in the spheres and have the right energy to bring about a certain healing. There are also butterfly gardens like this for adults. The female Light Being took the form of a little girl for her work with the children.

I could not take my eyes off of her, she radiated such love. Ohan told me that the other children I had seen were also such Light Beings, with the same tasks. Many severely damaged children are arriving, from countless countries. Fortunately, this is not the only butterfly garden available for children and there are many Light Beings who do their work there, with success and unending love.

7. Jonathan

Leviahnarah: After our call in the spiritual world, Jonathan approached us on behalf of a whole group of people. After his self-chosen departure from physical life and after reading his book of life, he was brought into contact with people who had had a similar history. His spiritual guide accompanied him during the first period of this contact. The Law of Attraction - like attracts like - plays a major role in these contacts. He learned from their history and they from his. They learn from each other's previous lives. Together they created energetic fields of insight and empirical knowledge, working in the earthly third dimension. This knowledge is used for the benefit of themselves and their own processes and for many of them in their work as guides. They form small collectives that focus on a complex problem, which for a large part leads to a function as a guide. This work is always done together with the personal guide of those they are trying to help.

Jonathan: To tell my story, I have to start with a previous life that, in Earth years, was a long time ago. Here in the spiritual world, however, we see the path of incarnations in its entirety. Our soul journey, our path of life after life, of stumbling and rising, of light and dark, sickness and healing, of positive and negative deeds.

Reading the book of life was great, no matter how hard and confronting it often was. At the end of this Earth cycle, I had to watch and feel everything of the past 26,000 years. Every part of the book of life passes us by, holographically, always in the presence of loving and empathic support from loved ones and guides. Later in my process I chose to allow others with a similar life history to look at my book of life, without restrictions. In this way a lot of learning material is exchanged about events that are 'real'. Never made prettier or more tragic. You see what *Is and Was* in all its purity.

I came to Earth 26,000 years ago with a whole group of souls. A new cycle began. Each soul came with several talents that were already developed, creating harmony in a world where darkness was already increasing. Neutralizing darkness was inherent in all our intentions and work. We were creative, sentient people, extremely loving. Our group came from the Pleiades to bring knowledge and inspiration that was intended to serve the development of souls on Earth. Seven Pleiadic peoples came to Earth with the same spiritual mission, each with their own uniqueness and talents. While reading my entire blueprint of life, the entire period of incarnations on Earth, it was wonderful to see the three periods of the Atlantic era. For many of us these were beautiful experiences. However, in the last period of Atlantis, more than ever before, Earth was flooded by darkness. One of the reasons we came here was to neutralize that darkness. Not to intervene, but to neutralize it. These creatures came from the empire of Anchara - an empire of darkness: Archons, Reptilians, Dracos, egocentric, self-serving, life and light stealing entities, greedy people, real evil. They became in many ways the parasites of the Earth, as they did in so many places in the universe. The stealing of light energy from humans; the robbing of the Earth's resources; enslaving humans, in many forms, letting others do the work for them.

In our spiritual collective we have studied these processes over and over again. We did this with other starseeds such as those of Sirius, Andromeda, Altair, Tau Ceti and Arcturus. In recent times we have reflected on our incarnations on Earth. It was the Great Evaluation of the last 26,000 years. We saw that there were different periods when the light prevailed and when the darkness reigned. A wave movement, that in this last part of this Earth cycle shows many escalations of accumulated darkness, not based on empathy and love. Everything that was so carefully hidden by those who served the darkness comes to light. For many who are now awakening this is a very emotional and shocking discovery, in spite of the fact that all the dark matters that are now becoming truly visible for the first time, were there for centuries. There is no need to elaborate on this, everyone can see and feel the effects of accumulated heavy negative baggage all over the world. Accumulated negative karma that for some people could only now be relived in this end time.

For myself, if I had made negative karma, which I attracted as energy in the next incarnation. It was an experience and lesson that my soul would never forget. Balancing energy with other people created wholeness. Each person could continue his or her life path in freedom. Where I came from in the Pleiades, there was no duality, no good and evil; the destructive that is common on Earth for so many people, we simply did not know about it. We did, however, experience it deeply in another place in the universe. Before we incarnated as souls on the

Pleiades, we experienced deep darkness when we lived in the Lyra System. There we lived in harmony, in farming communities, until the planet was conquered by beings that belonged to the empire of Anchara. They were obscure, dominant invaders; giant Reptilians captured us. Men and women were separated. They were after the resources of the mineral world and the light energy of the people who lived there. We became miners. Pain and suffering in all its forms were energetic nourishment for them. They loved sexual energy en thus we were abused, both men and women. They also forced us to be present at their sexual misconduct. They harvested the energy of fear we sent out under those circumstances. The energetic climax for them was eating an abused and completely exhausted human being. The body that was eaten was full of vibrations of fear and it was for those who ate these people, their necessary 'food'.

Many had to wear bracelets, high on the arm. Others wore collars. We were not allowed to speak and if we did, we were given an electric shock, which instilled even more fear. Sadists as they were, a 'slave' was occasionally sacrificed by administering a fatal electric shock and then eaten, creating another wave of fear energy. Whatever form these parasites took, they created misery, wars, fear, hunger and disease. The Light Beings that were held captive by them in all kinds of forms were their energy supply, their batteries. This is eloquently shown in the film 'The Matrix'.

Everywhere in the Milky Way they wreaked havoc, a process that was reversed several years ago. The Great Reversal is now underway. Whole areas have been freed, each at the end of its own cosmic cycle. All of this is happening on such an enormous scale that it is incomprehensible in Earth's 3D consciousness. In the spiritual world we are monitoring this process very closely. Every planet that has been liberated from the darkness, every freed area and freed system, is closely monitored here. The inhabitants may not always look like humans, but they are always light-bearing beings that through fear cultures in many forms serve as nourishment for those who lack light. Cycle after cycle is now coming to an end. The parasitic beings have to leave.

Procyon

According to earthly 'time', the people of the planet *Procyon* were liberated at the end of the 20th century from a very long period of darkness and slavery. These people are very similar to Earth humans. In a number of ways they experienced what we as a group of souls in the Lyra system have experienced. They rarely, if ever, saw the light of day. In their bondage, they ended up like livestock. Those who were selected for that purpose were herded to a form of factory, where they were processed into food for the various Reptilian peoples. That sounds awful and it was. Many will not be able or willing to picture it, but it is similar to what we do on Earth with animals in the meat industry. After all, animals are also spiritual beings, and if we could see the suffering that is inflicted on these, light-bearing creatures, we would stop it immediately. And we soon will in the New Age.

At the end of the 20th century, earthly time, the Procyon were freed from darkness, a heavy spiritual process. Now they are helping other peoples in their processes of liberation. We learn a lot from them and work with them in the Cities of Light. Their empirical knowledge is great with regard to processes as they take place on Earth.

So my own group of souls came from the Pleiades, where we also had a deep knowledge of parasitic creatures that lacked light. Having lived so many earthly lives and always wanted to see the very best in people, we did not always see through the appearances, the false light that was spread in so many different ways. In this age of great tribulation and of the wrongs that came to light in their individual lives, the souls who once incarnated from the Pleiades so long ago often longed for home. We are all light-bearing multidimensional beings, but we have forgotten who we are. Our inner light, our God Spark, was darkened by trauma in various incarnations. The material layer of the Earth, which we think is so real, is actually the least real of all the dimensions in which we live. It is the last dimension to reflect changes that we co-create with our Father-Mother-God in the Realms of Cause.

In my line of incarnations, I took on the task of loosening rigid beliefs in people. I was able to offer insights into what we could accomplish for the benefit of a society based on love and empathy. I was never a docile type, no matter when I incarnated. Feeling, thinking for myself, was an innate part of me. Whenever whole groups and crowds blindly followed what was taught to them as truth and necessity, I would 'see' the lies and false light being spread. Being able to 'see what is' clearly sometimes made me extremely lonely. It has led to my persecution in a number of lives: as a writer, as a teacher, as an organic farmer, as a doctor and as a politician in ancient Rome.

In my last incarnation I didn't recover from the many traumas I carried along in my soul; there were just too many of them. I became depressed, had very bad dreams. This made my functioning in daily life extremely difficult. Yet in the quiet, more positive periods I tried everything that was possible to seek healing. However, my encapsulation through trauma, which you could see as shadow layers over my earthly body, was great. A gifted healer and medium 'saw' the dark layers in my cellular consciousness of past lives. For a long time we worked on my process, for the better.

I always felt strong resistance to chemical medication, which is often prescribed at the diagnosis of 'depression'. Intuitively, therefore, I did not opt for that. Now I know that souls like me react badly to pharmaceutical drugs. I have been able to see and study a lot about this in the spiritual world and how it is very harmful for such souls.

One day a certain event was triggered in me: an old trauma that had never been processed and healed. I was at a place where a fire broke out. There was a lot of burning wood and that gives smoke a very special smell. That combination of flames and smell brought all kinds of hidden memories to the surface. Everyone was taken to hospital by ambulance, myself included. My burns were taken care of. They turned out not to be serious physically, but mentally something inside me went completely wrong. In the weeks that I was hospitalized I kept dreaming about the flames while I 'saw' a howling crowd. I saw myself standing on the stake. Then, in the hospital where I was recovering from my burns, I was given antidepressants. In no time, I was heavily addicted to these substances. One drug followed after another. I don't think the doctors themselves knew what a devastation the medication caused in me: it changed me completely, I was aware of that.

Stopping the heavy medication was strongly discouraged by my doctors. I was told over and over again that I needed them. The doctors were convinced that what they were doing was right. They strongly believed in it themselves, I now know. These doctors, modern medicine men, were in no way open to my strong desire to stop with what was completely destroying my body and mind at the same time. The desire to end my life became very strong due to the medication; something that had never happened before, not even when I had such terrible nightmares. I loved life and wanted to do as much as I could in this special time. That desire to die became an obsession at a certain point, as if there was no other way possible. I longed to return to my open-mindedness and clarity of thinking. I felt nostalgia as I looked at my childhood photos and those from my college years. With these photos I tried to regain the positive things I had lost. I wrote a letter to my father and a letter to my brother telling them that I couldn't go on like this. I still had some kind of communication with them, I though they would understand me.

With a body full of medication and after drinking a bottle of vodka, I stepped into the ice-cold water in the middle of winter. With so much alcohol and pills in my body it all went fast. My sister collected me together with my mother, who had both been in the spiritual world for some time. I went to a healing chamber where I was lovingly cared for by my loved ones. Their love was healing, nowhere was there any judgment on what I had done. That period in the healing chamber was important. After that I began the process of reading my book of life or blueprint, as everyone now does after they have transitioned to the spiritual world. I saw all the persecutions I had experienced but also all the good and beautiful changes in consciousness I created by being involved with this in many lives. Waves of consciousness by writing books in certain lives and by other forms I had chosen. From my soul frequency I could not help but live my passion.

In the collective of souls where I now feel at home I work as a guide, healer and teacher. Here we work closely together with many doctors and therapists, who are still on Earth in their physical bodies and who visit us here in their light body. Each of us is fully aware of the physical and mental damage caused by certain medications that are administered on a massive scale worldwide. Together we seek and find solutions. We search for alternative ways for people on Earth and we do that in the many Cities of Light, in other dimensions. Prescription drugs seriously contaminate many very sensitive people. For starseeds, chemical, non-natural drugs are very bad. It keeps them in a state of low vibration that prevents them from performing the tasks intended in their blueprints of life. This has slowed down the global awakening process. It should not come as a surprise that their use has been advocated for decades.

The collectives of guides who deal with these sensitive people give gentle nudges that can lead to change. Thus we see people, of all ages, looking for methods of detoxification; looking for food that is as pure as possible. In their search we see that what they send out they also attract. *"Seek and ye shall find,"* is a cosmic law. It gives the spiritual guides at such a moment more opportunities to offer solutions. As guides we should never force, only give gentle nudges which more and more people experience as help. Free will is always respected.

In the study of the collectives, such as the one in which I work, we see changes. There are more and more people looking for pure forms of living and finding them: the Law of Attraction works. Social media are instrumental to this. More and more people who choose not to eat meat anymore, for example, and who are also aware of why they no longer want to do so. They are appalled by the massive consumption of meat and the awful way in which animals are treated. Every day masses of people eat food that is filled with vibrations of anxiety from what is happening at the slaughterhouses. Apart from hormones and antibiotics, used on a large scale in meat production, these vibrations keep us all in a low frequency. There are many sensitive people who can't even walk past the meat department of a supermarket without feeling unpleasant. Small children who start crying there, because of the energy they feel and can often even see.

In the spiritual world we see the hundredth-monkey effect on many levels. That is the explanation for the greatly increased need for pure food and clean water, for example. The detoxification of all chemical substances in our bodies: additives in food, water and air, pollution and medication. We see and experience that what is created in the different dimensions of the Immaterial Realms of Light will manifest itself in the 3D Earth, in the material world. We see the subtle creations of people in the Realms of Light come to manifestation on Earth. A mass awakening is underway: an increasing awareness of awakened people who see through everything that is not based on love and empathy. Everywhere on Earth we see waves of awakening in all walks of life. The awakened, the conscious people, are attracting so many positive things, again due to the Law of Attraction.

Despite opposition from the old, the consciousness that is not built on love and empathy, this process cannot be stopped. Huge waves of light now reach Earth from the universe, which sometimes causes a dramatic change of old negative consciousness. Under the influence of these waves of light, the DNA of mankind also changes rapidly. In the Realms of Light we see mankind with all its twelve strands. In 3D, where we only have two strands, we see things changing. We regain what was once stolen from us. It kept humanity in a certain captivity that has now ended. Many children have already come with multiple strands of DNA. They're a promise. As the process in which Earth now finds itself evolves, the mechanisms created to stop this process of awakening, of the development of full human consciousness, will disappear. The ancient parasitic, dark, Archontic energy is completely in the light and is crumbling away.

The people of Procyon who assist us in different dimensions serve for many of us as a shining example of how we can and will transcend mental and physical limitations. As humanity, we will get our strength back. For example, only a small percentage of people on Earth are fully aware of the power of thought. We see the powerful fields of positive energy that people create together. The number of people who create this in so many different ways is increasing in waves. For example, initiatives to form circles in which people share goods with each other, put positivity in the field. Within these circles we see a feeling of 'enough is enough' arising. Willingness to share and exchange knowledge, goods and services, creates a positive field that is already permanent at the moment. These fields grow by leaps and bounds, which is visible and measurable in the spiritual world.

Showing global news reports in the media of all the positive energy that is now building up, instead of emphasizing reports of wars, disasters, terror and personal suffering, hour after hour, day after day, would bring about major changes. Many people think that negativity is normal. The images of the divide-and-rule techniques in wars, political circles, films and series with a lot of bloodshed and violence, it is and remains incomprehensible to us in the spiritual world that people can enjoy these miscreations so much, every minute of the day. It lowers the frequency and keeps people rooted in third density. We know that an increasing number of people watch less or no TV or movies anymore. We see that many are focusing more and more on the listening to and playing of music. Being more focused on art and artistic expressions, taking creative hobbies and wanting to enjoy nature. We can only stimulate this because it is increasing the frequency.

8. Ronald

Leviahnarah: Ronald told us his incarnation history as part of this book: a history of repetitions that runs like a thread through his various incarnations.

Ronald: In many of the incarnations I can now look back on, I was a positive person who was able to develop a different aspect in each incarnation. Trading goods was my life. I have had many beautiful positive experiences and developments. As an example I would like to mention the trade in spices in Asia. Spices were my passion and it was nice to see how this trade flourished. A long time ago, in China, I was engaged in high quality fabrics in three consecutive lives. I have been involved in a lot of merchandise. Anyway, in many lives I was a wealthy man, sometimes also a hardworking street trader, but I always worked with great pleasure. There was always enough. Sometimes I travelled with caravans.

In an incarnation in the Middle East, however, I came into contact with a negative energy. I now know that it was an extremely dark loveless energy. It all started innocently with arranging and transporting people from one area to another. Just a job at first. My talents were highly praised; caravanning people from one place to another under my protection. It went gradual; being sucked into that dark energy. Inconspicuous, because before I had actually realised it myself, I had ended up in human trafficking, unaware of what was going on. I was encapsulated energetically, spun into it. Only much later, when I had fallen deep into the human and child trafficking, did I see what I had been involved in. Pedophile networks are not new, as many people now think, because so much comes to light in this day and age. Unfortunately, it is all already many thousands of years old. They are deeply ingrained tracks in certain elitist circles; among others in the ancient Draco and Annunaki bloodlines. For years I worked in human trafficking, male slaves, women and children. It became quite common. I didn't think about what happened to these people. I delivered my 'merchandise' and made my living.

I traversed the entire Middle East. Until one day, after I had a road accident, my veil disappeared. This event made me realize with a shock what I was working on. Especially the trade in children for elitist pedophile networks shocked me deeply. It was as if a dark veil tore open. At that moment I could no longer live with my past in this trade. In a short time I developed great self-hatred. I blamed myself for my blindness, and for my looking away from what was happening right under my nose. After waking up from my concealment, several attempts were made to blackmail me. What happened then can hardly be described.

To contemplate on my life and find inner peace I went to a place I loved very much. Looking out over the landscape I decided to end my life. I could not and would not go on. I threw myself off the cliff and died instantly. I was 'collected' by a lady in blue and a tall thin man who I immediately recognized as my grandfather. Both looked young. I experienced this part consciously, the rest unconsciously. I 'woke up' in a healing chamber. Thinking that there was nothing after death, it was quite a surprise that there is still 'life': subtle life in a spiritual world. The chamber in which I awoke was the kind of 'nothing' I had longed for; the thought that everything would stop. The woman in blue turned out to be my mother who had been in the Beyond for a long time, not long after I was born. As soon as I woke up and thought of the woman in blue, she immediately appeared. There was no judgment on my self-chosen death: as always, help was offered by Light Beings.

I began reading my book of life. Reading is the 'seeing' and 'feeling' your own way through life; your talents and the use of them, both positive and negative. You feel the pain you inflicted on others. It makes a lot of difference whether you deliberately hurt another person, and enjoying it, or totally unconsciously. There is still no judgment. It is the hour of truth for you when you read your book of life. It can be an extremely painful and confronting process.

I saw very clearly how I was sucked into the darkness with all my talents and how that had happened to so many people. Then a situation develops that we consider to be 'normal' over time. I moved on. I was assisted in every possible way during that process. In a next phase I decided to make up for what I had done wrong in my own eyes. This is how I incarnated in Africa. There, all sorts of things passed me by that I had unconsciously experienced in the Middle East for so long and had only understood much later. My commercial spirit developed again and before I knew it, I was encapsulated again. Those who served the darkness 'saw' my talents, and all my old undissolved issues, linked to those former lives. Although I was a trader, I actually became the slave of that negative energy through that work itself. The slave trade was very cruel and caused great suffering. It was that energy of suffering that fed the darkness and those who were attuned to it. Simply put, in these places, everywhere on Earth, nourishment for the darkness was created. In many places blood sacrifices and cannibalism took place, which I have witnessed: dark energy. Self-hatred flared up in me again and I ended my life again. The same thing happened as the first time.

Then I incarnated in Africa as a slave and was shipped to America. Experiencing what one did to others creates a conscious knowing: a soul never forgets that. In the eyes of the slave owners, I was a rebellious man. After a public beating I had infected wounds on my back and legs and became very sick. Somehow I knew I could heal: our people brought so much wisdom from authentic herbal medicine. However, I didn't want to fight for my life, because I intuitively did not want to go any further. I let myself slip into the fever caused by the infected wounds.

In my next life I was the child of a plantation owner in South America. In that life I improved the living conditions of the slaves as much as possible: better food and living conditions. They got small houses and a place that could be used for group activities. That became a little church. In that life I became an old man who supervised the living conditions of the slaves with an iron hand, in such a way that it became normal for my descendants. Each of our family group was balancing old karmic baggage. We also formed a small collective in the awareness that things had to be done differently. Only much later slavery was abolished.

After this, there have been three lives in which I have been tested with respect to my talents in relation to old karmic baggage. Again and again that old piece of self-hatred emerged. Sometimes it was difficult to do 'good', to treat people with dignity. Those were triggers to previous experiences that brought that feeling to the surface. It was mostly unconscious. In one of those three lives I lived as a monk in a large monastery in Italy. That's where I once again encountered the awful situation of pedophilia and trauma-based soul splitting, soul theft. This was done to children who had been given to the monastery. People gave unwanted children to the church anonymously; a small barred window in the wall of monastery where people could deposit their infants. These things have actually been going on for centuries. Fortunately, things like this surface all over the world. Nothing can remain hidden under the increasing cosmic Light that is now flowing to Earth.

The care of severely damaged children was entrusted to me; I was but a simple monk. Negative loveless things come to light on a large scale in this time of change and reversal. However, in that period, centuries ago, that was not possible. It was as if you lived in a separate world in which these things took place. They were reservoirs of the energy of suffering, food for the darkness. Those reservoirs were always full, overflowing even. Self-hatred jumped on me, just out of nowhere it seemed. I jumped off a cliff again at a time when I couldn't go any further.

Does suicide solve anything?

Everything that concerns karmic luggage is never solved by suicide. That which needs solution and balance simply remains. Often, suicide creates new karmic baggage because the people who are left behind are confronted with all kinds of negative consequences. Many relatives are in shock, as are those who find people who have chosen to kill themselves. Think of people who jump off a building or in front of a train, or those who kill themselves with explosive weapons. In such processes there are people who have to take care of the often horribly mutilated corpse. These people also receive help from the spiritual world. This is often done by souls who during their earthly mortal life were doctors, nurses or other professionals in healthcare.

My life now

In total, I've ended my life five times myself. History always repeated itself. I got new tests and trials in subsequent lives, but the urge to end it myself, fortunately, disappeared. In my last incarnation I was a general practitioner, a man with great care and attention for his patients. In that life, the care of a family doctor was still very much old school, hands-on work. I was concerned with the care of the soul rather than with medicine. In that life I was able to balance a lot.

In the spiritual world, where I have been for quite some time now, I welcome people who put an end to their lives for whatever reason. Of course, in addition to everything I learned in the spiritual world, I am at the same time an expert by experience. Everyone who chooses suicide is lovingly welcomed, cared for and guided further along ones path. I chose to work here in the spiritual world because the number of suicides is greater than ever in earthly times. In the spiritual world we see the energetic damage of stress, drug use, alcohol and medicine. Because of the many forms of medication given to people with depressions, we see this as the main cause of suicide: every person with his or her own complex history. It is important to realize that the influence of such chemicals is taken into your subtle body. It can take a long time before this is purified. The misery is that addictions are taken to the next incarnation, in which a person finds new bumps and potholes on his way. Even moments of small triggers can persuade people to give in to those addictions again, in spite of the good intentions set out in the new blueprint of that life. These people need to be strong, sometimes unimaginably strong, to resist old patterns of addictions.

There are groups of souls who want to help others stay clean on Earth after their own suicide. When they enter the Spheres of Light of the spiritual world they can get any kind of training they want, in order to be able to help people on Earth as a guide. Because so many people choose suicide because of alcohol and drug addiction, we see a strong increase in such help from the spiritual realms to those on Earth who need and want to accept this help.

Recently we saw a woman who died of a brain tumour and the usually in large quantities administered chemotherapy. She chose to help her loved ones on Earth, wanting to assist them in their processes. Because it is pure love energy and people can have very strong love bonds and friendships, we see rapid changes in people on Earth who accept this help. While she was regularly in the vicinity of a dear friend, we saw that in a few weeks time he was able to stop smoking. He also stopped taking drugs and reduced his drinking. Unconsciously he felt her loving presence. Every time he wanted to grab something, he intuitively looked at her portrait. He also dreamed of her, at least that's what he thought. In reality he was with her in the spirit, in what we call Summerland. That is a Light Sphere where material people can meet deceased loved ones in their light bodies and where people can make plans together, for example, to get rid of addictions in the physical body. It seems impossible to many people in 3D reality, but it happens. People usually don't tell about such experiences.

The groups of helping guides, who themselves are experienced experts in whatever field and are now in the Light Spheres, are steadily growing. Something you have little or no insight into in earthly 3D life, becomes crystal clear in the spiritual world. Of course this is very confronting in the beginning, and often painful: knowledge that works to balance old negative energy. For next of kin it is important to know that their departed loved ones are lovingly cared for.

We cannot pass on words of comfort even if we would like to. However, we can offer insight into how processes can take place. One of the ways this happens is through the meetings in Summerland. Knowing that it is going well with your loved one is an important and healing thought. Listen also to the many young children who can see people in their light bodies and are passing on a message to family members. Children who can tell what their departed family members now look like. In the spiritual world the physical damage is no longer there. The light body is whole. Someone who misses a physical leg, for example, will have two of them again in the spiritual world, who is blind and deaf on Earth, can see and hear in the spiritual world. This knowledge has been passed down in many old books and it is important to do this again.

There are people who at some point during their mourning process have an inner feeling and knowing that their loved ones are doing well. Personal guides of people will always help. Only those people who rigidly cling to, often religiously inspired beliefs of hell and purgatory, are very difficult to be reached.

9. Peter

Collective healing

Leviahnarah: In recent years, large groups of people have awakened. In the physical three-dimensional reality so much is happening as a result of which old energy, which no longer serves us, can be transformed. As the old dark forces become visible and people turn more and more towards the Light in their growth processes, we see increasing and visible chaos on Earth. This seems extremely disturbing, but it is not. Everything that is not of the Light, and which was able to hide itself for centuries, becomes visible. The energy of purification through the white-golden ray is affecting more and more people. Nothing can remain hidden. From the Galactic Centre, Light Forces are working to places of darkness, including this solar system and our once beautiful Earth. You would almost forget, but our Earth was and will be a fantastic and beautiful planet again. Light Forces, including the Silver Legion, belong to the Galactic Federation of Light Peoples. This federation offers many kinds of help for the liberation of darkened areas.

Many starseeds on Earth have received help from these Light Forces through the ages. In the Light Spheres - the dimensions of Light and Love - and the Cities of Light to which people are attuned, all kinds of groups have been forming for quite some time now. These may include specialists who were starseeds, who have been able to secure souls throughout the Earth's 26,000-year cycle. These people often went into very dark places to neutralize dark unloving energy. They prevented the stealing of Light Souls by beings of darkness. These souls were robbed by those in whom Light is lacking. Thousands of Light Souls also did this work in between lives. Now, since 2011, a Field of Unity has been created, collaboration between the starseeds and our extraterrestrial family, with which more and more people in the Cities of Light were able to make contact. It is a great coming home to each other. They can directly approach the starseeds in the physical domain. In the Cities of Light where people in their light bodies can go to, areas have been set up for this cooperation. It is everyone's own free choice to join these networks.

One of the peoples that work very closely together with the people of Earth are the aforementioned people of Procyon. They have been freed from the darkness in the course of our earthly nineties. They are eight different peoples, all fully liberated by now, who have been working together with each other and with us for several years now. They share their technical and empirical knowledge with us.

The people from Procyon look a lot like Earth humans and many (earthly) clairvoyants perceive them as helping, guiding beings in the work they do on Earth in 3D. This help and guidance, together with their own guides, has brought about many positive changes. For example, various collaborations with the extraterrestrial family have come into being. When we wish, they help us to stand in our strength, strength that was often lost during our earthly lives. This, in turn, is closely linked to the important work of finding and bringing back stolen souls and soul fragments.

It is the people from Procyon, the Sirians, Pleiadians, Tau Ceti, Andromedans, Arcturians and many others who, from the Galactic Federation, who have collaborated vigorously with Earth specialists and scientists, and together have developed programmes that have been used intensively since 2011. Often it was one step forward and two steps back. Indeed, it is very difficult to work in a world where a heavy, low frequency prevails. For people and beings with a high vibration of Light it is as if you are wading through the mud and your feet can hardly move forward. However, the perseverance of the Earthlings is great: their inner knowing of a global liberation from that low frequency as well. The great awakening continues, step by step.

The Reptilians of Alpha Draconis, the Hydra constellations, the Greys, renegades of Zeta Reticuli and other parasites, have largely been removed. They are negative malignant, egocentric, self-serving, life-depleting entities. The last phase in the space war was at the end of January 2011. In the course of the following years, the Earth has been cleansed of them, layer after layer, by among others, the Silver Legion. An immense quarantine area was created at the 'edge' of this universe where these entities were taken.

Tens of thousands of life forms, hybrid crossbreeds of the Greys and humans, specially bred and programmed from birth to serve the dark, have been removed from Earth. In the dimension in which they have been captured they have been reprogrammed so that they can evaluate themselves and their actions with their own free will. Through the quarantine area, they will flow to a 3D planet of their own. Dark forces previously destroyed such places. It is also a karmic process of reversal. Stripped of their 'programs' to serve the darkness, they create their own society in a beautiful energy.

After 11-11-11, we saw the hybrids living on Earth and their associates weaken. They were usually very arrogant prideful creatures, unable to accept the ongoing reversal. Their inner conviction that they are right and cannot possibly lose is a huge pitfall: narcissists with psychopathic character structures, who were often implanted with a certain technology to 'enhance' themselves. The knowledge of for example the Procyon, to weaken and increasingly disable inserted chips, immediately made them weak. This technology was developed together with Earth's scientists, people who, unfortunately, often left the material life prematurely in a certain period of time. Those among them who were, as they say, 'suicided' - i.e. murdered but of whom they suggest that they have taken their own lives - are lovingly welcomed and cared for. Most of them join this important work, no longer in the physical 3D world but now from the spiritual world. They support their colleagues living and working on Earth through which powerful fields of light, invisible to the darkness, have been created. They energetically transmit the unity in diversity that they experience in the spiritual, subtle world to those who are open to it.

Anyone with the spiritual attunement to the Light travels at night to the Light Sphere of his or her attunement and/or to the different Cities of Light. Here spaces have been created that serve especially for coming together in oneness. The Hall of Oneness is a place where one connects to the Source, the One or whatever one calls it according to one's own conviction or feeling and experience. People increasingly feel the need to connect vertically with the Light, a feeling that has been taken from the nocturnal astral visits to a Hall of Oneness.

Peter: The coming together of small and large groups of people in the Light Spheres and Cities of Light is a development that developed rapidly. I was attracted to one of the groups of which Leviahnarah is also a part. Longing for wholeness and harmony in a higher frequency, we humans seek opportunities for collective healing. I am fully aware that we are living at the end of a cosmic cycle, and that there is a need for a great purification of our soul after that 26,000-year journey. We are all working on it in this end time on our way to a new beginning.

My desire to process and purify my earthly baggage was great in my last physical life. Coincidence does not exist, but in one of my final years I read Thea's book, '*The Cycle of Life and Death*'. My contribution to this book is not by accident; I knew her in several incarnations. Among others in different eras in Egypt, Atlantis, the Celtic period and with the Cathars in France. Later, we were connected by the spiritual work we did together with many during the Second World War. That was above the prisons and concentration camps of the Nazis. There we tunnelled with a group of about a hundred people in our light bodies in which we brought souls to the healing chambers. Concentrations of starseeds, using light energy together, preventing souls from being stolen. We prevented these traumatized souls from being harvested in areas of great human suffering. The energy of suffering, including the vibrations of fear, was nourishment for the darkness. It was a collaboration of the Realms of Light with many people in their light bodies.

With the group to which I belonged I also worked for a short time above the Normandy coast where a terrible drama took place on D-Day. Drugged, mainly very young men, boys in fact, who stormed the European coast and made the transition en masse. Just like the boys and men they fought against. In our tunnel work we picked them up from both sides. Everyone was convinced in that war of the good work they were doing, but they were all unconsciously part of the terrible and deliberately created theatre that fed the darkness in enormous quantities. There on that beach and in the dunes they were all physically and mentally traumatized. Fortunately, they could all be taken to the healing chambers. Through the work of many groups of Light like ours, souls have been prevented from being stolen by darkness in different eras.

After I felt attracted to a certain group of souls, all were starseeds, the meaning of it unfolded. In my last incarnation, I was a doctor. I had been a doctor many times in my long line of incarnations. After working many lifetimes as a natural doctor, I now became a man trained as a modern physician. This had a purpose: to get to know the rapidly developing pharmaceutical world from the inside out. But in the end my intention proved very difficult. In all my previous incarnations, natural medicine, in all its beautiful forms, was connected with divine nature to help man and beast. Life after life I gained knowledge and was able to bring it to a higher level and frequency. With my whole being I helped people in need, based on natural medicine. It was all so self-evident. In ancient times I still knew that I came from Andromeda. Later that awareness disappeared as the energy on Earth began to become more and more dense. Now that I am in the Spheres of Light, after that turbulent life as a modern physician, I am fully aware of that lineage again.

The group I was attracted to during my last life, were all souls who had come as starseeds and we all had the memory of our origins from the stars. Each of us had our own contract in this earthly cycle. One of our self-chosen assignments was to help neutralize the dark energy on Earth; energy that was spreading in this solar system. We were not allowed to intervene according to the Cosmic Law of Free Will that existed on Earth.

Starseeds came to Earth in many thousands after each of us felt a telepathic call that resonated with our being. In the book 'The End of the Circle', it is described how that went for souls of the Pleiades. The Starseeds from Andromeda also experienced such a cosmic call in their worlds. Also in the last decades many new starseeds came to create, anchor and hold an increased frequency in the end time of this earthly cycle and period of reversal. We are on our way to a society in a high frequency, loving, human, full of compassion, living on a clean Earth. In this age of reversal we see an almost unimaginable chaos of the darkness, which is visible to everyone who can but above all wants to see it. Much of that darkness floats to the surface: the enormous pedophile networks, the big lies in politics, the manipulations, the dark intentions of the pharmaceutical world and the world food supply, the poisoning of the environment by chemtrails and agriculture, the private creation of money, etcetera. The list is unbearably long.

In this age of the Great Awakening, it is hard for many to deal with what comes to light. The enormous lies in all parts of society; the divide-and-rule that has been going on for centuries and centuries, it all become visible in the incoming Light from the heart of the Galactic centre. People now see the lies that were actually there for so long, but that were carefully covered up with beautiful words and appearances. Much of what appeared to be light, was in fact deep darkness behind a often brilliant façade.

In one of the spheres I witnessed the effects of false light. Like sheep, a group of several thousand people followed a man. They worshipped him and believed everything he told them: sincere people seeking light and truth. When one day his mask fell and more and more people looked through his carefully constructed exterior it gave them a collective shock. It caused enormous traumas. Fortunately, everyone could be healed in collective processes in the spheres. People, who felt attracted to certain groups in the spheres, were staying there during their sleeping hours. These are often collective processes, experienced by a whole group of souls, and often in different incarnations. Such processes of collective elaboration and healing belong to this end time. A lot of help is available from the Light Forces. Following false light is never condemned in the spiritual world, which many people think when they wake up. If we see in the spheres, how ingeniously that false light was built up in these places and how it served the darkness, then a collective understanding arises. See What Is Without Judgment. The moment people see through the false light, both personally and collectively, its force diminishes significantly, before it vanishes completely.

In my last life as a doctor, with sadness I saw how false light in the medical world developed. A pharmaceutical idol came into being and sick people became more and more a means to earn unimaginable amounts of money, while at the same time keeping the frequency of those people at an absolute low level. Where beautiful developments did good work in the beginning, it was immediately taken over by darkness serving forces, degrading the positive changes in the field of healthcare.

But isn't that the way it always went? In all layers of society we see aspects that were positive, healing and friendly in origin and which were gradually turned into inhumane systems. It is well known that darkness in all its forms feeds on suffering, drama, war, pain, sorrow, poverty, injury, hunger and misery. The most miraculous thing is that in the groups I visited it was always said, again and again, that we have become so used to it. Now that all this is unmasked and people are learning to see the true causes of misery, fields of consciousness are emerging. Darkness serving people are weakening noticeably. This process of collective awareness is lovingly supported in the Spheres of Light and the Cities of Light. It is like an old festering wound being healed: the dirt can be drained away and the old can be transformed. These collective healing processes are supported by a powerful foundation of people of light on Earth. The carrier field is measurable and becomes noticeably stronger. In the Spheres of Light and the Cities of Light, we can track all of this as light energy.

In a previous incarnation I worked as a doctor with seriously ill people. The art of medicine of natural remedies and treatments, love - the positive universal life energy - was a popular topic of conversation for a small group of doctors and herbalists. We supported each other and exchanged experiences. Each of us was a descendant of Cathars, aware of the immense lies of the ruling church with its dogmas, its false light and soul theft through the ages. On a soul level we had known each other for a long time and we were able to do healing work for a number of generations. As a group we chose to incarnate once more in order to be able to do our healing work, but this time in silence. The secrets of the spiritual world, its loving help and presence, remained within our group. Only a few of the people who needed our help were aware of this. After all, many people were completely trapped in the carefully constructed web of power and control of the ruling church and its servants.

We saw, in addition to an all-pervading, deeply felt fear, a lot of unnecessary suffering around us during processes of illness. We also saw how the servants of the church especially wanted this suffering to continue. Young and old, educated in the dogmas of hell and purgatory, were trapped in an inescapable web of fear. In our daily vertical connection with the Source and the spiritual world, we were assisted to do our work, together with loved ones who preceded us and continued their work as guides in the spiritual world. During those periods I was completely clairaudient, in the development of which I was guided by one of the wise women in our group. Thus moments came when we could help people to let go of material life, at the right moment for the souls. This can still be done with help from the plant world, such as blossom remedies. Every human being who in those periods of earthly life could go to the Beyond without extreme fear, was a victory.

From the spiritual world I have worked with many others to save souls from great suffering during consciously created blood sacrifices, like the American Civil War, both World Wars and so many other unnecessary wars. We never did this work alone, but always with others in carefully formed groups, together with people who worked in the physical world as doctors or nurses, intuitively or consciously knowing.

Reservoirs of suffering

The darkness has, in all its forms, scattered throughout the Earth, created repositories of great suffering through an unimaginable bloodshed in wars and genocide, during the entire 26,000-year Earth cycle. Reservoirs of suffering, with the low energy of insufferable misery, have been created in many places on Earth, resulting in an enormous lowering of the total Earth frequency. Technologies are available in the Cities of Light to make images holographically visible so that they can be 'viewed' by millions of people in this time of reversal. There you can see, energetically, how and where this beautiful planet was put and kept in a low frequency by, among other things, enormous bloodshed. This low vibration is the precise attunement in which the darkness, in all its different forms, can maintain itself. Here we see why in our world history one drama follows another tragedy and what the consequences are. This is also the reason why darkness does not care about the large-scale pollution of the planet. It fits its low frequency.

Many converge in the Cities of Light. In the great process of awakening in the incoming light, there is a lot of help from the spiritual world. We are working on the earthly dogmas in all their various forms and of all times. Dogmas leading to the famous words 'that's just how it is', with as a result a world that has become so used to violence and suffering.

So after my transition I joined a group of people from the healthcare sector: doctors, nurses and therapists. In this group we are concerned with the care of people who have died in deep fear through by the imprinting of all kinds of dogmas. It doesn't matter where they lived; there are dogma's to be found all over the world, which is part of deeply, ingrained traditions about life and death. I find it particularly important to tell you that in this place in the Spheres of Light people come together with different faiths, religions, races, sexual preferences and ancient traditions. Here, if people want to, everyone can exchange experiences with one another.

After leaving the healing chambers in which people had gone through all kinds of healing processes, it turned out that many people had gotten completely different insights. It is often very shocking when in that process they discover that on Earth people have been set up against each other in so many different ways. They feel cheated.

Thea: I came to visit a friend in the hospital who had had surgery. After I had been with her for a while I went to the hallway, looking for some more magazines. I saw an old lady standing outside another room. I walked in her direction and she said to me: "Oh it's not you, your footsteps sound different." I asked what she meant and she told me that she waited for her brother in the corridor every day; that she could hear from the footsteps that it was he. She turned out to be blind. We got into a conversation and she asked me why I was in the hospital. I told her about my friend. She walked back into her room and kept talking. When I asked her why she was in the hospital, I didn't get an answer. I respected that. I wanted to excuse myself and walk away but she said: "The Lord makes me wait until he thinks it's my time." I asked what she meant by that and she said she had to carry on with her life even though it was often difficult. She had had a child but it had died and also her husband was no longer there. I said I felt sorry for her. "That's life, that's what I have to bear," she said and asked if I was religious. I said I was. "What church do you go to then?" she asked. I said I believed without going to church. She'd never heard of that, surely that's not possible? I said: "Do you have support from the church?" She replied: "You have to do what you're told, first by your parents and later by the church. What the Bible says, that's how you have to live."

I said: "And if something bad happens, do you feel supported? When your child died?" She said: "If something bad happens, it's my own fault." She sounded like a little girl now. She was sitting in a chair by the window and fiddled with her hands on her dress. I said that I think differently. That the idea is that others should comfort and support you and that you should enjoy life. No, she's very firm and stands up: "It's not like that. You live your life because you have no other choice. You suffer everything that happens to you, you don't complain, you don't seek support." I'm asking if she thinks she'll see her child and husband again, after her own death. "No, I don't think it'll be very nice. I haven't always done everything right. In that case nice things don't happen."

I said I couldn't imagine she'd done things so bad she'll be punished for it. She says it's because I don't live according to the Bible. I notice that she is getting restless and wants to go back to the hallway to wait for her brother. I say I enjoyed talking to her and that I don't think she needs to be afraid. She reached out her hand and I take it. We say goodbye to each other. I walk back to my friend's room.

10. Lord Kumeka

The healing chambers

Leviahnarah: Healing chambers are special spaces that have been created to work on processing past lives in groups, in optimal conditions. There are beautiful healing chambers to purify the old. Lord Kumeka, whose name is mentioned several times in this book, uses large groups of helpers for this work; without exception all masters from different hierarchies. The help from the Realms of Light for the total purification of all negative vibrations on Earth is dealt with on a very large scale in this end time, at the end of a cycle.

Margaret: I was a guest of a special group of people. They found each other while working in and around the hospitals, here in the spiritual world. Here we call these places *'healing chambers'*. In many spheres there are healing chambers, each with a specific attunement and purpose. Some are especially created for small babies and children. People work there who are qualified for that specific kind of work, people that usually were nurses or doctors on Earth. They often chose to work there after they have arrived here, after which they get a very specific training. In a particular section of the Hall of Wisdom, a campus of schools and universities in every Sphere of Light, people who truly desire can receive a specific education. Studying here is so different from studying on Earth. The knowledge you wish to acquire is to a large extent already present in your soul being. That is why people have chosen it in the first place. There are classes together with groups of like-minded people, but there are also ways of studying individually that I can best describe as a kind of 'radiation education', 'vibrational' or 'light education'. Such education can take place in spaces where in shielded areas there are small holographic screens, where knowledge simply flows in via a kind of headphones. There is also a kind of 'home education', where you sit in a comfortable chair and let the knowledge you are looking for flow in. A prerequisite for study in these ways is a complete and sincere interest in the subject. Without that, such a study would be pointless. This is not really different on Earth, although there is a lot of coercion within education and people have to process a lot of unnecessary information. This often goes hand in hand with enormous demotivation among young people. It is literally a waste of time. Here, the subject of study is always a reflection of what has already been developed in the soul.

In several previous lives I have been a nurse myself and although that was a long time ago, there is a lot of empirical knowledge available. People here pursue an inner calling and choose that which suits them. Because of the cancer I had on Earth, I was in a special kind of healing chambers for some time. Those spaces are pleasant, light and airy, areas without windows, because in the healing chamber you go into a kind of state of sleep. Every person gets the colours and vibrations that are necessary for him or her. It is a beautiful sight to see a human being in such a deep tranquillity, surrounded and immerged by a certain colour. In the healing chambers for former cancer patients there is always a certain amount of gold present. I was in a chamber where the colours blue and green dominated, enhanced with white-golden particles. In other chambers I saw a warm golden haze that penetrated everything. The white-golden energy is from the eighth ray of purification.

Lord Kumeka

The Chohan (or administrator) of the Eighth Ray of Purification is Master Kumeka. In this period of the Earth, his Ray is highly effective in all healing chambers. Its white-golden energy gives a total cleansing of old aspects from all previous lives on Earth.

The process of humanity, now at the end of a 26,000-year cycle - a transitioning to a new cosmic era - is deeply connected to the work of Kumeka. It was not until the early 1990s that he was able to gain access to the Earth, when a certain amount of light had grown into the collective consciousness of humanity. Before that, it was not possible for him to work here. By the way, all other rays are connected in this great plan of purification. Kumeka is a brother of Jesus, but has never incarnated on Earth. He serves all people on Earth and in the spheres. People on Earth who perceive his light appearance - by directed meditation on his help - recognize him with their hearts. People who originally come from other places in the universe and whom we call star people or starseeds also recognize him. Through conscious meditations they soon come into contact with him. Clear-hearing and pure channelling people have already made contact with him many times. As a result, the starseeds wake up at a rapid pace and begin to remember their origins and their tasks on Earth. Kumeka shows these people the way in their purification processes and the channelled messages find their way to the people for whom those messages are intended.

The recognition of Kumeka was a revelation for me as well. I am coming from the stars as well; I am a Pleiadian soul by origin and from those lives I know him very well. What Jesus meant to us on Earth, Kumeka was to the Pleiadians a long time ago. On Lyra he first led them through hard times, until they ascended as a people to the worlds of the Pleiades, and later on the Pleiades he was their teacher.

I was deeply touched when I first met him. That was in the period after I had read my entire book of life and, even more than on Earth, became aware of my soul's origins. Seeing and understanding all this gave me an enormous inner peace. Kumeka knows the essence of all starseeds from their evolution. With the people of Earth evolution he now works in soul groups. Every human being who consciously chooses to ask for his help, becoming aware of his tasks to the Earth and its people, gets that help.

Rapid purification is the result. Also here in the spheres, people are searching for fast, effective ways to greater purification of all previous lives. There are special classrooms for that. Although every person now has to read his or her book of life after the transition, due to the new transitional laws, connecting to the white-golden energy of Kumeka - the ray of purification - is entirely voluntary. Fortunately, these classrooms are being expanded as a result of the great need for people to balance all their past lives now. More and more classrooms are being added. It is like a wave of deep longing to flow on the waves of light into the New Age. Never before so much work has been done on healing and purification as in this transition period to a New Age in which this Earth is going to become a World of Light. There is an atmosphere of hope and expectation in these places and that is highly contagious. These places have an enormous attraction to many. From these centres people will start working again with newly arrived people in the spheres.

Everyone focuses primarily on his or her own soul group. This creates waves of change in processes that at first were very difficult and laborious. There are so many people who are committed to the changes to the new era. I meet many starseeds who often work together with countless others from their own soul group. One of their tasks is to help them wake up to who they are, because many have been working on

Mother Earth for so long that they have forgotten their origins. Especially many people in Europe and Asia are still unaware of that background. In America, proportionally more people are aware of this soul-origin, there are also most of the channels that, connected with their Pleiadic companions and teachers, help people to awaken. They also write books that find their way all over the world. Many people spontaneously begin to remember this information. It is not yet socially accepted to talk about it, so these kinds of feelings often remain dormant in those people for a long time at first. In the world, about 4 to 5% of the souls come from the stars, the largest group of which has been returning here regularly since the beginning of the Atlantis period. That group has become physically trapped on Earth. They once came as teachers, parents, artists, builders, architects, doctors, healers and so on, with the intention of transferring knowledge in the broadest sense; to give new impulses in all parts of society. Because in many times 'renewal' was met with fear, many of these people were severely persecuted. Their good intentions were not always understood and people reacted with fear. Their often very open connection with the spiritual world of light - what people on Earth call 'the paranormal' - was very often condemned.

Truly special was my meeting with a group of people who turned out to belong to my own soul group. I was in a healing chamber, in a beautiful place in a landscape penetrated by a white-golden haze. People can go there who have come to realise who they are. First, however, you have to read your book of all lives on Earth. Some take a long time to do that. When the time comes to take the next step, you can certainly call that a milestone. At least it was for me: a real "coming home" although I already felt so at home. The feeling of recognition is extremely intense for some people. Just seeing the Light Beings of the Pleiades stirred up my whole being.

One of them was Ohan, who was my spiritual teacher for seven years. He taught me who I am and how to regain my old talents. I looked at that possibility with him on the holographic screens. Many people who are in such an open connection with the world of Light have all made their books of life available as teaching material, and so there are books of life by artists, doctors, musicians, administrators and so on. Ohan helps people who can see and hear him on Earth, which in turn allows them to pass on a lot of information to their fellow souls.

All of the starseeds who have incarnated here have now set up these systems in order to be able to receive each soul in an appropriate way and to show them the way: for each soul at his or her own pace. Once people are in balance with all of this – and the process of recognizing and remembering goes quickly at this level - then they go on again and become guides of souls of their group still living on Earth. This work is so specialized because the starseeds who chose to return after the great transition first need to balance all their earthly karma.

Others choose to work with the people of the Earth evolution. They will always be people with whom they were connected in one or more lives. Once the connection is healed, it is very touching to see how people were originally connected in love.

The beginning of our stay in Lemuria was so pleasant and fulfilling. It was all worth it, even though it was hard to be drawn so deeply into matter. Many of us descended into dark areas on Earth to help darkened souls rediscover their light. These lives were often hard. Ohan has shown us all, through his many teachings, how good the Pleiadians were and still are at this.

I now know that the young woman, who was able to show Bernard - who we will meet later in this book - the way to the light, has been doing this for an eternity. Bernard was an earthbound soul, wandering around in the cathedral. She had been practicing it in many lives and took it with her to Earth as deeply lived knowledge. Over the years she taught others, often quietly and in inconspicuous lives, how to show earthbound people the way to the light. More and more people from all soul groups are beginning to remember this knowledge, which everyone once possessed. A lot of forgotten knowledge is now coming back into the consciousness of mankind in leaps and bounds. It goes fast because also here the principle of the 'hundredth-monkey effect' is working.

It is time for the knowledge of all those peoples in the universe who incarnated on Earth to come out. The time is certainly right for it. Only a certain group of people, who have been reading everything on the topic for years, find these ideas normal. In the last twenty-five years many souls of many Light Peoples from all over the universe have incarnated on Earth. With the light they possess, they help Mother Earth in her birthing process towards the Light. These souls are focused on the Light, but live inconspicuous lives. It suffices that they 'plant' their light on Earth. Some, however, are teachers or writers with a certain task. In the New Age, new teachers will also come from the Light Worlds and everyone will be able to choose the teacher who fits his or her evolutionary path.

This was also the case in Lemurian and Atlantic times: people chose the learning system that best suited their own soul's path. People would incarnate in places on Earth where the specific teacher they had chosen on a soul level was located, such as Peru, ancient Mexico, Egypt or Palestine. Sometimes images in stone were made of their teachers from the universe, like the cosmic Maya's, also a Pleiadic people. Everybody knows that feeling of seeing a culture with which they feel connected, and which gives a warm feeling inside. Those earliest times were beautiful and nourishing, until dark forces brought darkness over the Earth. This is a world of duality and we all had to deal with it. With the transition to the New Earth in the fifth dimension, duality will also disappear.

Not everyone is ready for the Light World. Each soul has its own process of growth, at its own pace. We always talk about a whole group of souls. Because I think that it matters, I would like to reiterate that everyone is taken care of and no soul is ever lost. As mentioned before, those who still need the experience of duality can incarnate on another third dimensional world. That will be a planet that has almost collapsed through far-reaching wars and pollution and has been uninhabitable for a long time. It is now ready to receive its new population: a beautiful place, beautiful nature and a special animal kingdom. I have been able to see that other third dimensional world on the screens in a space above the Himalayas.

Those who once came from the stars as teachers, who have been stuck here for so long, work very consciously in the lower astral spheres to help souls in darkness to regain their light. They teach all those who feel the need to do this work, and many choose to do so because they are aware of its great importance. It is beautiful to see how all the souls here, once they have arrived in the higher Light Spheres, work together. The higher you rise in the Light, the more the differences that were present on Earth disappear. Here all the souls from the federations of Light Worlds work very closely together. All those nuances that are visible here are no problem at all. The Earth alone has such a variety of people that you can safely say that variation is the fundamental theme of the Divine plan, coexistence, living together in diversity.

I like the Pleiadians. With their long, slender stature, they look most like the Dogon, a certain people of black people in Africa. Those beautifully formed bodies move like gazelles. Their almond-shaped eyes give me a familiar feeling, their beautifully shaped hands with one thumb and three fingers; to me look as if that is how it should be. Almost all men wear long hair, hanging on their backs with a tail. That hair is held together with one or more straps from which you can read someone's status. The women also wear a band in the hair, but their status can be seen by the band around the upper arm or by the necklace. Status is really earned by them and built up through many lives. People belong to a certain clan and that goes back centuries. Someone from the clan of governors can connect with another clan if he or she needs it for work and development. I belong to the healer's clan and the tasks of that clan are broad and cover all possible areas. This includes, for example, writing this book, which has the intention to remove the fear of death.

There are people who are ministers or clergy on Earth, but originally have a Pleiadic soul and originated from the healer clan. They assist the sick and the dying. They have a healing task. In the course of many incarnations they often had souls who were younger in their evolution, as disciples. This could be as a son or daughter, because from a parent one can learn a lot for the rest of one's life. In this way peoples of very different backgrounds became intensely intertwined. In the healing chambers all these different souls work closely together, it is a constant stream of learning from each other, an interaction that does not stop. All distinctions between all these different peoples have already been eliminated here, now this has to happen on Earth.

The work in the healing chambers in all spheres, with all the different levels that are there, is taken extremely seriously. They work very hard. Every conscious human being chooses a task that suits him or her. If there is a need for rest, it is taken. Just like the Light Beings who work on Earth in areas of war and famine, who sometimes opt for a period of total rest at a place of their choice, either in their own home or in a healing chamber. Lying in the frequency of light that suits them, after a period of time they return to the work floor, healed and refreshed, back to Earth to continue their work.

I wish hospitals on Earth could be as they are in the spheres. Without a shortage of staff and without the enormous workload that this creates. And with the disgracefully low pay that somehow should go with it. I remember very well what it's like to be in need of help. How scarce domestic help is, how limited the allocated time is to do the work properly, the enormous work pressure. That needs to change. It certainly also applies to nursing homes, fortunately I was spared that. I admire everyone who is trying so hard to make something of this underfunded healthcare. There is the consolation that the people who arrive here are well and lovingly cared for.

The unity in diversity here is like balm for the soul. All those different soul groups that work together seamlessly here, I enjoy that. I see my own ideals come to life here.

Sometimes there are occasional confrontations in Kumeka's healing chambers. Very old soul connections of people are involved that cross each other's path again in this end time. I am allowed to mention one such confrontation here.

A man who stayed in the group of newly arrived souls later spoke to us about his experience during his confrontation at Kumeka's. In a war in the Middle East he had been tortured and died of his wounds. The person who had tortured him was present at the confrontation, now also in the Beyond. Reading both their books of life, they saw that their path's had crossed many times: they were once brothers in a loving relationship while later they were enemies. Reading his book of life this newly arrived man discovered that he in turn had tortured the other man in the Second World War. He himself was then a high-ranking officer in the SS and his victim was a Jewish man.

People often ask what cosmic laws are. That question is easy to answer because those laws are so simple that anyone can understand them. So here we see a cosmic law at work: don't do to someone else what you don't want to experience yourself.

In this end time a lot of confrontations take place that show people their history and shared experiences. A lot of hard work is being done to complete such processes in the old 3D world. History, by the way, does not repeat itself when a 'lesson' is learned. By peeling off the encapsulated God spark, layer after layer, often after an incarnation period of 12,000 to 26,000 years, the soul can continue on its way. Many know how and in what way they once ended up in those shadows. An important story is told by the scientist:

The scientist and the legacy of Atlantis...

Margaret: In the healing chamber of the Pleiadian souls, which I wrote so enthusiastically about, I met a scientist. He had been in the spiritual world for a long time and had made a long journey before he was able to enter the spheres of Light. After Kumeka's healing chambers, he could now devote himself, together with other scientists, to a scientific project. In a certain sphere they meet and exchange ideas with each other.

The scientist: 'I came to Earth at the beginning of the first era of Atlantis. I came from the clan of scientists and would make my contributions to the evolution of the young Earth. My tasks were fixed in my blueprint of life and through contracts I had entered into. In my early years on Earth I was still strongly connected to the Light Worlds. I could fully communicate with them, it flowed easily and it was as normal as eating and drinking. At first I had a very Pleiadic body, long, more subtle and slim than that of the Earth people. We looked most like the Dogon, a people in Africa. Our skin was slightly bronze. My hands had a thumb and three fingers. That seems to be an anomaly by earthly standards, but it was supposed to be like that and they were beautiful, slender and graceful. I wore my hair in a long tail on my back. Usually I opted for male incarnations, although later, in the third and final period of Atlantis, I lived as a woman a few times.

In the first Atlantic period I regularly went back to my world of Light, which was still possible then. You could say that I went to 'recharge my batteries', like we do in the spheres in a light or healing chamber. I was happy with my contract on Earth. I had committed myself to serve as a parent for Earth souls, souls who were brought to Earth after the great explosion of Maldek. All these soul fragments were collected and brought to the seabed of the young Earth, where the dolphins took care of them. Dolphins are our noble brothers of Sirius and they brought love and healing to these souls. I was part of the plan to take care of the parenting of these souls, a function I had already fulfilled in other places in the universe. Many of us were engaged in this plan of healing on Earth, and with success. These souls, who had previously lived on Maldek, poured out over the Earth and went their way in evolution. The memory of the destruction of their world was gone and they all entered a new, very hopeful phase of their evolution. The Earth was then a wonderful place where it was good to be. I worked as a teacher at the temple schools we had built and enjoyed that wonderful initial period, which lasted more than three thousand years.

My contract ran until the third period of Atlantis, after which I would return home. But it went differently: I made karma. I had been too generous in passing on knowledge. I was naive, because I assumed that the given knowledge would be used for the good of man and planet, in the service of the entire evolution, like we had experienced in many places in the universe. We have never before experienced abuse such as on Earth in that particular period of time: never to this extent. The polarity on this planet was very strong. More than I have experienced in other places. People started to abuse the knowledge I gave them for their own benefit: to gain power, to oppress and dominate other people and above all to gain great wealth.

Earth is a planet of free will. Many of us made the mistake of passing on too much knowledge, so we unintentionally created karma. I have had the bitter experience that someone, with such wonderful knowledge, chose for the deepest evil. Many of us lost our naivety on Earth. It was so painful to see what the people of Earth did with the knowledge; knowledge that could have served all and not just a few selfish people gaining wealth and great power. That phenomenon was new to us. No matter how hard we tried to balance the karma we had created, it often turned out to be irreversible. The technology of the end time of Atlantis was very special. Initially it had created a great deal of beauty, but eventually society went completely insane in the course of those three periods, especially in the third period. I now know that without our given knowledge that state would have been reached as well, but for me it was unbearable that I had had a part in it. My integrity as a scientist was very important to me in those days. In our culture you earn status through purity, integrity, and intentions that are fully attuned to the Light. We don't even think about doing things differently, that's our state of being. More and more people on Earth, of all soul groups, are going to see this and live accordingly. It is the only way home, to more and more light.

I longed more and more for my home world and went to one of the temples when my time had come. Via a dematerialization chamber I was transported to the mother ship. There were about 20,000 new Pleiadians who would come to Earth. That was after the destruction of Atlantis, and was meant for the next period of the Earth Revolution. Our first group of 10,000 souls was scheduled to return. It had been a long lasting contract for us, longer than we would normally enter into. I yearned for my home world, my cosmic family, after all my hectic incarnations in the third and final period of Atlantis.

I only wanted to go home. Life after life I carried the memory of the world of Light where I came from with me. Even when I had this earthly body like everyone else here, that memory always remained. And that memory now becomes back stronger in this end time - the end of the 26,000-year cycle. Likewise in people with the same background as I have, and in people from other star systems. And because we have forgotten so much, it is very confusing for many people to remember things that do not exist here on Earth from time to time, and in fact never existed here. Such memories belong to the unique features of our distant places of origin.

In that last period of Atlantis, on the mother ship, all the people of my clan helped to dismantle the dematerialisation rooms that were scattered all over the Earth. Nuclear power plants, some of which were located in the oceans, were rendered unusable by us in order to prevent even greater doom. What had happened to the planet Maldek was not allowed to happen to Earth. On Maldek the whole process with the dark forces had escalated to such an extent that the entire planet was destroyed.

In those last seven years, the abuse became more and more serious and many were completely under the influence of the dark powers, which were doing everything they could to get the Earth entirely under their control. All instruments, such as the ankh and crystal tools, were brought to the mother ship by special teams. For seven years, many of us were involved in these operations and we did what we could. I did everything with just one idea. I wanted to go home.

Homesickness began to take hold of me in a serious form; it had been too much, more than 12,000 years of incarnations on Earth. When all the people had gathered on the mother ship, on all levels of 'being' and vibration, a great conclave was held. This took place in a huge hall, surrounded by holographic screens, in which we could see that the representatives of our Light Worlds were also present on the Pleiades. It felt very much like home again; it was wonderful to see their familiar shapes, to hear them speak our language. I was touched by this meeting.

Most people in my group were tired of the difficult last years, in which so much horrific things had happened. Together with a dear friend, a doctor, I was intensely concerned with the care of certain people in those last thirty years. I am now talking about 'people' who were created by the Atlanteans through genetic manipulation to serve as workers. This slave race of workers was manipulated in such a way that it needed little sleep and not much food. Their scientists did all kinds of things to clone away the ability of these creatures to have feelings and emotions. They were not allowed to reproduce, and if managed to do so, they were severely punished. Anything but work was actually punished. They only wanted to create machines. Scientists are doing this again right now, by the way.

A very small number of Atlanteans who did not agree with this formed a silent resistance. They saw an opportunity to sabotage a lot; slowing down or crippling processes, destroying equipment and files.

These suffering artificial 'people' were taken to the temple complexes of the Pleiadians. They worked very closely together with sister souls, teachers of Andromeda, who by the way were and still are fewer in number on Earth. Confrontation with all this misery, with deformed clones, with people suffering unbearable pain because of a deformed gastrointestinal system, brought us to ever-greater efforts to take care of them. It was a harsh society, even tougher than it is now. Before I began the seven years of cleaning up dangerous technologies, I worked in a large temple complex. This temple area was inviolable. It consisted of many buildings; it was like a small village, with a huge hospital and it was completely self-sufficient.

First we cleared the large buildings where the older priests lived. For them smaller rooms were built next to the temple. In this way every large space was made suitable for the care of these sick people. Elsewhere in the area medical facilities were created for those who suffered from a disease that in many ways resembles what we now call AIDS. Sufferers from this disease were normally thrown outside the immense city walls, without mercy, without food and drink and after they were stripped of all their possessions. Many died of hardship. Elite troops of the Atlantic government were regularly chasing these people. This was done from the air, using special, low-flying vehicles. They saw it as an exciting distraction in their highly material existence. With laser weapons they shot the pariahs who lived outside the cities. It was quite an honour to join one of the elite squadrons on such a mission. The government let them have their way.

There were mortal remains everywhere, scattered all over the place, because someone who is dying is not going to lie next to a corpse. It was horrible to see. We disposed of the mortal remains through a form of dematerialization. That was necessary because many of them were already in a profound state of decomposition. The living were taken in and brought to safer places.

The disease I was talking about was deliberately spread to reduce the numbers of certain groups of people and that happened 'successfully'. They called it 'purification'. In the last thirty years, the shelter became bigger and bigger. I often flew along with small vehicles with which we would pick people up on the outskirts of the city. Our vehicles had an elliptical shape, a silver colour and with sliding walls on the sides. They were propelled by an inexhaustible source of energy, the same energy that would later be rediscovered by Nicola Tesla. I worked closely with my friend, the doctor, and many others from my soul group. We searched for methods to make life liveable for the people created by the far-reaching genetic manipulation and cloning. When all possibilities were exhausted, we offered them the opportunity to go to the next existence through a purpose-built dematerialization chamber.

We worked together with every other discipline imaginable. We were shown a path to the greatest possible spiritual wholeness and were guided in this by Lord Kumeka - our teacher through the ages - who assisted us in this process from the Light World. Before these people departed, we tried to provide as much spiritual assistance as possible. It was always made clear to us who were ready for the next phase, for a passage to the fourth dimension. Most of them died in their sleep at night, others chose the dematerialisation chamber. In these shelters, of which there were several in Atlantis, a high frequency of love and care developed. Clones who were able to do so took care of those who were less well off. It went naturally, and always in the best of relationships. I will never forget this love and togetherness, which are etched in my soul being. Also in what I will call 'AIDS patients', we saw great solidarity between them. People took care of each other as best as they could. Hundreds of Pleiadian souls devoted themselves to these people. Their doctors and spiritual helpers did what they could. They worked closely with the Andromedans. The cooperation was wonderful, but the human misery we saw there was terrible. Some of us asked too much of our own bodies: there was so much work and new people were brought in all the time. They became ill: their immune system would deteriorate to such an extent that the virus got hold of them.

Due to their many negative deeds in that end time, Atlanteans brought great negative karma upon themselves. Later in the Earth's history they drew the consequences of their actions to themselves; much was worked out in the twentieth century. Many scientists of that time are busy again working on genetic manipulation and cloning: nowadays also on robotisation and artificial intelligence. It is one of my tasks, together with a very large team, to guide them from the spirit. Unfortunately, many are not open to our positive inspiration; in their material existence they are completely cut off from this energy. Some are just as obsessed as in the time of Atlantis, and I can assure you that quite a few plans are being developed that look very similar to ones in those terrible days. This is instigated by the invisible leaders of the world; also referred to as the shadow government or the deep state. The Realms of Light won't allow that to happen this time.

Many new incarnations of Light Peoples came to Earth to serve as catalysts of positive energy, just like our mission at the time in Atlantis. The people of my soul group who came to Earth at that earliest stage now remain in the spheres. From there, they help the starseeds; they are their guides.

The Federation of Light Worlds has brought together very powerful Light Beings from different galaxies. All these incarnated Light Beings are accessible to us in spirit, and we are just as 'audible' as if we are standing next to each other in the material world. Through this communication, important negative developments can be strongly slowed down, stopped and questioned. In this day and age, a lot is exposed that could not be seen before, let alone be discussed, and the starseeds contribute to this to a great extent. I can tell you now that at this stage of the Earth-evolution the horrors of the end of the Atlantic era cannot be repeated. That has really been rendered impossible and it is good news that I can share with you.

Lord Kumeka told us that in June of the year 2000, a golden-white grid was created around the Earth. This was partly due to the efforts of many light workers on Earth. It consists of many intricate little grids of golden-white light, which are interconnected with each other. With the help of this grid, people can work together in a better way, in their attempts to let go of duality. Now that this energy is anchored, this process will run more smoothly and everything will be brought into a state of balance, without 'good' energies escaping from the Earth's surface. The energy that is present between the Earth and this grid will continue to serve and can no longer be influenced by external forces. The grid is also intended as a source of energy. It consists of higher frequencies of light and is attuned to and co-designed by the light workers on Earth who made this anchoring possible. The people on Earth laid the foundation on which it is now possible to built. It will also serve as a beacon for the coming period. Many people have waited for this, because it was so difficult to balance the controversial energies on one's own. Because of the anchoring of the light energy, every individual who chooses to go up to higher frequencies will feel carried by the light grid, without having to fear a relapse into the old. Everything is dominated by purification and transformation and for many there will be a period of renewal, much quicker even than many think possible. This grid is nourishment for many positive change processes. Intuitively, a growing number of people are tuning in to this grid in their daily and weekly, global meditations. On a soul level this is recognized and through channels tuned to Kumeka and Archangel Michael this information will quickly spread.

Faith

Faith is the bridge without pillars
That carries what we see
Up to the spectacle we can' t see

Emily Dickinson

11. Tobias

Leviahnarah: We've seen the Earth complete its 26,000-year cycle. It has been a hard journey for many souls. This end time is even more difficult for many Light Beings who are going through their last earthly life. The number of suicides on Earth has increased dramatically in recent years: especially among young people. This is only marginally discussed in your media. There are many misunderstandings about suicide. It is therefore important to listen to a number of departed souls who would like to share their personal story with us after a telepathic call in the spheres.

Tobias: I was a hypersensitive boy. The depressions started in high school. My parents and other family members were always there for me, they helped me to get out of that depressive darkness. As a child I liked to be in nature, looking for tranquillity. Our holiday house in the Ardennes in Belgium offered all the possibilities to experience that peace and quietness. Between the animals and the living nature I was able to calm down. I felt great outdoors, in nature as opposed to the metropolitan environment in which I grew up in Brussels, in Belgium.

I was born into a family of academics and I was expected to pursue an academic career as well. My parents, uncles, grandfather and my brothers and a sister were presented to me as examples. Ever since I was a child, this has been put into me as a matter of course. Two of my brothers studied in Leuven and were very successful. When I was in high school a sister of mine was studying in Paris and was also very successful. But my youngest sister wanted to become a nurse and I too dreamt of a different kind of job, one in nature conservation. In the Ardennes I often spoke to the people of nature conservation and felt very much at home to their stories and plans. At home, that dream was kindly dismissed as a child's fantasy. Something like kids wanting to become a fire fighter or a pilot.

High school was a drama, full of the kind of excitement that made me very restless. It was during this period that the depressions began. They came and went, alternating with periods in which I was able, fortunately, to do a lot of schoolwork. Whenever my teachers and parents felt it was necessary, I was given tutoring.

During my time as a student, I moved from Brussels to a small dormitory in Leuven. I was lonely without my caring and sociable family around me. Life at university proved hard for me. A specialist in the hospital prescribed me antidepressants and that's when I began to feel suicidal. I talked about it with my teachers and also with my family, but they were all convinced that the medication I got from a specialist was good for me. They meant well, but now I can see that within a year I had become heavily addicted to these drugs, the antidepressants especially. In a profoundly dark period, I ended my life with pills. My death caused a huge shockwave through my family and among my friends.

My grandmother from my father's side was there to welcome me, together with two other Light Beings. They reassured me and took me to a healing chamber. I have only little recollection of being there. My grandmother had passed away when she was eighty-two years old but here she looked like in her pictures from the earthly years in which she was entirely in her strength. Beautiful soft brown curls in a face that looked so familiar to me.

She accompanied me to my family on Earth. They were sitting together in tears. Of course they couldn't see me, except for one of my nephews. He pointed at me and told me that he could see me. He looked at me with his shining eyes. This little boy could also hear me and I asked him to tell them that I was fine, which he immediately did. Only my father felt that this was true, being the open and spiritual man that he was. His own mother, my grandmother who guided me, put that feeling into him. Here with my family I learned that departed souls always try to give a message to their next of kin in one way or another. Unfortunately, there are always people around an 'open' person who are laughing it away or are sometimes even unpleasant about it. Hell and purgatory are deep convictions in many people, programmed in during their upbringing, education or by their religion.

I want to stress that the loving words and thoughts of my family and friends have helped me a lot. Outside the physical body you see and feel real truths. You can see and feel it immediately when the tears that are shed are only crocodile tears. False light is clearly visible in people's energy fields. Fortunately, many people are now evolving intuitively and emotionally. Seeing and feeling what is real and what is not.

I wasn't present at my own funeral service, but afterwards I was able to see everything in detail. Seeing so much love and friendship was a light experience that lifted my soul.

In the meantime I have read my book of life: especially of my past life and a number of previous lives. I had no idea that this was possible. I take every opportunity to balance that what has caused the deep depression in me. It was beautiful to see cause and effect. In many past lives there was a well-intended pressure from my family to make career choices that were not of my own. I was born into families that thrived in such circumstances. There was a gentle and sometimes downright harsh coercion; they were convinced that this was best for their son. In ancient times, the family was obeyed. In my book of life I have seen how profoundly unhappy I was in a life as a notary in the nineteenth century in France, where I had to succeed my father and grandfather in that life in the family business. I became a barren, joyless man. There were more of such experiences in other incarnations.

I am now being prepared for my next incarnation with my youngest sister. I am often with her in spirit. She is a loving person as is her partner. We meet in Summerland during her sleep and discuss what we want. When she wakes up, thinking that she dreamt about me.

The cause of my depressions is now crystal clear. In between other lives I refused to look at them, but I'm past that stage. Convinced of the possibilities that lie ahead, I am positively looking forward to my next life. Following my heart, making my own choices in life is in my new blueprint. I will become a little boy.

12. Liana

Leviahnarah: Liana attended her own funeral service.

Liana: I incarnated into a fine family. In my blueprint for life I had several intentions, possibilities to heal my soul with the right people. Through actions in a previous life in which I was a loveless mother, the children from that incarnation hated me. I understand that now. I was completely disinterested in my nine children. Every year another one came along. My alcohol abuse, tantrums and the physical abuse of the children marked my life in that family. We were very poor. I was loveless and in many ways cruel to those who needed all the protection a mother could give them. The children left when they could, which was often at a far too young age. They sought and found their way into old London, the London of the nineteenth century. Some of my children had stolen food, hungry as they were. They were arrested and eventually deported to Australia as criminals.

In the spiritual world you can trace all the lives and lifelines of the people you are deeply connected to. This happens clearly and visibly when reading the book of life. You then fully realize what you have caused by your behaviour. The consequences were devastating, I know now. Somewhere along my incarnation path I chose power, prestige, money and material possession. I sold my soul to the darkness and served it in the many lives that followed. Creating suffering of any kind is nourishment for the darkness.

After London I incarnated once more, this time in Australia where I had five of the earlier children again as my children. It was a life of hard work on a farm. My husband was one of my sons of that earlier life in London. In the Australian life I did my best to be a good mother and wife. However, despite my best efforts, it was never good enough. There was something that made them wary of me. As if the insults, the outbursts of verbal and physical violence of that life in London would be repeated. Every now and then I had a tantrum, but not at all comparable to those of the previous life in London. Intuitively I felt that alcohol wasn't good for me. A few times when I saw someone who was completely drunk it disgusted me tremendously. In the course of that incarnation I started to feel very much unloved.

I created that myself with all those negative traits in many of my incarnations. That started much earlier than London: it was in an earlier incarnation in Italy. A life as a wealthy man in the 16th century, in which I thought I owned the entire world. My great wealth gave me power, which I abused. Whereas in so many other incarnations I had provided well-being and harmony, in that Italian life I had become a very selfish man. I caused great poverty to a large number of people in that life.

Male staff I expelled from my home and land with the slightest wave of my hand: people with families who all lived on the estate. Many young women who were employed in my palazzo became pregnant of me. I used them and then threw them away like garbage. These pregnant young girls and women could not return to their families. Sometimes these girls went to an abortionist, an angel maker. Many of them died of infections and blood loss.

Power; I enjoyed my power intensely. It was extremely addictive. Power *is* very addictive. My dominant character and short temper caused a lot of misery again. I died an old man, totally abandoned by everyone. Loved by no one, hated by all.

Incarnations of experiencing, of balancing negative energy followed. It was a laborious process. My soul was searching for my lost self in wholeness, my lost light. The choice to sell my soul to the darkness had completely changed me. The spiritual fall I made, through lusts for power, prestige, wealth, made me a loveless man, only serving the darkness. I saw them in the spiritual world, all those wonderful lives I lived in harmony with All That Is. But addiction to power is hard to transcend: it can be a strong connection with a tremendous pull. I had to develop an even greater spiritual power to do what I intended in my last blueprints of life: to transcend the energy of darkness. But if people didn't do what I told them in those subsequent lives, I would get really angry and mean. Some lives were accompanied by great alcohol abuse. It became a long way to transcend the addiction to power and the abuse associated with it. Life in nineteenth-century London finally gave me the soul lessons to reached the turning point.

When you start to see cause and effect for yourself, what you have done consciously or unconsciously, only then you can begin to do things differently in life. In our various incarnations in which we undertake things to balance old energy, we can heal each of those lives. Many people succeed; others are still on their way to healing in their incarnations.

Elementals

Through our thoughts and strong beliefs in life we form elementals. When they are powerful enough, they start to live a life of their own. In this way you take that which has not healed from previous incarnations with you to your next life.

With me there was a self-created elemental of my conviction that I was that great and very powerful man in the 16th century in Italy. Thoughts that were constantly present. I was completely convinced that I had real power over many people. I therefore took this strong elemental with me for a long time. I later saw my tantrums as a dilution of that old power to get my way. In one of those subsequent lives, after the 16th century, I developed asthma, literally something that was breath-taking.

Another elemental that built up life after life was the thought: 'no one loves me'. That elemental was not easy to dissolve and transform either. I managed to transform my power and dominant behaviour, but I brought the thought form 'nobody loves me', along to my last life.

As Liana I incarnated in a loving family: souls who had been through a lot with each other and were healed from previous loveless incarnations. It was a musical family in which a lot of instruments were played, and there was much singing and laughing. Lessons presented themselves that I overcame with the help of the family. Being loved was once difficult, however strange that may seem. But within my family I was able to receive love, sometimes in tempestuous expressions of it. I could also give love, unconditionally, learned on that long road full of bumps and potholes.

When I was eighteen years old, I fell in love; a marvellous period in my life. He was sweet and caring. We did a lot of fun things together, music, sports, holidays. I enjoyed it intensely and radiated happiness. Then one day he said he didn't love me anymore. He had fallen in love with another girl. From one moment to the next he disappeared from my life. I was completely in shock. He doesn't love me... he doesn't love me... he doesn't love me... it got stuck in my mind. It triggered something very old. In a haze of sadness, I went home, threw my bike into the verge and bent down under the railroad-crossing barrier and jumped in front of the train that was arriving at that moment.

With this self-inflicted death I brought much grief. After a week I went back to the third dimension, together with the guides who came to get me and brought me to the healing chamber. One of them was my grandmother. She had passed away when she was eighty-five years old, a sweet old lady. I recognized her in the healing chamber. She now looked like a woman in the strength of her earthly years. She stayed by my side uninterruptedly. In the healing chamber she always appeared immediately when I thought of her. She expressed no judgment. Together with her and my personal spiritual guide, I visited all the people I had caused great grief that week. I was with them in spirit. My whole family sat around the table in disbelief and bewilderment. I could hear and see all their conversations and their thoughts. Some were angry, very angry at what I had done. No one knew at that moment that my relationship had suddenly ended in a shocking way. Also friends from my school were sad. I saw that they really cared about me, because of all my good and despite my less good qualities.

Elderly family members, an uncle and a grandfather, had constant thoughts about hell and damnation, about purgatory and other imprinted beliefs. Those beliefs were old and had become powerful elementals for them with regard to their own beliefs. I could feel every thought. Those were hours of truth.

I was present in spirit at my own funeral service. Two boys, sons of my brother, could see me. They were three and five years old. One of them waved at me and told out loud to the others that he saw me. My parents listened to them later that day. Their descriptions helped my dear parents a little in the process they were in the middle of. The boys described what I looked like and that was with a (subtle) body without damage. I know this happens regularly. Children and animals see us when we visit them. At a young age children see both people and animals from the spiritual world. For them this is a very common experience. That talent is quickly lost in a world where children are told that this is all nonsense. At school, at an early age they are forced to start focussing on the left-brain hemisphere.

I wasn't earthbound then, as many people might think. Indeed, some souls cannot get away from the Earth after their physical death. However, I continued on my way and read my book of many lives. My own truths gathered in a line of countless incarnations. I realized that I had thrown away the great opportunities I had in this last incarnation, with this beautiful family, soul connected people, in a short and desperate moment.

However, my desire to go back to them was enormous and I have since reincarnated. By the way, this is always carefully prepared, together with the spiritual counsellors in the spiritual world. We then see where we want to balance energy and choose the right people and environment where that is possible. It was precisely this wonderful loving family that could mean so much to me. My parents from Liana's life know on a higher level in the spiritual world that I would again reincarnate into their family.

I incarnated with my youngest sister; with her, whom I loved so much in my life as Liana. We were inseparable, our mother used tot say. On a soul level, she also made this choice. The veil of forgetting descends at birth and a new live begins.

At the time I am telling this to Leviahnarah I am one and a half years old. In my nocturnal hours, when I am outside my body, I work together with the group from which I felt the need to tell about my experience of suicide and its consequences on others. In my life's blueprint lies the intention to give and receive love: new lessons to increase my light frequency.

13. Francis

Alcohol, drugs, and sex.

Francis: Also, with me there were lines that led to a self-chosen death. Lines that I had a hard time transforming. Looking at it in the spiritual world, I see my accumulated weakness: a weakness that in different incarnations led to laziness and irresponsibility; a weakness in which I could not and would not take responsibility, nor for myself nor for others. Here I see and know that I once was a powerful soul that long ago made a huge fall in frequency. So many lives I had before, which I lived in light and harmony, some in simplicity others in prosperity but always in balance. I went a long way before I found my lost light again.

With me it was the love for a man that heralded my decline a long time ago. It was in a period in ancient Egypt. From a simple rural family I went along with a wealthy man. He took me to a big city, which I enjoyed so much. He was a handsome man, charming, captivating. I fell in love, loved him and couldn't live without him. Now I know he sedated women energetically and I was completely encapsulated by him: my free will was gone, it became an imprisonment. I would do everything he expected of me as a woman. Soon I ended up in a luxurious brothel. There were many women and girls recruited by him. At the time I and the other women were well taken care of: clothes, baths and perfumes, food and places to rest. From my simple upbringing in the countryside where I had to work hard on the land and in the house, my new situation was like heaven on earth; laying on the couch, all I had to do was please the men. Dressed in beautiful robes, I was admired for my great beauty. It was like a dream, the house and the clothes, the whole setting. I was fifteen years old when I got there, but at twenty-three I would be dead.

I became ill, infected with a venereal disease, syphilis. By then I had experienced enough in that brothel to know that this was the end of my life. I was shunned by everyone; also by the other women. The man who had conquered me showed his real dark face behind his beautiful mask. Through black magic and drugs I went into a trance and walked to the river where I went into the water. I drowned.

I crossed paths with this awful man several times in my subsequent lives. Each time I fell for his charms and the luxurious life he offered me. With some variation it became a repetition of what happened in Egypt. Only most of the time *I* made the decision to kill myself when life became too hard for me. In total I committed suicide no less than six times. It became a habit for me when life became unbearable. In retrospect, this was a clear signal of a far-reaching laziness to solve life's problems. I was extremely lazy and used other people to do the hard work for me. In addition, I was often heavily addicted to alcohol and drugs. I became so disconnected from the Source that I needed the energy of other people and for that reason I laid chords to them to drain their energy. It took a long time before I found my way back to my lost light. My laziness had become an ingrained trait, the naturalness of letting others do the work as well. Over and over again drugs and alcohol decreased my frequency.

However, in my second to last life on Earth I made a good start, and my blueprint for life offered good opportunities to make steps to a higher frequency. I had dear and caring parents, a good, solid upbringing, and an education with which I could make a good living. But once again I opted for the temptations and started using drugs. Now I know that addictions from previous incarnations, which have not been transformed, are taken to the next incarnation. So, once again, I was addicted to sex, liquor, drugs and the attention of men and I gradually became more and more irresponsible. I avoided difficulties and always chose the easiest solution. That went so naturally that I always look back at it with amazement. When things got difficult, I thought of a way out, an overdose. Now I know better than anyone else that such a flight solves nothing.

So I incarnated again and together with my personal spiritual guides I consciously chose my last life. I ended up in a rural community in the mountains. The man who seduced me over and over again would be my father this time. He had lived through a whole series of incarnations in which he himself experienced what he had always been doing to others. His accumulated baggage of many lives made these lives very tough. But his soul experienced and learned and he was able to change. In one of those lives, for example, he was a deformed boy, hideous by the notions of the time. Nevertheless, his parents and family loved him unconditionally: a soul lesson with regard to the correlation between outside and inside.

At a certain point he wished to balance old negative energy. Thus he began his way back in which many women crossed his path again.

They came in different incarnations on his path as grandmothers, mothers, sisters, and lovers, but he took good care of them.

His own reversal had once begun with the Maori in New Zealand. They would often take in souls to help them regain their lost light, through strict but righteous upbringings. They were often hard lives in which you had to be able to build on each other as a group, as a people. There he learned to respect women again. The shamans of those times 'saw' and 'knew' the old deformities of a soul; its ingrained traces of negativity. He devoted himself fully to that healing. From two Maori incarnations he chose nature in later lives. Thus the mountains were important to him, lives in which he could give and receive love again from his heart. Lessons that were laboriously learned and never disappeared.

So in my last life I was one of his five daughters. In that life my recovery began. I loved my father very much. We had to work hard on the farm. The energy of nature and the mountains carried me. Before I incarnated, I followed a program in the Hall of Wisdom, together with many human souls who suffered from addictions in their earthly lives and fell into the repetition of laziness over and over again. You do this spiritual program from your own conscious choice. Initially it was quite difficult. Reading my book of life, however, I was in my own truth. That is something you can't ignore. You see What Is And Was. So I saw how I chose suicide in all those lives when life became too hard for me. I also saw that I didn't make any effort to look for solutions myself even though they were offered to me over and over again in those lives. In my last life I made it: no alcohol, no drugs. It became a life with two children and a sweet man. Harmonious.

Well, I enjoyed that last life so much that for once I actually became an old lady; something that didn't happen very often in my previous incarnations. I now work in the spiritual world as an expert by experience, working with people who have a similar background as I did back then. The consequences of alcohol and drugs are disastrous. Creating severely damaged souls that can end up in a downward spiral. However, they must ask for help themselves if they want to get out of it. It has to be their own choice to get out of the automatic repetitions; a cycle that one must break oneself. That is possible in basically every life. If that's what you want as a soul, help is always available. You have to ask for it.

There are also many doctors working here in the healing chambers who, after their mortal deaths, choose to do this work. They see and know a lot about what alcohol and drugs do to the body cells: to the liver, the kidneys, dying brain cells that cause some form of dementia. Alcohol and drugs as silent assassins, addictions from which one cannot easily get rid of. They often worked with these people during their physical lives and are aware of their problems. In the Light Spheres, however, they are the experts by experience who always listen to those that are struggling with old addictions.

About believing in hell and damnation

I must say that
relatively speaking
people from ecclesiastical circles
very often get completely trapped
in the dogmas imposed on them.

To think that all Earth's religions
might share the same foundation
to them is often
a very heretical thought.

Leviahnarah

14. William, Paula, and Rose

William: During my last life as a doctor, I met many people in my practice with symptoms of depression. My profound interest was in the field of mental health. I always examined the patient with an open mind, willing to gain new insights, in various forms. Depression was not always recognized as such, because people in periods of depression often led quiet, somewhat reclusive lives. Relatives and friends at the time saw that as part of a person's character. They only saw that something was seriously wrong when the depression manifested itself in an extreme way. My search for the spiritual cause of depression was a fascinating path that I went together with like-minded people. During that search I also learned a lot about myself through a number of personal regressions with a gifted man and teacher in this field.

This special man taught me a lot that I could later use as a doctor in my clinic. Through him I got to know people with whom I resonated beautifully. One of them was a woman I worked with for years. She was a lovingly inspired medium and regression therapist. In that clinic we discovered among the patients we worked with that there were causes of their complaints in previous incarnations; something that, unfortunately and unjustly, is not part of the curriculum for doctors and therapists. We worked closely together. My communications with other doctors, who worked in the same way, formed a 'Field of Awareness'. It is not appropriate for every human being to see past lives through regression and possibly relive them again. Things are never black and white. Intuitively I was always very sure when I could or could not. Mainly sensitive and empathic people came to us; attracted by the way we worked. A matter of resonance, you might say. Paula came to us with severe depression and suicidal thoughts. She wanted to find out where they came from. The regression brought her to a previous life at the end of the 19th century.

Paula: Indeed, it was an incarnation in Sweden at the end of the 19th century. I lived with my father, mother and younger sister in a big but gloomy house. However, the large garden where I played with my younger sister was lovely. When I was eight years old, father started sexually abusing me. I was afraid of him and I would often hide with my sister in the big garden. This incestuous period lasted until I was fifteen years old. Mother knew about it but never did anything to prevent or stop the abuse. Father had a position that made him respected within the community. People looked up to him: the minister in black. I realized very clearly when I later read my blueprint of life, that he enjoyed his high status tremendously. To the outside world he would behave like an eloquently charming man; in his own family he was just a child rapist. Now, one would say he was a sociopath, a narcissist.

I was often overcome by fear when he satisfied his lusts on me. He would always repeat statements like: "...if you don't do what I say, you don't love me..." and "...this is our little secret..." Repeating over and over phrases like 'our little secret' terrified me. During the abuse, he cried out that he loved me. He repeatedly called me his 'sweet girl'. Under the pretext of 'love' a lot of damage is and has been done in the world. Because he was so strict and we, the children, imitated the slavish kindness of our mother and the people in our church community, it determined our upbringing. We also regularly took quite a beating, as corporal punishment was not uncommon in those days. That is why we tried very hard be 'loved' by our father instead of getting his anger. We did everything to get 'love' from the man who was so cruel to his daughters and his wife.

His words full of fear made my now gloomy, depressed moods worse and worse. I lived in an incessant state of fear. It never stopped. When I was fourteen my body changed because of a beginning pregnancy and that was very frightening for me. Without ever having been sexually educated in any way, I intuitively knew what being pregnant meant. Also because of the experience we had with our cat, her fat belly and then the little kittens. There my knowledge stopped. Talking about your body was a taboo at home. My mother said nothing when she discovered my pregnancy. Instead, I was sent away to an aunt up north; she lived on a remote farm. I was going to give birth there and then come back to the parental home. The baby would be given up for adoption and it would be as if nothing happened. Father and mother had arranged the adoption through the strict Calvinistic church to which they belonged. At home we kept keeping up appearances of course.

At my aunt's house I hoped to have a good time, away from father. She turned out to be very much like my father. She told me I had to work hard on the farm because she had to feed an extra mouth. Her words were extra depressing in this fearful period of pregnancy for me. Every day she told me that she prayed for my 'depraved soul' and called me 'a bad girl'. She beat me as often as my father. She believed the lie told by my parents that I had become pregnant by a soldier stationed nearby. The words 'bad girl' constantly echoed in my head. It gave me suicidal thoughts, but then I was terribly afraid that, like I was taught, I would end up in hell, in a place where all the very bad people would end up. Here in the spiritual world, I know that the fear-and-pain-related trauma of sexual abuse had divided my mind.

When I was six months pregnant, I didn't feel the baby move anymore. When I told that to my aunt, she called it 'God's punishment'. My health was bad because of the deceased foetus, but no doctor was consulted. Sometimes I felt that my aunt was hoping I would die, together with the 'shame' for the whole family. I constantly picked up these strong thoughts. After all, everything is energy and a pregnant woman is extra sensitive.

I was unwanted, a disgrace, a fallen girl... and that's why I wasn't allowed to go to the church my aunt went every Sunday, with her horse and cart. I was not allowed, but 'she would still pray for me', she told me every week. One day I walked onto the ice of the lake. I had heard of people in these northern regions who sometimes walked into the ice-cold water of a fisherman's hole. Stories I had heard from an old servant. I didn't think about hell but about not being able to and not wanting to live any more, and I stepped into the hole.

My life passed me by like a movie. A saw a woman in a light blue robe, and then I was unconscious. It was only in the healing chamber that I saw her again. I was lying in a soft blue space and the woman who had met me stayed close to me all the time. Whenever I thought of her for a moment she appeared. She caressed my head and hands. I was not in hell, she told me in a healing chamber. She said that hell is a place that was made up by a few people on Earth to instil fear as a means to exercise power over many.

My subtle body was no longer pregnant. Later, by the way, while reading my book of life, I learned that the baby's soul had left much earlier. Fortunately, she was also well taken care of. At the place in the spheres where I was then, I heard that my sister was in shock after she had learned of my disappearance from our aunt in the north. My body was never found. My sister was also abused and suffered an anxiety-related trauma. She was a year younger than I was. When she was fourteen years old, she also became pregnant by her father. My sister had a dream about me then; our soul connection was strong. On the day that her suitcase was packed for the journey north, she too put an end to her life. Mother found her that night in a bath with cut wrists.

Her funeral was heartless, with thick crocodile tears from father and a great sense of guilt with mother. It was a display of hypocrisy; nothing was said about the real cause. Because of this there was no scandal and her body could be buried in the family grave. After all, that was denied to people who had committed suicide.

Now it was I who saw her in the healing chamber. We were happy to see each other again. I was with her a lot, enjoying our being together. We each embarked on a process of reading our blueprints of life shortly after our transition. Later we 'read' our shared experiences at our childhood home together. In doing so, we learned a lot about our parents, their own soul deformities, incurred in their own childhood, in their own upbringing, and in previous loveless incarnations. We saw that each of them had experiences of abuse: father with paedophilia in a monastery and within several families where they were members of black orders; mother in different incarnations, including experiences of incest.

I incarnated again, but this time in Finland, together with the soul that was once more my sister. After a wonderful life in complete harmony in Finnish nature, both my sister and I chose to give 'father and mother' another chance and thus to balance our common process. Our commitment was great. We knew during our stay in the spiritual world that such incarnations were often successful and we wanted only one thing, to balance old negative energy. Of course this has everything to do with old soul connections where everything was still in balance during loving lives. The search for wholeness, rediscovering lost light and the deep desire of souls to balance old energy is great at the moment, but is actually something of all times.

Anyway, with my 'father and mother' I incarnated in England at the end of the Second World War. My sister also incarnated there and once again as my sister. The family was less well to do than in the life in Sweden in the 19th century. Father had to work very hard to support his family. Mother was again a slavish type, a woman who did everything in her power to keep her husband happy. With each angry mood and the raising of father's voice she shrank and went to her private sanctuary: the kitchen. Father's loud voice triggered strong but unconscious memories of the preacher in black at the time. He often spoke in the same vein, with a roaring voice. In that life in England my father was repeating himself. From the age of eight to fifteen I was abused. Again my mother did nothing about it while she was very well aware of what was happening. My sister, two years older in that life, ran away at the age of sixteen. Her father also abused her for years. She sought and found her way in life and I found my way too. But that didn't end the trauma of our childhood. On the contrary, it was tucked away very deeply. Because this is how the mind works: the trauma of youth creates a splitting and the experiences are buried so deep that it seems to everyone as if they had never happened.

During the sexual abuse I would flee from my body. Sometimes it seemed as if I looked at my body from a distance and saw what was being done with it: a self-created temporary escape, away from the violence that my young body had to endure. But certain events triggered my memories. It then seemed as if a door that was shut for a long time, was suddenly and completely thrown open. I got depressed again in that life. Thoughts about not wanting to, or being able to continue, popped up every now and the. My sister looked for help for both of us. She found Doctor William who took us on as patients. Through regression, all the experiences of my childhood came to light. He did these sessions together with a gifted regression therapist. I discovered that during the years of abuse in that life in England I also had severe suicidal thoughts. Rigorous thoughts of escaping from that life burdened with incest. The previous life in Sweden came into my awareness a little later and I realized that I was in a life full of repetitions. Our intention to give our parents a new chance had failed miserably.

In the end, my sister reported the sexual abuse. However, they did nothing with it. Partly because of that, it became a long and difficult road on which nevertheless we both healed. Both my sister and I married and had children. I cherished the peace and safety of the house where I lived with my family. For years we didn't see our parents, we couldn't stand their energy. Later in life, we went there together.
Mother thought it was cruel of us to mention the enormous damage father had inflicted on us when we were young. We also mentioned the fact of her remaining silent during these long years of abuse. We concluded that we could not expect any understanding or empathy. We went back to our own families in the awareness that both father and mother will have to carry their own karmic baggage.

When we read our book of life, we see such truths. In the holographic looking back to that past life you see every aspect of it. The loving and loveless contacts, the false light, and every detail of the film we can observe, halt and examine it more closely. This is how I 'saw' the long road we went to be healed. I 'saw' mother's disinterest in my life as a mature woman, with my dear husband and our two beautiful children. I chose not to meet my parents again.

The physical and spiritual consequences of my incest past, with all its lovelessness, I worked out later in life through cervical cancer. I was only fifty-three years old. But I took warm memories of a happy family life with me to the Beyond. My sister became an old lady. We found each other again after her transition in the healing chamber where I visited her. We are together a lot.

William: Events in past lives can have a great influence on a subsequent life. For the large group of disbelievers; in the coming period there will be more and more awareness of how this works and how insight into their own history of incarnations can bring clarity: insight into soul life, especially with regard to old traumas, because that is what can prevent us from living a life in harmony and energetic balance. People with limiting old traumas and old negative beliefs can heal with the help of skilfully guided regressions. Physical complaints can sometimes even heal completely after reliving and explaining what caused them in a previous life.

In modern times, many people are convinced that there is a pill for every complaint or disharmony in life. These are also the people who take this for granted in the conviction that they actually need it. And for many of those pills, it is true that they will continue to be needed once they have started using them. We call this addiction here and we know that this is also the purpose of those pills, which in the best case only sedate, but in most cases do not remove the cause.

When a person searches for their hidden truths in past lives and childhood, regression therapy can bring up memories that provide answers to what you are looking for. Related to the physical or mental complaint or the unconscious memories hindering the current life. That offers healing.

Rose: In my last life I had a nice childhood, which I remember with great warmth. Now, in the spiritual world, I am strongly aware of the importance of such positive memories. I went to a Montessori school and later I became a teacher myself at one of such schools. Relationships, however, were less successful and after having a few occasional boyfriends in my childhood, relations always ended in disappointment. I didn't understand that because these boys themselves weren't the reason for my aversion when the relationship went a bit further than holding hands.

The bottom line was that I didn't want to be touched. Violence towards women in films, on television and in books, for example, often completely upset me. In my search for answers I took a course in intuitive training and intuitive massage. Every time I was touched my body reacted very violently. It was very unpleasant for me while nothing negative actually happened. During one of the massage sessions there was a wave of fear that overwhelmed me suddenly. I now know that our body cells have memories and something was triggered in me that provoked a negative experience. I sought help and found a dear doctor in William, along with the woman who was a gifted regression therapist. I went looking for a damaged piece of myself.

During a session I relived a previous life in Germany before and during the Second World War. I am telling the story of that period from the spiritual world where we have insight into all the details of previous incarnations. I was a teacher and worked with toddlers. I saw how these children were brainwashed by parents, other family members and a rapidly changing society, due tot the rising Nazi regime. Over and over again, the repeated words that so many people heard during that period damaged and deformed them. During these hypnotic mass speeches, this repetitive flow of words created great energetic thought forms: *elementals*. Elementals take on a life of their own and create a reality of their own, not least because the environment and circumstances change as a result of them and become the helpers of these hypnotic words. Almost all people seemed to go along with what was forming there. The people who were aware of what was unfolding were a relatively small group within the total population.

Both my parents decided to leave for the United States of America in the mid thirties. However, I decided to stay in the hope of making a positive contribution to the upbringing of the children under my care. Unfortunately, I now know that the evil of deformity had already happened. It had all became so common. When the masses had been made docile, an era of horror and dehumanisation followed. Together with a group of fifteen people, both young and old, I worked on an escape route for the persecuted and on organizing hiding places.

At the same time, I was in love and thus I was able to handle the whole evil outside world. Together with my sweetheart, one of the men in our group, we managed to bring people to safety. The Nazis who dominated the streets of Berlin harassed his brother, a gay actor. Using his acting talent, he travelled to our home and workplace, together with two colleagues who were also friends of his. They arrived there, disguised as three somewhat older ladies in rather unflattering clothes. They often laughed about it later on, but in all seriousness this dressing up party saved their lives for the rest of the war. These bold men helped many on their escape from the Nazi terror by changing their appearance to suit them. Much of the men's acting talent was shared and practiced with people for as long as it took to be convincing. After all, old harmless mothers and grandmothers were seen everywhere in the country and no one paid attention to them.

Even though it was a horrible and dark time, we experienced a lot of humour among ourselves. But the tide turned. Part of our group was betrayed. A traitor was given money for everyone he reported. Betrayal is a form of energy and its soul frequency is very low. It works through all time, even to subsequent incarnations.

I was taken to a castle in the middle of the country. I knew the place from pictures. For three years I was trapped there and escaping was not an option. A stream of high-ranking soldiers passed me by in those three years. Some of them were nice and friendly men in need of a bit of 'fun'. Most of the visitors, unfortunately, indulged in all forms of perversity a man can think of. Sadistic satanic rituals were regularly performed on calendar days that were important to them. As a result of these black magic rituals, many women and little boys, whom they also kept imprisoned in that place, were severely damaged.

A trauma-based splitting of the soul took place within me. Repeating negative words, which pulled me down as a young woman, struck me in my subconscious. I retreated when they hurt me and sometimes I 'saw' myself lying there when I was outside my body. There I had no pain and I began to yearn for a permanent life outside my body where physical pain is absent.

There was a lot of drinking by those in power, the high military and we, the imprisoned women and little boys, had to suffer the consequences. The man who I was 'given to' that evening was a man who was welcomed with much display and an excess of excellent food and drink. He belonged to a group that periodically attended the satanic rituals, in which people were sacrificed as well. These blood sacrifices were part of the worship of the power of darkness.

My fear of having to go through these rituals again, knowing what would happen to me afterwards, was enormous. I jumped out of the highest window I could find to find my freedom. Through that jump, the encapsulation they had energetically made 'tore'. That same evening four other women followed, who also realized what horrors were on the menu.

Spiritually I expected nothing, but through my upbringing I was aware that the soul lives on. Outside my material body I saw the five female bodies. Seven Light Beings came to us and formed a circle of light around us. They used streams of beautiful light around our bodies to heal us. In my immaterial body, it was like a vortex of soft colours whirling through me. We saw whole streams of dark energy coming out of our bodies, energy in which we had been trapped. One of the Light Beings took that energy with it. I now know that this was done to transform it. Most people are picked up by acquaintances, loved ones, but in our case there was a special team of Light Beings. They cleanse what pollutes man and Earth so much: black energy that turns humans into energetic slaves, into batteries of evil.

I went to a healing chamber, and I was there for a long time; in Earth time, about five years. After that period I intensely longed to help people with similar experiences and there were a lot of them. In places of the elite for example, as I had experienced myself. But also in prison camps and in places where women were used as so-called 'comfort girls'. Working in the spheres had a healing effect on me. In my next life as Rose I brought with me things that I had not yet been able to heal. By intensively cooperating healers in the spiritual world I was already free of the feeling of always being dirty. That feeling had become very strong at the end of that previous life. It fortunately did not get stuck in a spiritual conviction of which I know there are people who took such a deep conviction to a next life; some resulting in extreme forms of mysophobia. What I did take with me was the fear of being touched, which triggered old experiences. Seeing blood was also a problem. Seeing violence towards women, real or played, totally upset me. Thus, there came a period in that life when I had suicidal thoughts.

I am now glad that I found the way to William to really solve those traumas and not just seek medication to sedate them. In a good life, compared to the experiences of the previous one, I have worked things out and was able to transform. Fortunately, I didn't bring any feelings of hatred with me. As spiritual baggage you can sometimes have a lot of problems with that in a subsequent incarnation. Hate is a low frequency that hinders our spiritual growth.

Through William I found a cranio-sacral doctor and therapist. Step by step I healed further and let myself be touched without any fear. Loving healing touches. The body is capable of wonderful things to heal you from old experiences. Our self-healing capacity is great when we find the right path that suits us. Consciously searching we find it according to the Law of Attraction. My suicidal thoughts have disappeared, which is what I wish for everyone who struggles with them.

The Resistance

The higher the vibration you emit,
the fiercer people of a lower vibration can react.

There is a great resistance to overcome at the masses.

Leviahnarah

15. Jasmine

Hell, and damnation?

Leviahnarah: Jasmine was a nun in her last life. She'd never had any possessions or a cosy place for herself. She works in the healing chambers on different levels. They call it a hospital and they take care of people who die from monastic communities.

Jasmine: Especially at the beginning of my stay in the spheres I was very motivated to do healing work with people from monastic communities. Later my work also expanded to other people who came to the spiritual world from closed Roman Catholic circles. The enormous dogmas that these people bring with them, dogmas that seriously hinder their progress in the spiritual world, is extremely disturbing. I am very upset that so many clergymen die expecting to end up in hell or purgatory, awaited by a punitive and vengeful Old Testament god. When I myself passed away after the First World War, such a conviction was very strongly present in people everywhere. But even now, people arrive here with these kinds of beliefs. The reception of these believers in the spiritual world requires special knowledge and guidance. That kind of care is my specialty.

There are many of us here, all souls who were once part of some kind of monastic community or religious order. We form a bridge to a new consciousness; to a 'real' spiritual world. It is quite something, when a man from the higher spiritual hierarchy on Earth, for example a bishop or cardinal, dies in great fear of hell and purgatory. We then help him overcome that fear. It works like this: if you die in the belief that you will burn in hell, you will create that for yourself after your death. The power of creation cannot be overestimated in that respect. Fortunately, there are many here who are attuned to the Spheres of Light who understand this from their own experience and are therefore the most appropriate people to help the other person to a higher state of consciousness. Fortunately, our help is usually accepted fairly quickly.

High-minded people usually need more time and attention than others, because they offer more resistance against the help that is offered to them. If they stick to their own conviction that they are superior to other people and for that reason or out of habit look down on anything that is (seems) beneath them, they will remain at the level of that spiritual alignment. However, that is an attunement that is not of the Spheres of Light, but of the twilight or shadow spheres below. If they accept the offered help, however, they will go through the healing chambers to attunement of greater light. There too, people are working who are specialized in this kind of thing.

Margaret: Jasmine wore a warm red tunic with very elegant long trousers made of a supple fabric that looked very similar to silk. Around her neck she wore beautiful silver jewellery with simple shapes. She clearly enjoyed beautiful, personal clothing. I felt right at home in her house. She offered me a huge armchair in which I could settle down in and brought little juices, in a kind of alabaster cups, filled with mead.

Curiously I looked around. I noticed that she had surrounded herself with warm, earthy colours. There was a simple, elegant sofa in the colour of red brick. Laughing, Jasmine told me that in her last life she had so often dreamed of a chair in which you could completely crawl away, in which you could sit and lean your head against. And there he was, and she enjoyed it immensely. Here and there were crystals, amethyst and rock crystal and a warm red chalcedony. On a small table stood a beautiful egg-shaped lapis lazuli. Jasmine told about it enthusiastically.

Jasmine: They are gifts from people that I have cared for and guided in the healing rooms. Because of my specialism in receiving deceased clergy of the Roman Catholic Church, of which there have been many hundreds over time. I enjoy my self-chosen place, my house and garden, both of which are exactly the way I always wanted them to be. The roses, the surrounding gardens, there are people who choose a place in a very quiet environment, with only their home surrounded by nature. I know many people who prefer that. I myself felt the need for people around me. When I stand in my garden I also see other houses. Further on I see the gardens of the healing chambers with people walking together with their guides.

During my last life I often fantasized about a place of my own in warm colours, a sweet white house with a red tiled roof and roses everywhere, in the garden around and along the walls. At that time I had an enormous need for warmth, both from a stove and from the sun. I dreamed of sitting in the sun and having my body heated through and through; to be 'in the Light'. I was used to a gloomy environment in a very old monastery where I rarely saw the Sun. Now I know I had a serious lack of light there. The Sun is a source of nourishment for mankind and I was almost completely cut off from it. Sometimes I looked dreamily out of the small window and imagined I was in a beautiful garden, a garden like this one.

I died in 1918 at the age of forty-eight. That was during World War I. I did not believe in hell and purgatory, although my parents had taught me otherwise, just like the school did and after that the nuns in the convent. It was my grandmother who taught me about a God of Love. I was still very young when she spoke about it with conviction. Grandmother was different from the rest of the family. Later in life, she didn't go to church anymore. Tragic things had happened in her life and her opinion about the doctrine of the Roman Catholic Church had changed dramatically. She saw how the lives of the people around her were completely determined by the Church. That was in nineteenth century France.

Her beloved brother committed suicide and she was very saddened by it. In an accident he had been so maimed that he could no longer live with it. She had nursed him and cared for him as best she could. But instead of offering help and assistance, the Church openly spoke about hell and damnation regarding him. He was a sinner and this was the punishment God gave him. The whole community went along with this, including the family. Grandmother was brave enough to go against all this and she continued to take care of her severely disabled brother. Together they talked a lot about faith, God, the Church, the attitude of the family and the community. One day she came home from the market and found her brother dead. He himself had put an end to his life. She understood him and did not condemn him, but she was the only one who reacted this way.

He was buried in a quiet place, far from the official cemetery, because his body was not allowed to lie in consecrated earth. That was a disgrace to the family. I know there are still places on Earth where clergymen refuse to bury a man who has committed suicide in consecrated earth.

Grandmother was then married off to a 'good Catholic' and forced back on the 'right track', but she was never the same after the events surrounding her brother. For her, the rituals had lost their content and she saw the negative compulsion of the way of life imposed by the Church. Life became very oppressive for her. She told me that she would have liked to have a small family, with at most four children. Twelve children - customary in Catholic circles - could never be given the love and attention they needed. But she had twelve children and had had four miscarriages. That's how it was at that time and in many places on Earth things are still going that way.

Grandmother always kept her faith in a God of Love and told me about it. I was the only one in our whole big family who wanted to listen to her and believed her. Her belief that there is no such thing as hell and damnation, and that an avenging god is a fabrication of people to exercise power, has always stuck with me. Grandmother incarnated twice again after that life. First she became a nurse in a life that also took place in France. In the second life she chose to become a doctor. So now she is a doctor at a place where having many children is normal. This is in a country in South America where people still have huge families under the great influence of the Roman Catholic Church. A country where contraceptives are not allowed to be used and where hunger and poverty are rampant. She is a courageous lady who is committed to better care, education and awareness of women. Because she gives women contraceptives and sex education, she has had many clashes with the Church in that country.

My grandmother and I have a deep soul connection. I see her every now and then in Summerland, a place where spiritual guides bring physical people in their subtle bodies, during the night. There she takes lessons in the Hall of Wisdom, after which we meet to spend some time together and talk about everything. And although she cannot consciously remember this afterwards, she has a lot of support in her work from these visits and from our conversations.

So my family decided that I was to become a nun. At that time a family was always proud when one of them entered a convent. That was honourable and gave a certain prestige. Now I can say that I was a very religious girl, but that had little to do with the Roman Catholic Church. I found God in all things, like outside in nature where I stayed a lot as a child. I spoke about that but my family thought that was heretical; I spoke sinful words in their eyes. They did not allow me to think like that and I was punished for it. When I turned fourteen, my father brought me to the monastery. It was a big and gloomy building where I stayed until the First World War broke out. I had nothing to say, I had to do what my family wanted. My grandmother's ideas were literally beaten out of me there. I had told in my innocence that we create our own hell and for that I was severely punished by the merciful sisters: lashings and solitary confinement, 'to reconsider the matter for a while'.

I sat in a chilly, half underground hole in the garden, with open bars at the top so that I occasionally saw someone walk by. I was only allowed to wear a rough shirt and didn't get a blanket or anything else to keep me warm. There on that spot I dreamt of a better place, of a heaven of Light and Love. I imagined a garden with roses and a white brick house with a red tiled roof.

They were thirty harsh, lonely years. I slept in a simple grey cell without heating and with only a candle for lighting. The bare floors and walls were cold and damp. I suffered a lot, had to work very hard and was poorly fed. In retrospect, it is a miracle that I survived at all. The 'normal' way of doing things in the monasteries was so very different in those days. It wasn't that bad everywhere. But during one of the times I was put in that half underground prison cell I got pneumonia. I had already felt sick when they took me there. I remember it was snowing and I had to go barefoot through the grass to that cell. I said I felt sick, but my superiors dismissed it as an act of posturing. Now I know that many have died from the hardships of such punishments and repentance; such a penalty has nothing to do with God's Love, it is pure lovelessness.

There in that place, when I felt and knew that I was going to die, a Light Being appeared to me. I was reassured and a wonderful and calm feeling came over me. The next day I became sicker and was on the verge of living and dying. However, no one saw that I was so ill. The water and bread I was given were put in a kind of hatch, down in the dungeon. I had to get that out myself.

Then I had a near-death experience (NDE). I saw my sick body lying on the bed, shivering with fever in no more than a thin rough shirt. Suddenly I was in a tunnel, surrounded by a blue light. I also saw other colours of the same deep intensity. And at the end of that tunnel I saw light, a very bright light, without being blinded. That's where I wanted to go, away from that sick body. Suddenly I found myself in that light, and I was welcomed by Light Beings, some of which looked familiar to me. Behind them a lovely undulating landscape stretched out. I saw flowers, flowers everywhere! I was greeted and reassured, but that was not necessary at all, I felt wonderful right away.

My whole life passed me by like a movie. I now know that these are holograms from your book of life or blueprint. My soul being had chosen this experience and images of a previous life appeared. The meaning of things became very clear to me. I received loving explanations from my guide, the same loving being that had appeared in my cell. Suddenly I knew for sure that I had to go back to accomplish the task I had taken on: to learn lessons for my soul that I couldn't possibly learn in any other way. My guide told me that I was a bearer of light and fulfilled a certain task in the spiritually dark world. He showed me that in many places light carriers incarnated with tasks of their own choosing. All of them, including me, belonged to the Family of Light. Then I returned to my body.

I was taken to the infirmary where I was taken care of. High fevers plagued my body. The sisters feared for my life. Sometimes I saw the Light Being who was my guide, and then I was lying in my bed with a smile. I called him my angel. Soon the sisters were talking about an angel who had appeared to me. I didn't have much to lose, so I told them about my near-death experience and about the beings of light I had seen. I told them that I was not afraid to die, just the thought of my experience made me shine. Now I know how important my story was to the other nuns back then. I changed visibly, was more sensitive than before and I had gotten healing hands.

At this time, thousands and thousands of people have spoken about near-death experiences. You can't get around it anymore. But at the end of the 19th, such experiences were referred to the realm of fables. Doctors told their patients they were just hallucinations. Clergy called it illusions and the devil. However, my fear of death was gone and that could safely be called a gift from God. As a result, the next few years were less difficult for me and it seemed as if my experience of what the people around me called an angelic experience had brought more light into that dark monastery. A kind of hope had been awakened in all those sour and gloomy women. I was put in charge of the infirmary, and we got another abbess; a woman of a more flexible regime than the previous one. Well, at least more humane. When the First World War broke out I was given the opportunity to go to the front and I didn't hesitate for a moment. Never before in my life did I function so well. For the first time in years I got enough and good food. I had a comfortable, warm place to sleep and the work I was allowed to do gave me enormous satisfaction. Even though I was a stranger to the world - I was forty-four years old when I went to work at the front - I was able to hold my own very well. I enjoyed being back in the world, among people, with all their pain and joy. I realized very well that I was in the middle of a war, but for me it was freedom and it seemed like heaven on Earth.

It was a very dirty war, although that goes for all wars of course. I went with the brothers to the battlefield to help pick up the wounded. It was all so double, the seriousness of the situation and my enjoying the Sun, being able to move freely in the world, driving around in the ambulances. They thought I was such a happy person and so was I, because I enjoyed myself to the fullest. Every time I went to bed in my modest room, I enjoyed the comfort, the softness of my bed, my pillow and the woollen blanket. I liked lying with the wool blanket under my chin, it gave me a feeling of incredible richness. The food in the hospital was good and I enjoyed every bite. Every morning the rising sun was a great miracle and gift for me. I developed the habit of eating my breakfast outside in the sun, others started to do the same. They were moments of rest and enjoyment in the open air. Other nuns who worked there also started to let go of the conventions. I went before them and they followed me. We never talked about it, we just did it.

Next to the hospital was a neglected garden. Nobody thought about maintaining a garden anymore, most men were at the front in the trenches. In the scarce free moments I had, I started to take care of and maintain that garden. I pruned the roses along the walls and in the beds, I hoed between the plants. All kinds of birds started to use the garden again. My enthusiasm also ignited others and at a certain point one after the other they came working in the garden. Some old garden benches were put down, the tiles were straightened; it became the place to relax for a while. Doctors and nurses came there to have their meal, to drink their cup of coffee. Those few moments of rest in that garden became very important for many people. 'Quality time' is what they call it nowadays. And you can be sure that when you're in such a war, the moments of enjoyment have a much higher quality than in other times.

Slightly wounded found their way to the rose garden before being transported to another place. A few times I drove a dying man to the garden. Or at night, when I was sitting next to a dying man's bed, I told him about the garden. How I had started in that neglected, completely overgrown with weeds. And how the roses were in bloom there now. Here, in this place, I know it was very good what I did.

In the early morning we looked at the garden with the roses, which seemed enchanted by the rising sun. Together with a dying soldier I sat there on a bed in the silence of the morning. Nobody said a word about that and it was a wonderful experience.

I was attracted to people who could no longer be helped by an earthly doctor. The injuries of the English and French soldiers were terrible. I watched over the dying and became, as it were, a midwife for life on the other side of the veil. I came into contact with theosophists, Rosicrucians, anthroposophists, people who all had their own ideas about life after death.

Dying, by the way, is a misconception. It is a transition to another dimension of life. I heard talk about reincarnation and that was new to me. Such a thought was actually heretical in my environment, but I absorbed the ideas of others like a sponge. In silence I let all these things pass through me and tested them against my feelings. That happened especially during the night when I kept watch next to the beds. My ideas slowly changed and I began to get a different idea from God. Slowly I let go of the old dogmas and returned at my grandmother's ideas, they started to resemble each other very much.

As time passed I became freer and freer in my thinking. For example, I didn't go to confession anymore and I liked that very much. Every day at my evening prayer I went to ask myself what those new ideas felt like. If I found negative ideas, the next day, in my hectic work environment, I practiced to turn negative ideas into positive ones.

I worked very hard for four years. I was very concerned about the dying people and gave myself completely in my work. I became exhausted because of that. To make matters worse, the food also deteriorated in that last year of the war. I slept badly because of the noise of the war and took too little rest because of the amount of work that had to be done. After all, it was always work that could not wait until the next day. Finally, fatigue increased to such an extent that I died of pneumonia and total exhaustion. My grandmother came to get me and after that all the pieces fell into place.

In the spiritual world I decided to devote myself to deceased people with severe church dogmas. And my dream came true: a place of my own, set up according to my own wishes and surrounded by flowers. I finally had clothes that I liked, both colour and material, but who were most of all comfortable. I chose to keep working on this side. I would like to incarnate on the New Earth again, after the big change. I long to have a family, a warm family, living in freedom with each other, without the dogmas I struggled with in my last life on Earth.

There is so much work here now in this time of rapid change. Never before have so many people been aware of the predominant negative role that the churches - the organised religions - have played. Mankind is waking up at a rapid pace. Many channellings published in book form have helped people to come to different insights. While everything is examined on the basis of people's own feelings, so many find the freedom to go their own way. A small conscious, awake group has led the way and now the masses are waking up. Many people are finding the God of Love on their own strength. They detach themselves from all limiting and dominant influences and see more clearly than ever between loving and loveless concepts. And there is no one who can stop that. The publication of books on these subjects on every conceivable level is a blessing in this day and age. That which was hidden comes to the surface in all its nakedness. What was shrouded in darkness comes in this end time in the light by the inflowing light. What used to be a secret mystery comes in full daylight after which it can be seen by everyone and that's good.

The arduous path of the soul

I just described my last lives, but in the lives before that I found myself in an all-consuming, controlling, dominant energy. For me at some point that meant that I also wanted to control others, which I wanted to have control and power over everything and everyone. I created an awareness of scarcity that resulted in loveless deeds in different lives. My way back to the Light was therefore long and difficult. But about three hundred years ago I regained the light within myself and since then I have been back in the Family of Light. By living lives of service, I redeemed myself of my heavy karma. My life as a nun as I described it included a series of experiences in which I experienced karma. The lack of freedom to decide about my life as a fourteen-year-old, for example, was one of them. Dominated and controlled by my family and later by the nuns in the convent, the loveless behaviour, it was all part of it. Now I can look at it very openly. That's the way it is when you're here in the Spheres of Light. You understand how and why certain events had to take place and you see how you made that choice on a soul level. In the same way I once opted for a sickness process in which I learned great lessons through which my consciousness grew by leaps and bounds. Also in a life of poverty I saw things that increased my consciousness. And the knowledge that every human being has had to experience every aspect makes me humble and modest.

My way back to the Light may have been long and difficult, but I now fully realize that I once made a choice for darkness, for domination, for abuse of power. By seeing and living every aspect, I have learned an untold amount of things. Mistakes I have made have been fixed and healed. My understanding of things has deepened and intensified and I share that experience here with all those others who speak freely about their experiences on Earth in various lives.

Everyone here in the spheres is an experiencer in their own way and every soul is looking for ways to use those experiences meaningfully. Many join forces and look for ways to be of service to the development of mankind. Serving that group of people to which their hearts are particularly attached. Nobody imposes anything on anyone else. Sometimes someone is invited to do certain work, or to participate in a study group, but everyone is free to choose tot do so or not. Some people need peace and quiet for a longer period of time and seek beauty in all things; in nature, in music that sounds so very different here, books and so on. Each individual goes his own way of development at his own pace. Some are eager to do something, to discover the 'new' life and to take on tasks. All this is of course closely related to how your last period on Earth was. Everyone's process is different. Nobody here is treated in the same way, as often happens on Earth. Every human being is unique in his growth and development and that is what makes the whole evolution so fascinating: every human being matters.

God is Love and it is people who, of their own free will, make a mess of things that can be so beautiful and peaceful. God is Love and doesn't judge; we do that ourselves. And believe me, we sometimes judge very harshly about ourselves, and our own actions on Earth. With the growing awareness of a spiritual world, man's attitude on Earth also changes to himself and to the world around him. I am full of good courage that the changes will continue. Much can change for the better considering the enormous pace of change we have seen in recent years. We will see small and big miracles happen. We will enjoy the positive changes because we carry with us so much knowledge of the many lives in which things were so completely different.

Margaret: Jasmine showed me a little statue of an elephant that she had received from a priest she had cared for and guided for a long time. She played with it and told me:

Jasmine: This man worked in a country in South America. He had become aware of the restrictions the Roman Catholic Church imposed on him there. He gave information in all kinds of areas and helped people on their way to a better life. It was a hard and hard life for him. At the end of that life he realized how he had dared to let go of the dogmas of the Church and go his own way in that distant place. He was loved by everyone because his commitment was so great and his intentions so pure. He worked with the people on the land when it was time for harvesting and he enjoyed it. He had developed into a very versatile man. In the remote place where he lived and worked he was the nurse, the doctor, the midwife, the negotiator, the lawyer and the judge. He mediated in small disputes between people and in big ones between whole villages. And he always carried with him the little elephant he had been given by an old village inhabitant. Once in the spheres he gave me a little elephant that he had made especially for me. It's these things that have great value to me. In the monastery I was never allowed to have anything of my own. That was an empty, bare and cold existence.

16. Brother Peter

Transcending the Fear

Thea: During the years in which I counselled the dying, a man came to me and asked for a meeting. I then stayed in the cottage of a dear friend of mine in Limburg in the south of the Netherlands. Our conversation showed that my friend had told him about my work, the regressions, the readings with a number of previous lives and the dying accompaniment. Outside in the sun on the terrace with a beautiful view of the valley of the river Geul, a wonderful connection started. For me it was important that our conversation was very organic, in the sense that this conversation had a higher purpose.

Brother Peter had come to the end of his mortal life. He was a powerful tall man but he told me that he had an aggressive form of cancer. His own choice not to start on chemotherapy was sincere and, he said it 'was told to him' during a prayer. At that prayer he also 'saw' for a moment the image of Harm, his deceased fellow brother (and during his life also his dear lover). When he told this to the other brethren he was shocked by their reactions and their words. They were unanimous in their opinion that he should choose for the proposed series of chemotherapy treatments. Two of them even tried to convince him that the 'hearing of voices' was the work of the devil and pure deception. He found it very confusing when this negative energy was poured out on him. He then came into contact with my girlfriend and told her about it. She herself had been writing books for some time about reincarnation and about life after this life; about people who 'see or hear' and then in a positive sense, to be of service to others. So Peter also heard about my work and our meeting was arranged.

He told me he met Harm a long time ago when they entered the monastery. It was recognition and pure love from the heart. They lived side by side during their life in the monastery and they were strongly aware of their love for each other. One of their fellow brothers was very jealous of their silent love and told him that Harm could not go to heaven after his death because he had sinned. The word homosexual was never said, but his message and his conviction were clear. It was a man, Peter said, who preached hell and purgatory, not only to him but also to those around him. Many in the monastery, however, were convinced that his words were true.

During a next visit to me Peter suddenly expressed his fear about that hell. That touched me deeply. This man had a beautiful loving aura and I 'heard' from Leviahnarah that Peter was the kind of man who had always been of service to others, and that throughout his long life. Leviahnarah explained to me for the umpteenth time that old imprinted programs from someone's childhood can return fiercely, especially at the end of someone's material life. Rigid beliefs that had influenced and shaped the child and boy he had once been. And because Peter had lived in a religious community, this was reinforced by similar beliefs of the others. These memories, by the way, only came in all their intensity after the death of Harm, a few years before.

Harm had read many books during his life about reincarnation and about life after death. Together they discussed these books, without the more conservative men in their community knowing about it. Harm experienced the attitude of these men as an imprisonment of thought, in which they determined for others what you are allowed to think and what you are not allowed to think. I asked him how Harm had died. Peter told me he had had a heart attack that he had survived in the first instance. He had had a near-death experience, which enabled him to surrender. Peter said that Harm had described it as a wonderful experience of light.

Leviahnarah: The consciousness of Harm, his energy field and their connection at heart level helped Peter through life and to experience their love as normal. When Harm passed away, Brother Sebastian, who was jealous of them, found an opening in Peter: a spiritual wound in which he would sprinkle his salt. Poisonous salt. Although there was never any guilt during Peter's and Harm's life, Sebastian, with his repetitive words of hell and purgatory, laid the poison of doubt in Peter. The other brethren, a bunch of cowards, agreed with Sebastian.

Thea: I saw the image Peter received during his prayer; it was a message from Harm from the World of Light. After intensive talks with Peter - a gathering of two people from heart to heart, his stories, my stories, my listening - something changed in his inner attitude. Afterwards he called me and told me that he contacted his younger brother, who lived in a beautiful small community in Switzerland. The decision to leave that stifling environment in the last year after Harms departure was difficult. One day his younger brother, a loving human being, just took him with him. He was a nurse and took over the care of his brother. Peter enjoyed his new loving environment. His brother called me at one point after that to tell me that Peter had died, in peace and without fear. How good it is to cross over to the spiritual world without fear. I realized again that ingrained traces from youth can play a important role and how deeply these beliefs, that are not based on light, have an effect on a human being.

Leviahnarah: Peter went to a Light Sphere. During his stay in the healing chamber Harm was always close to him. Peter only had to think of him and he was there. He later met others who had been clergymen during their earthly life and told him about their own transition. Those who were convinced of hell and purgatory experienced a more difficult transition than those who were convinced of the Spheres of Light. Their being together was often about guilt, the kind of guilt that was preached by servants of the church and how that keeps people in a low frequency. A few of those people lived in a boarding school for boys where paedophilia was widespread. They watched together in the Light Spheres on a holographic screen the dark energy of such acts and the negative consequences for the children concerned. And of course they also looked at the consequences for the pedophiles themselves. Many created heavy luggage in their books of life. Especially when this happened life after life, over and over again. A connection with the energy that is not of the Light, that made them again and again darkness-serving people who increasingly derived meaning, pleasure and power from it.

They also study the consequences for the often very severely abused and damaged children: their split souls and the often very negative consequences for their various subsequent lives. Every relation of love between two people, whether it is man-man, woman-woman or man-woman, is pure when it is entered of one's own free will. In the dimension of the spheres after the transition, there is no judgment about these things. When a relationship is based on love, it creates beautiful and pure energy. In small groups of people who resonate with each other in the spheres, there is a lot of talk about imposed celibacy and the frustrations one experiences. Everybody exchanges his or her personal experiences of a celibate live.

The ego

The need for being worshiped
is the frequency of power on Earth.

Modesty in what you can do,
is explained by many people as
'not being an expert'.

Leviahnarah

17. Cardinal Bernard

Cardinal to a god full of wrath

Margaret: Jasmine appeared with my spiritual guide Elize as I walked in the fields around my home. I enjoy the freedom after all these years of being sick and sitting inside. I can't get enough of it, of the space, the beauty, a beautiful silver haze that surrounds everything in this sphere. Really, I can't tell you often enough about it. Sometimes Elize is there and then we talk. I got quite used to telepathic communication. I communicate like this with Thea, who writes down my words and it is as easy as if we have always been doing this.

Jasmine said we were going to meet a man. He wanted to tell his story to me as a contribution to this book. Everyone here is so happy that knowledge and information can flow from the spheres to Earth. A lot of people feel the need for more information, the veils are slowly disappearing and that's good. Everyone is excited to participate in this project to remove the fear of death. Providing clarity is their intention. On pure thought power I travel through the spheres and that is an experience I could never have imagined. But I am a realist, it doesn't all happen by itself in the spheres, but I already knew that on Earth. There are so many layers and intermediate layers. Every human being comes to the place of his or her spiritual attunement. I would like to try to show something of all these facets, to give an impression of life in the spiritual world. To give a hint of what people on Earth can do to work as much as possible on their spiritual attunement.

Bernard: In my last life, I was a cardinal. When I died I was spiritually attuned to 'hatred' and that was sphere where I was pulled into. A mask shielded that hatred during the last years of my life on Earth. In my youth there had been no freedom of choice for me. At a young age I was sent to a seminary without me having any say in the matter. I stayed there until I was an adult. I missed my brothers, sisters and mother terribly. Above all, I missed human warmth, because I came from a warm family, which I had enjoyed so much. Although I didn't have such a good relationship with my father, we were a close family.

Once I was an adult, I accepted my fate. I was moulded and shaped for a life as a priest. It was only much later that I began to realize that I was being lived by others and had never been able to make real choices. However, I did not doubt the sincerity of my faith, other ideas did not occur to me. The faith did not leave much room for one's own views, one was formed according to an age-old concept. It didn't even occur to me that there might be another truth. I believed in 'hell and purgatory' and in a judging and avenging God. I believed that an indulgence could shorten your time in purgatory, that people are sinners and unworthy in many ways. Speaking and thinking about things like reincarnation was considered sinful. I was very strict in my teachings and did not tolerate aberrations. But I did begin to realize at a rapid pace that I was being lived: others determined my positions and promotions.

At the age of thirty-five, I fell into a deep crisis. I was sent away to a place to reflect. There I was also pushed and influenced from all sides, but because this had been the case since my years at the seminary, that had become very common for me. I dismissed my deepest feelings about the meaning of life as fantasies.

In my childhood I had certain dreams about what my life was supposed to be like. My parents knew early on that I would be a gift to the Church. Like supple dough they kneaded me the way they wanted me to be. Around the age of fifteen, I had resigned myself to their expectations and those of the family and the teachers at the seminary. On the way, however, I had lost myself. After the breakdown at the age of thirty-five, when I seriously thought about leaving the Church, I let myself be pressured by influential family members. In hindsight, this was outright blackmail. After all, all that was at stake for them was the family honour. Everything revolved around that ambition, a desire for power and prestige, even though they already had so much of that without me. I was nothing more than a pawn in their game of chess. I had to continue an old tradition and they didn't look at what I needed in life as a human being.

In my childhood I dreamed of a family and a sweet woman, of a simple life on the land and a large garden with flowers. I longed for the estate managed by an uncle of mine, where I loved to be as a child during my vacations. The thoughts of that region are dear to me, as are the smells and the colours. I hoped to succeed my uncle later on, but that was not to be. My life was aimed at advancing in the church hierarchy. I was not happy and as my life progressed, I began to hate it all. I saw many people around me wearing masks and I saw with increasing clarity how hypocritical they were. 'Holy' means 'whole' and you can learn a lot from really 'whole' people. With some of them I had a deep and warm contact, with them I could talk about what touched me inside all these years. But most of my feelings were hardened.

There was a lot of hatred and envy in the church hierarchy, also in the Vatican. That may surprise you, but it's true. There was so much mutual hatred and envy that it nauseated me. Now I know that it was a nasty, low-vibrating energy that caused my aversion. At one point I got sick and lying in my bed I started thinking about my life. And my God, I was so lonely. I was well taken care of, but very cold and loveless, without a trace of human warmth, and I felt such a need for that. I hated that fake life and I hated the people who participated in that charade. I hated the hypocrisy, the flattery, the tricks to gain favour with others and me. I saw how they were all nice and sweet to each other and especially to their superiors, how little by little they created their masks of hypocrisy. There were more and more moments when I looked through those facades and I was shocked by what I saw. I had more and more trouble with the hypocrisy and judgmental attitude of most of them. I know that there were 'special' relationships between them, while this was so strongly condemned in the outside world. Very often situations of power were also created in this way. Now that we are entering the Age of Aquarius, you can see that all that is hidden is coming to the surface. It is obvious that a much needs to be changed and that is actually already happening.

I estimate that only about ten percent of the clergy choose to live a celibate life from the heart. If someone really chooses to do that, they will succeed and it can definitely serve a higher purpose. But if it is not done wholeheartedly and is not a choice of the soul, then that celibacy will prove to be very difficult and it will not serve a higher purpose. I think it is no coincidence that so many excesses in the Church were reported in the media in recent years. Clergy have rightly been called to account by groups of victims, as was the case in America in the 1990s. Victims, now adults, have been sexually abused in schools and boarding schools. And even in spite of the fact that so many people from all states of America found each other in their shared experiences, these 'incidents' were covered up after which the accused clerics were often transferred, after which history could easily repeat itself.

However, the changes were unstoppable and began to become visible everywhere. And that is desperately needed; the whole system is rotten and cracking at the seams. The Church's scenarios of fear less and less impress people. Less and less people believe that you are tried by God and condemned to hell and purgatory. No one is ever condemned, we all come from the same Source of Light and we will all return to it. We all do this in our own way and there are many ways that lead to God and the Light, which is what is so special about this planet of free will. And guides who are patient will never give up helping the people who are spiritually attuned to a shadow sphere, as I was, in a very loving way. Often also by people who themselves have had that experience at the deepest level.

My hatred was deep but also for the most part unconscious. As one approaches the time of death, more and more veils disappear. Especially when dying, it is so important that you have people around you who are honest and sincere. I was regularly out of my body and floated through the room, only connected by the silver cord. There were many prayers around my deathbed. I observed the thoughts of those present.

The hours before your death were the hours of truth. There was not a single person by my bed who prayed a truly sincere prayer from their heart. They were mumbling habitual prayers that were empty and without any content. Because hate was my attunement, I hated that whole bunch that came to my deathbed: faces with masks on, without any expression. All the movements around that bed were rituals without substance and empty gestures. I say this mainly because the truth around your deathbed is so important.

One day I suddenly saw a being of light at the head of my bed. I couldn't help but be afraid, because I was sincerely convinced that I was a sinner and would go straight to hell. At that moment I could not open my heart to the experience. However, when I told one of my colleagues about it, he said that it was a delusion, caused by the medication. Of course he talked about hell and purgatory and that was it. I hated the man in silence for what he said.

I died in my sleep. I went to the sphere of hatred and stayed there until I could accept the help offered. Jasmine was there again and again, but I was not accessible in the beginning. I went through my own hate and relived those hateful things over and over again. I stayed in a place where hate is concentrated. I was earthbound and went to the places where I had felt that hatred during my life. Of course, no one could see me, in spite of my many attempts to attract attention. I wanted them to know that I still had a 'body' and that I could see them and hear their thoughts.

I often went to a cathedral where I felt good. It was familiar territory, but even there I wasn't noticed. Nor was I the only earthbound soul who wandered through for example the Vatican, and I can tell you that even in that spiritual sphere they were not all equally kind. Some even thought they should scare me away, because they believed it was their place. I now know that Jasmine led me to a certain place where mostly 'ordinary' worshippers came. Several times I was drawn to that place without knowing why.

And one time there was a young woman there who could see and feel my presence. She spoke to me telepathically. I cannot express in words what it meant to me that this being could notice me and speak to me as well. She began to tell me telepathically that I had nothing more to do in this place. She told me about the Light, about the spheres of Light. "Let go of your hatred and ask for help," she said. There are people who want and can help you, they are around you," and she described Jasmine who was there to help me go to the Light. Then she visualized an image of the Spheres of Light and immediately a beautiful landscape with flowers appeared.

I was terrified, however, because there were so many negative beliefs in me. I returned to this place a number of times and each time the young woman sat there she spoke to me over and over again. She radiated a certain light where I was drawn to. After that it didn't take so long for me to accept the help. I now know that you create your own hell and that was exactly what I had done. Love and Light heal everything and the loving efforts of Jasmine and others made me choose that help. And so I slowly ascended into light frequency.

I began to read my book of life and received help from very sweet and especially patient and knowledgeable people. I reacted very vehemently to people dressed as clergymen. When Jasmine approached me that way I chased her away angrily. It is important to approach people in the shadow spheres in the right way, everyone has their own story and many are full of fears. As long as I was convinced that I deserved hell, I stayed in a depressing environment. Jasmine took me to the healing chamber and there began a path up into the Light.

Reading my book of life was complemented by a visit from my father, who was already in the Beyond. He told me that we should go back to see what was in our past lives. He pretended that that was the most normal thing in the world, while during his life as my father he wanted absolutely nothing to do with reincarnation, a thought that was heretical and sinful at the time!

And there we were, with the help of both of our guides, looking at experiences from our past lives. Reading your book of life is like a hologram. You see every possible detail, every choice you made, the pain you inflicted on others, everything. You feel what you did to someone else. You can look at all the positive and negative aspects bit by bit. Now I also understand that certain people have been connected to the Akashic Chronicles in their material bodies through time and can read them; that they form a network of spiritual workers, together with the spiritual guides and the Higher Selves. These things will become more and more common and understandable to people on Earth.

Until some time ago, you were free to read your book of life or not. Apparently, many people refused to do so and therefore barely made any progress in their soul evolution. They would incarnate on Earth again through the mediation and advice of the Lords of Karma and their own spiritual guides and soul mates. As we enter the New Age, those laws have changed. Now every soul must read his or her book of past lives. As a result, as people begin to understand why certain things happened in their lives, enormous leaps in growth are being made. People will begin to see the causes and therefore the consequences, which can quickly lead to a change. Acquiring insight and understanding about your own processes, under the guidance of beings of Light who are extraordinarily patient and loving, without anyone calling you to account or condemning you. You can do the latter yourself.

I began to understand the laws of cause and effect and found them to be just. I discovered cause and effect in my own lives. My father was already familiar with all this and had prepared himself well for my arrival in the spiritual world. Together we went through this process. It was a great karmic process. What I experienced in Bernard's life was what I had previously done to someone else. I was living in a previous life with the same souls that were my family members in my last life. The composition was different, but we were all there. My father used to be my son. I was a landowner and, against my better judgment, forced my son to live a life as a clergyman. I left the boy no choice, so I was hard and rigid. I was loveless towards the boy.

No matter how much my son had begged, I was unwilling to listen to him. He was punished for his disobedience. I forced him to bow to my will, his father. I thought it was a great honour for our great family to give my son to the Church. I was all-ambitious and did everything I could to give the boy a high position, which I did in that life. I was rich, very rich even. Our family was held in high esteem and we were influential in the Church. However, my son was never happy in his later senior position. His attempts to leave the Church and live a secular life were then thwarted by my great influence in that life.

Now I am working with Jasmine and have come a long way to achieve this sphere. I have chosen to do the same work as Jasmine. With my past I qualify as an experienced specialist here. I take on the care and guidance of people who, like me at the time, were forced to live a certain life. Usually these people come from the same circles as me in my last life. And they sometimes leave those lives full of hate and can then often only very gradually transform back into more light and love. Whenever I can help someone regain the light in themselves, I am so incredibly happy that I can do this work. Together with Jasmine I have formed a group of people who, coming from certain church professions, make a study of their own experiences. There are many negative experiences that further distract them from their light and deepest feelings, from their essential 'being'. Here there are no masks and people are open and honest, which is a refreshing experience. Some are preparing to incarnate again. They bring the spiritual impressions of the spheres of Light with them, but also the knowledge of the lower spheres. One cannot see the one separate from the other.

The awareness of mankind is growing enormously. Many children of Light incarnate in this time, beings with a message, beings also with the knowledge of Light and Love. Just by 'being' they bring light to Earth. One of the Light Beings who teaches us in this Light sphere told us that there are now many children coming from the stars with very specific soul tasks. Earth is in a transition phase and these beings, coming from areas of Light from the Milky Way, assist the Earth as a living body in her birthing process to the New Age. Among them are teachers, many of whom are ready to give open-minded people knowledge and insight into all aspects of life on Earth.

This time, which seems so full of chaos, is truly a time of hope. More and more light is flowing to Earth, a process that has been going on for years. Gates of light that have been closed for centuries by the controlling negative powers are now being opened. With the growth of consciousness on Earth, this whole process is rapidly approaching completion. All of us here are focused on this great event, which will transform the Earth to a world of light. Anyone who wants to go along with it will be included. This process can no longer be stopped. It is a time in which everyone will have to make a choice.

I know that people who will not (yet) be able or willing to go along with this will go to other places in the universe. They will incarnate again on a planet of the third dimension and live and experience what they still need for their personal evolution. Jesus, the great master and teacher, already said: 'My father's house has many rooms'. I know now that it is so and that it is good as it is. No soul will be lost, no matter how much some religious denominations claim otherwise. No one can claim the heavens, for they already belong to everyone.

Understanding spiritual processes helps people on Earth to free themselves from pride, hatred, jealousy, greed, and envy. Also cleansing negative feelings towards yourself and your surroundings, as I experienced in my last life, is very important. A remarkable woman, the Swiss physician Elisabeth Kübler-Ross, has done enormous work in this field and her lessons to the living about 'dying' are invaluable. Her work was truly a gift to health care, with insights applied by many people in the here and now, such as sorting out unfinished business, with yourself and with others. I wish I had had that knowledge back then, together with the people around me. Just confessing and then three Hail Marys never solved anything. You have to solve it yourself and become aware of your own negative aspects, without another human being judging you.

Change yourself on your own strength; make the right choices that are important for your soul's path. That is why it is so important that man comes to his own feelings and core of God and therefore can make inspired choices. Also feel that your choices are right and do not let that depend on the opinion of others, because each goes a unique way. Parents often force their children to do what originates from their own soul desires and that is not always nourishing for the growing child.

I would also like to dwell for a moment on purifying addictions related to food, drink, tobacco, alcohol, drugs and medicines, sex and violence. But that also applies to addictions to money and goods, to power and similar matters. I know that this book is also meant to give insight into what these things do to a human being, in order to understand the deeper meaning of what almost all religions on Earth have tried to make clear. Also in certain forms of yoga attention is given to control of lower desires.

Good food is delicious and necessary if you have a material body, but overkill is of course harmful. If you can't think of anything else but food and keep stuffing yourself with too much and the wrong food, you have become fixed in your mind and have become dependent. You do not control your food, but your food controls you. I once had an addiction to food myself and that completely dominated me in that life. In my last life, it had long since healed. With all the other addictions I mentioned, it's the same.

Being dependent on alcohol or drugs is really awful. Even when a soul has arrived here - but is still earthbound - addicts keep looking for alcohol and drugs. It's awful to see how they try to get hold of alcohol or drugs. They look for places, without being seen by others, where alcohol or drug addicts hang around. They nestle in the auras of drunk people and often encourage them to drink even more. In this way they get some of the energy of the intoxication of the alcoholic. With drugs it goes the same way and so drink or drug addicts get an extra push from souls of the lower astral spheres. And many find it difficult to break away from that; they create openings for these seeking and wandering souls.

Also in psychiatry many are surrounded by elements from the lower astral worlds and more knowledge about this could help a lot. The often far too strong medication that people are given also contributes to this. Thank God more and more people are starting to read and feel the sincerely loving messages from the spiritual world. Always read such messages with your heart, because there are so many levels from which one can pass on information. They can also come from dark spheres, but then they are cold. The reality is that there are lower and higher spheres. Knowledge of this can only bring awareness into life on Earth.

So feel with your heart. Channellings of Light are always warm, loving, even if they sometimes mention negative aspects. Such messages always feel warm. The Earth awakens and man is looking for answers. And also here the law applies: 'Seek and ye shall find'. Many have the deepest intention to find the truth, and there are beings from the Light Worlds ready to help you gain that awareness. That help is offered in everyday life; tailor-made insight because everyone's path is and remains unique.

I would like to say so much and there is so much to say. If, like me, you have been trapped within a certain dogma, then all this is such liberation, such an unspeakable pleasure. I now also know that many of my previous lives were lived in Light and Love, living with respect to Mother Earth and everything that lives on her. That is how I lived with the Hopi Indians a long time ago and there I learned to live in love and respect for everything that lives. I was allowed to experience the love of a family to the fullest. It is terrible that many of those wise indigenous people have been so persecuted and exterminated. This was done deliberately.

During a life in Egypt I was involved with the mysteries in a school in Alexandria and in Atlantis I experienced the love for the teachings of the Light. I had teachers there who originally came from the Pleiades, tall slender people. They were wise teachers and now I also know that my soul being chose to explore countless areas, both in the Light and in the darkness. I taught at schools in Egypt. Again and again I look at aspects of my soul being and it is like threading beads, one by one and with each bead comes another piece of insight into who I am as a being and what I have gone through to learn what I had intended to do at the higher soul level. More and more understanding flows into me about the past and how and why I had to experience those things.

My last life as a clergyman brought me a lot of insight, precisely because I experienced it from within. I gained insight into aspects of power, in all sorts of areas. And now I also understand, with the insight of many past lives, why my spiritual freedom is so important. Also the pain and sorrow have had meaning. They are pieces of a puzzle that fall into place.

Margaret: I asked Bernard why he only surrounds himself with the colours purple, blue and white. Inside his house there was a large piece of amethyst.

Bernard: It gives me a supreme vibration of happiness. My garden with purple, blue and white flowers gives me what I need. It has a healing effect on me and I can't get enough of those colours. You also have an unspoken question about the wicker chairs, don't you?

Margaret: I'm laughing, yes, I am, but I didn't dare ask, it seemed so trivial after all the wisdom he shared with me.

Bernard: There used to be chairs like that at my uncle's house. In his big house in Tuscany. There was a sort of conservatory - a half open porch - where we sat in the early evening hours. Then I would enjoy sitting in that big wicker armchair, with my head against the high banister, looking at the setting sun. These two chairs refer to that, they make me feel at home, a warm and familiar feeling. Everyone has something like that. Just like Jasmine felt such a need for a home in warm earthy colours, cosy and comfortable. Seeing her white house with the red tiled roof makes her enjoy it intensely.

Margaret: He stroked his hand over the back of the wicker chair and I understood. We left. It had been an intense encounter and I wished to retreat to my home for a while, in the peace and quiet of my bedroom. That's necessary now and then. Refreshed and full of energy I start another day. Although day and night do not exist here, it is possible and often desirable to retreat into your own space where you can let your mind rest in a kind of sleep. When I lie down so deliciously in the soft peach colours of my resting place I am so intensely aware that after my repose I can get out of my bed again and do whatever I wish. Such a long period of bedriddenness in my last life, in which I slowly became more and more dependent because of my illness, makes you extra aware of the liberation of the physical body.

I met Jasmine and Bernard regularly in the healing chambers, where they both work. They had developed a deep friendship and love for each other. They had known one another for a long time and had also lived some previous lives together in different ways. There had always been this unconditional love between them. In the spiritual world their love had become one of marriage. You can see and feel their love for each other. There are no marriages here, people choose for one another and the form in which they want to experience it. Some start living together in a home, but Bernard and Jasmine have both kept their own home, which is the choice that suits them best. Living apart together relationships are not an invention of the twentieth century. They spend a lot of time together; I meet them at the concerts that are given here in the music centre. They visit many friends and family who are also here. The quiet experience of the beautiful nature is important for both of them. They are more outside their home than inside. This has also to do with living in closed communities in their last life. I also feel that very strongly. Having been bound to the house for years, I enjoy every moment of the beauty here.

The limit

It is one of the commonest of our mistakes,
to consider that the limit of our power of perception
is also the limit of all that there is to perceive.

C.W. Leadbeater

18. Helene

Leviahnarah: During a meeting in one of the spheres of Light in the spiritual world, people came to answer to our call. Such a call resonates with an individual or a whole group of souls. Sometimes there is a call for a music concert. When it is music that resonates with you, you decide whether or not you will go there. All this happens telepathically. Our call was specifically focused on a certain theme. It was about traumas, incurred in wartime in connection with satanic rituals. We share our experiences and together we can see how others came to be healed. This can be done in the spiritual world, by helping newly arrived people in the healing chambers and in the vicinity of them, or by a new incarnation in which healing was sought according to the self-chosen blueprint of that life.

Helene: My great trauma lies in the Second World War. I grew up in a German family. We were outcasts for our environment because we did not allow ourselves to be influenced by the mass hypnosis built up by the Nazis in the 1920s and 1930s.

It was important for my family to think independently. Every change we observed was discussed in the family and at home. My family and our circle of friends were interested in the spirit and spiritual life, in the purity of life and thought. Among them were anthroposophers, theosophers, Sufi's, and people who, regardless of any doctrine, had their own thoughts about life. They were not under the influence of an ecclesiastical doctrine, which dictated what to think and what to do, as was common at the time for many people. Several members of our family were teachers or academics in Leipzig. My mother taught primary school children and also taught her own five children.

I was a very sensitive child, could see the energy field around people, animals and plants, and I was not the only one in the family with this ability. We talked about it openly, as well as the negative energy I sometimes observed around people and felt in their words and environment. I played with other children simply because I liked them, without distinction of race, religion, or lineage. We never talked about Jews or hatred of Jews, gays and lesbians or the Roma. Nowhere was there any hate in this group of people. I also came to some friends' houses to play and that's how I came into contact with people who thought completely different from us. And that' s how it happened that we brought the words and the energy of the hatred that was building up in German society home with us. If that happened, our family would talk about that. My parents and uncles also had to deal with it at work. A clever process of divide-and-rule developed insidiously in Germany. One drop at a time, the poison flooded into a society that had already been disrupted by the First World War. You don't usually see something like that when you are in the middle of it, but later you see it very clearly.

My mother became ill after she experienced hatred towards Jewish children in her classroom and saw the Nazis terrorizing them and their families. A befriended family was beaten up, their shop attacked and badly damaged. One of their children died as a result of that attack. My mother could not bear the fact that no one did anything but watch, or sometimes even participated in such atrocities. Nowhere was there any justice for these people. So we saw the carefully dispersed poison beginning to do its work. It was creepy to see how people who used to have nothing to contribute in the positive sense, chose to let a hidden negative inside come out. This is how eternal gossipers suddenly became traitors and we have seen many of them in those days. In my conversations with others I understood that many people with dark insides developed in these negative circumstances, everyone with his own dark part that could grow out into a true monster.

My parents decided to go to Switzerland. My brothers and sister were the first to leave for the Vosges where an uncle of ours lived. I took care of my mother who at that time, to make matters worse, had cancer. Father, however, insisted on taking mother to Switzerland and so we began a difficult journey. During a check-up I was taken out of the car and interrogated in a very unpleasant way. My parents were ordered by armed men to drive on. When my father refused to leave without me, he and my mother were also taken out of the car and shot in cold blood in front of my eyes. I was terrified, but I could not do anything for them.

I was taken to a large old country house and there I had to 'serve' the officers. It was a walled-in area. Many young girls and women were imprisoned there. We were allowed to walk in the garden once in a while, but armed soldiers always guarded us. The arrogance of those men was great. We were seen as their toys.

In my youth I had heard a lot about negative energy, about elementals and earthbound deceased people and how they could attach themselves as energy sucking elements to the energy fields of living people. There was a growing awareness that many of these dark soldiers were controlled by elementals that, through them, could satisfy their energetic needs. Whether it was violent rape or any other negative sexual expression, each of these elementals steered the very people who could provide this for them. Like attracts like. Later, in the spiritual world and after their own violent deaths in the war, I saw many of these sadistic immaterial and earthbound men, wandering the Earth, looking for 'batteries' to satisfy their energetic needs. They were looking for people through whose energy fields they could experience negative things.

I saw many elementals in need of liquor and encouraging people in a material body to consume a lot of alcohol so that they could join the hitchhike on their intoxication. In addition, during the war many drugs were given to soldiers for the purpose of making them feel invincible. My sensitivity allowed me to feel how these drugged people were able to satisfy their desires, enjoy describing their acts of terror, and turn killing and bloodshed into a true religion. I saw how Satanism worked and all these people committed horrible acts as servants of the dark: the gigantic energy of suffering, as nourishment for those who lack the Light.

Because of my sensitivity, I was able to perceive many 'invisible' negative things. For example, I saw the larger thought form, or elemental, which due to the perversity in that mansion could grow into a large energy field, which in many cases led to enormous damage.

It occupied me intensely. Every day I connected vertically with the Source, the One, and with the core of Mother Earth. Thus, seeing the great suffering that was created in this place, I asked for help for the people around me. I saw a young girl of ten years old energetically change in a very short time. Everyone was allowed to use her. Again and again I saw that she was not quite in her body. She told me she could fly during such a gang rape. So she left her body in order not to feel the pain. This girl told me, in her own words, how her rapists also verbally abused her. That way her mind was brought under control. This was later called mind control and in the Second World War the dark developed this method into a powerful tool, knowledge that would later be used all over the world.

I realized the girl was starting to believe their evil words step by step. There were men who were very sweet and fatherly with her, making her feel safe, only to abuse her young body like animals afterwards. Because they knew that I was a friend of hers, I was appointed as her nurse. Thus certain women were used in the house to take care of their fellow prisoners. Sometimes girls could barely walk after being 'visited' by a group of officers, many times because of serious injuries on and in the body. Pregnant girls were forcibly aborted while black rituals were performed. After such an abortion, some girls allowed themselves to be carried along with the fever that followed because they didn't want or couldn't live any longer.

The little girl was taken care of by me once again. She bled heavily after such a satanic ritual. I helped her to let go of her life. I connected with the One and asked for help and felt how she was taken away so that her soul could safely reach the spiritual world. There was soul theft on a large scale among these people. With the help of black magic souls were prevented from making the transition into the Light. In this way souls could not move on and the place where they were incarcerated became darker and darker.

I began to dream of the spiritual world every time there had been such a satanic bacchanal and my body no longer could endure the pain of the abuse. Suicide had never crossed my mind before, but I longed for a way out that was not there in this imprisonment.

During my daily walk through the garden I was summoned by one of the officers to halt. Apparently, because of my painful body, I did not react fast enough to his shouting after which he shot me in the back. Outside my body I could see my father reaching out his hand to me. Two other Light Beings took care of my soul and my body. They brought me to the sphere of my attunement and I immediately went to a healing chamber that had been specially created at the right frequency for traumas like mine.

After having been there for a period of time there was the choice to incarnate again. However, I chose to stay in the spiritual world and go a way in which I could help people on Earth who had fallen into a network of satanic rituals and severe sexual abuse. My family members of the last life chose to reincarnate. After their lives I saw them again and that is always wonderful: we never lose each other, our souls are immortal.

Thus I became a spiritual doctor, and I have been a spiritual doctor in a number of incarnations on Earth: among others in ancient Egypt, Atlantis, Ireland, Cornwall and France. Lives in which I gained great knowledge through the use of healing plants, healing water and frequency therapy with sound. Being aware of old traumas through regressions, seeing where the causes were and making them aware; such regression therapies were quite normal in certain periods on Earth. I had such lives both as a man and as a woman. After my transition I entered an area that is intensely concerned with soul damage as a result of sexual violence and satanic rituals. As long as there is darkness on Earth, such things have happened. The first group of starseeds came some 26,000 years ago to help neutralize negative energy; another group about 12,000 years ago. I came from the Andromeda system and came to Earth in the first period. There were many of us.

I love Earth, this beautiful planet with heart and soul. It was difficult and often very hard to see beautiful souls being sucked into the darkness. How they were enslaved energetically. From my perspective it is in miraculously brilliant how this negative plan to use the Earth and its inhabitants as a kind of 'battery' came about. Trauma-related damage meant that time and again, even after a new incarnation, there was a weakness for those who served the dark. Those who serve the darkness can use an old impairment in one's energy field as a hook-in point. Strange to see how people were pulled towards each other again and again in successive incarnations so that history could repeat itself; over and over and over again.

Within my group I worked with young people who did auto mutilation or self-harm. For example, by stabbing themselves with a knife. These are often severely damaged souls, with a history of sexual abuse and satanic rituals. Some in their present life, others in previous lives. There are those who once were perpetrators themselves and now end up as victims in a certain group or order. However, it is extremely dangerous to generalize in this field; for every soul the narrative is different, as are the causes. From my passing in 1942, I chose to follow the path I have taken until now.

The Reversal

We have entered a phase of the end of a whole series of cosmic cycles. A Great Reversal is now underway. Things that had been hidden for a long time are coming fully into the light. In this period of an exponential influx of light, people are waking up en masse. Some experience this awakening as waking up from a long nightmare, which for many it actually was. Many New Age children incarnate, many of which will be system breakers. From basic to university educated. Sometimes it seems that things are going terribly slowly, but we in the spiritual world closely monitor every positive development. An invisible stream of energy brings everything that is not based on love into the Light. It raises awareness and creates a great longing for a truly human society; it positively changes an entire planet that has experienced darkness for so many millennia - a win-win society, a society without losers.

19. Jan

Leviahnarah: Through our spiritual telepathic call in the spheres to pass on knowledge regarding a self-chosen departure, Jan entered our group. Jan works in different atmospheres with journalists and others from the media world. After his departure and the reading of his entire book of life, he naturally returned to teaching. Along his line of incarnations he was a researcher and a bringer of truth. He was a starseed with a sincere desire to bring to light, that which is deeply hidden. Truths and purities that have been reversed and abused by those who serve the dark. He has brought much false light to the surface in his various lives, waking up, as far as possible, the groups of people who had gone along with it. The telepathic call in the spiritual world touched many people and so various workgroups came into being who exchanged all their experiences of the past earthly cycle. While collecting material for this book, Jan asked to be allowed to tell us his story, precisely because so many truth-seeking journalists are gagged or bribed.

Jan: I was an inspired journalist in my last life. My interest in what is hidden has a long history. Along my line of incarnations as a starseed I felt a strong inner urge to bring hidden darkness to light. Both here in the spiritual world and during my incarnations I have observed the energetic damage that comes with the rituals meant to control people; rituals to keep beautiful light-bearing people under a lower ceiling and use them as energetic batteries. To prevent them, with their higher frequencies resulting from their individual spiritual growth processes, from surpassing those who had power on Earth. In this way, many people were told that they were insignificant, and people were also told to be afraid of everything. Fear that they didn't originally have, which made them perform considerably less compared to the possibilities they had as free, light-bearing people. With the group in which I work I learned a lot from how oppression of humanity was created on Earth and then developed.

We exchange everything in the spiritual world that can serve the whole. It is all open here as well. We 'read' the Akashic Chronicles, the world' memory, together with like-minded people and we learn a lot from each other.

In a period in ancient Egypt I was able to bring a lot to the surface about hidden black rituals, wrapped up in a beautiful creation of false light. This was during one of my lives as a woman, and I worked in a temple and initiation school, where I took care of the clothes of the girls and the women. I took care of their overall wellbeing and did so inconspicuously. Hardly any attention was paid to me because I had an old and ugly injury to my face and I never spoke.

I noticed an energetic change in the girls who were initiated. They were needed as sex slaves of the ruling elite and had to participate in occult rituals. I could read their traumas in their energy field. Once initiated, few of them saw the world outside the walls of the initiation school. Parents 'gave' their girls and boys to the temple school, which was considered a great honour. These very deeply secretive orders, with magnificent facades, were at the service of a hidden darkness-serving elite whose servants sold their souls to the darkness over and over again from generation to generation. In this way they retained their power and prestige in a deceitful world.

So in that period of my life I was able to expose what was happening there in secret. That was also the intention of that life. When as a result my position had become untenable, I responded to an inner urge to flee the temple school and thereby disappeared from view. I was led to a Pleiadian temple community, into which I was admitted.

In that short period of time many truths about certain temples came out, partly because of me. This was seen by many; people with young children, both girls and boys. In the spiritual world we can see how certain families came loose from that deeply ingrained track of automatically handing over their children to such a beautiful temple on the outside but one of false light on the inside. It was very painful for those who for generations had given up their children to the temple in good faith. In spite of this, some people continued to hold on to these family traditions. They considered it an honour to donate a child to the temple, no matter what would happen to it. That, by the way, is something of all times.

In other lives as a man I have also described energetic damage and soul splitting of people as a result of paedophilia in hidden societies for example. Here and there on Earth there are still ancient books of mine, handwritten manuscripts from which many have gained knowledge.

In a life in Ireland, I met a man whom I had exposed as a false prophet in another life. He masked himself as a so-called bringer of light. However, he was a black magician. I was ten years old and lived with my mother in a castle in Ireland. The Lord of the castle had a son who was severely disabled both physically and mentally. My family was of a lineage of healers, herbalists, and they worked with healing energy. My mother knew how to give the boy a reasonably comfortable life with her herbal skills. If the boy suffered a rage, her presence alone calmed him down. I was trained as a healer by her and my grandmother.

One day, the boy's father heard of a great magician from the east of whom he believed would be able to completely heal his son. He sent for the man to be brought to the castle. Raised in the simplicity of a family of herbs and energetic healers, it was astonishing to see a man and a woman arrive with a whole entourage. Decorated with a brocade cloak and turban, with large ostentatious rings and jewels on the clothes of both the man and the woman; all was meant to impress the people who saw them.

What we as clairvoyants saw, however, was that the lord of the castle, hoping that his young son would be healed, opened himself completely to the magician. He was then energetically captivated by him and became like a fly in a spider's web. He firmly believed in everything the magician said and did. The only thing we saw was false light that was worshipped. The magician blinded almost everyone in the castle. As a ten-year-old, I observed the dark rituals from my inconspicuous hideout. I recognized the energy of this darkness serving man from earlier lives.

Our habits, the simplicity of our lives, our simple clothes, they were all ridiculed by the magician and his wife. The lord of the castle, enchanted as he was, said they were right. The magician saw in my mother and me, her son, an enemy of him and made us suspect. We were falsely accused of diabolical practices and the lord of the castle believed him. After all, he was blinded by the promise that his son would be healed. We were locked in a dungeon and tortured. Our pain and fear fed the darkness. In a ritual, attended by a whole group of people, our tongues were cut off.

Later, I met this dark soul in other incarnations. Every time I came into contact with him, I got pain in my mouth. In World War I, this man was a senior military officer who gave orders to torture people. He called it acts of war but in fact they were satanic blood sacrifices that had to be carried out on certain, very specific dates. The man enjoyed his work; he was a sadist.

Within the group we had formed in the spiritual world, his actions came to light in the holographic books of life of several people. Souls like him were brought to a low-frequency area by the prevailing darkness after their transition. They were sparing of souls like his: souls in which Light and Love were largely absent and who did what was expected of them by the ruling powers. It was impossible for such a soul to go to the Light after death. Throughout time, only in a physical body was this man able to present himself as a brilliant light. It was false light, however, that blinded masses of people.

He incarnated again in the twentieth century. My mother from the life in Ireland was now a good friend of mine and we recognized him immediately. She told me that she felt a profound disgust when she entered the room where this man gave a lecture. Worshipped by many, using wonderful words, a beautiful entourage, few saw how deceitful this 'Master of Light' as he liked to present himself was. People surrendered completely to the whole act he was playing. They saw it as a great honour that he wanted to answer their personal questions.

As part of my job, I had to interview this man. On the railway platform on the way to his hometown my mouth started to hurt as I was thinking about how I wanted to do the interview. My friend had warned me about him, she told me about Ireland and other places where he crossed our path of which we were both aware. She talked about the euphoria we had seen in many people during the lecture in the room, the pure adoration people had for him, complete surrender.
But she also told about the energy of the false light she had observed. She had listened to her deep sense of disgust and had left before he would do a healing with the whole audience. She did not connect with his energy. I was stubborn, as I have been in so many other lives over and over again. I wanted to see with my own eyes exactly how this man worked. I shouldn't have done that. During the interview I felt a pain in my mouth again. It took a lot of effort to formulate my questions properly. What I now know in the spiritual world is that I made a new connection with him because of my great curiosity. The mother in Ireland had already warned me not to spy on the magician like I did in the castle from my hiding place. But I did not listen.

The universe works in such a way that I was warned again for this man not to make a connection with his energy. My drive to expose what was not of the Light became a trap in that way. The whole thing had actually become an obsession. Here I know that he recognized me too, though on a subconscious level.

That's when the psychic attacks started at night. I was besieged by dark entities; one attack after another. It got worse and worse. I ended up with a psychiatrist. However, whatever I told this doctor about my experiences during those night hours, he didn't understand it. He prescribed me antidepressants and other medications that were supposed to alleviate my fears. I started hallucinating. My immaterial assailants, directed by the old magician, gratefully made use of the openings created by the heavy medication I was on. When I ate, I 'saw' creatures walking across my plate. I saw very scary creatures crawling along the walls, just as the famous painter Hieronymus Bosch depicted them. The frightening shapes made me very scared, something they enjoyed very much. I barricaded my windows thinking it would help keep those horrible entities out of my house.

I was eventually locked away in a psychiatric hospital and then given even worse medication. So it all got a lot worse because of that. I know now that a lot of people were experiencing such things there, it was horrible. I had completely lost myself in a dark cocoon that enveloped me. A cocoon of energy carefully created by the black magician. Packaged, as many have described this phenomenon.

One day I walked to the railway and jumped in front of the train. Outside my body I saw the havoc I had caused. I was welcomed by a small woman whom I recognized as my grandmother, together with a whole group of Light Beings. I 'saw' how the Light Beings removed the black cocoon that had been ripped by the collision. Other than that, I made my journey to the Beyond unconsciously. Only much later I became aware of life on the other side of the veil.

The 'bed' in the healing chamber floated in a white-gold-blue-green energy. Loved ones who were already in the spiritual world visited me there. When I thought of them they were there instantly. When I started to read my book of life, I was given loving specialist help. My soul journey, through all my incarnations of the past 26,000 years, shows a relentless need to uncover occult control of people, both whole groups and individuals. In these chaotic times large groups of people awaken, they see through the large and small lies that have been told for so many centuries, to the greater glory of people serving darkness.

Recently, the man who so besieged me in my last life died. In his last days on Earth, his hypocrisy had become even worse. Later, as a group - people who had all been severely damaged by this man in pedophile networks in different lives - we were allowed to examine his life path after his transition. This is very rarely allowed. As a group, we learned a lot from the state of mind of this soul; a soul that tortured and raped others in different incarnations without any empathy or even remorse.

He believed in what he did and saw himself as a true Messiah who brought healing to many people. Outside his body, at night, he stole a lot of light energy from people through an energetic cord that he had carefully attached tot them. He lacked a natural vertical light connection through which energy can flow endlessly so you wouldn't have to steal it from others. He wasn't able to generate it himself. Please know that there are many such energy robbers out there who aren't able to get light energy naturally. Often charming charismatic people, usually very successful, living on the energy they draw from their 'walking batteries'. That can be partners, children or colleagues. When they are well known in a certain circle that admires them they get a lot of energy from their worshippers. This also happens with 'gurus' in front of a crowd of people. These are major pitfalls for the soul.

Discovering and developing for oneself what is real or unreal, loving from the heart or loveless, that is what many people are doing now: making a distinction - people who only take care of themselves versus people who also take care of others. It is seen, shared and exchanged in awakened states of being. Much has surfaced in the area of false light and lies.

We could 'see' that this man was part of a pedophilia ring for a long time. He was a very violent man. When he passed over he could not go to the Light, his spiritual baggage was too heavy due to his many lives in darkness. In this time of transition, souls can no longer go to the lower spheres when they have such attunement. Those lowest of spheres are dissolved as we already heard. Curious as I was, we asked what would happen to souls after their transition. Some go to very special Galactic healing chambers but most are taken to the great Central Sun. There is a whole stream of souls who have committed very serious crimes against humanity, animals and the planet. They are removed from the planet and will not incarnate here or anywhere else. They will go to other places.

Our joint work in the spiritual world as guides and teachers in the spheres to work with people still living in a material body is picked up by people everywhere and it helps people to wake up in the great process of planetary awakening. For many people it is a difficult path to develop and see for themselves what is pure and true from the heart. We are with many to assist them in that great process of awakening. It is happening and can no longer be stopped. That is the Reversal.

Beyond matter

Beyond matter
lies man's true being,
that cannot be tainted by sin,
that cannot be smeared by crime,
that cannot be infected by desire,
that cannot burn by fire,
that cannot be wetted by water
and also, cannot be killed by death.

Vivekananda

20. Steven

Leviahnarah: In the earthly Spheres of Light are places where like-minded people meet. Like-minded people in the sense that they have empirical experiences in previous lives, which eventually led to a self-chosen departure from the material world. For some it has been many lifetimes since they chose to do so, for others quite recently. They create their own place where they can exchange insights with each other and where they can see where they have been able to resolve darkness. They are people, souls, who chose suicide a long time ago and have now gone down a path where they learned how to balance their old energy, which was unbalanced. Here it is not about finger pointing, but looking for answers and solutions.

Steven: My experience with suicide was, by human standards, a very long time ago. I have lived many lives in balance, in which I managed to balance disharmony before that life ended naturally. In incarnations in ancient Egypt, I also learned lessons and gained experience in temple schools. I did this when those schools and temples were still pure. That would be different there later on. Everything a soul learns belongs to you. Apparently we cannot understand this in our daily physical life on Earth, but my experiences in this are clear. In the spiritual world we see and know who we are, in all our wholeness and disharmony. We can fully see our shadow side here. By looking at this openly, we can work on ourselves. With the necessary help we choose for incarnations in which we can learn exactly what we need. Sometimes these are experiences of which we, in earthly life, in a material body, cannot understand that we would have chosen this ourselves. In the sleeping hours, when we are outside our bodies, we have a full view of our blueprint of life again. That is, if we want to see that ourselves of course. Not everyone wants to look at his or her shadow side. If, for example, someone is addicted to drugs or alcohol, the process will be much more difficult.

In the spiritual world I am aware of my earlier incarnations. When you read your book of life immediately after your arrival in the spheres, you have a lot to 'see' and process of what your personal life journey has been. We see our life holographically, we can feel, know and see. See what Was. Seeing how you tackled the bumps and potholes on your way. Where did you confront, for example, your fear and where did it come from; was it ever created by you and if so, what kind of ancient history is associated with it.

In ancient Egypt, in the still pristine first period after Atlantis, I was born into a family of rulers. My upbringing was strict, my childhood delightful, but completely focused on preparing for the succession of others. This was already clear at birth. A seer at the court where both my parents worked saw what talents I had developed from my earlier incarnations. He also oversaw the possibilities for the new life. It was wonderful to develop talents incarnation after incarnation, to gather knowledge and to be able to go to the limit of my abilities in such a life. My teachers always lovingly guided those lives. I was aware that my teachers came from a different place than Earth. Mine came from the Pleiadian system. Their radiant love I will never forget. Until my last life I experienced that the bonds of love cannot be broken.

We learned the cosmic laws and acted upon them. Living like this, life was in balance, the energy was in balance. In several lives, I became a governor. From my different teachers I was taught the different degrees of human consciousness and how to deal with it. I learned about the differences between the races because I would have a lot to do with them in my later work. I loved these studies and continued with them in my subsequent lives. In one of my future lives during that first era of Egypt, my Pleiadic teachers told me about the different peoples in the universe. Sometimes she drew images of different people and beings with a reed pen and ink. Beautiful loving creatures for example with amber almond-shaped eyes, shining like gemstones; others with blue crystalline eyes; people with long hairs on their necks, bound together by golden ribbons; strong long slender appearances, radiating strength and love. I became very old in that life.

The end result of all these lessons made me see the people on Earth as 'Unity in Diversity'. Being able to look at people that way has brought me a lot of good in the course of my lives, mostly in administrative functions, but also in a series of subsequent lives as a doctor and therapist. The different incarnations I lived in a harmonious society, next to the structure of my classes in the temple schools, level after level, made me strongly aware of what was pure and impure. In a certain period of incarnations, when darkness increased in Egypt, I searched and found the right teachers on my path. I wanted to learn how to energetically make the right distinction. It happened so often that people had a beautiful shining mask, but underneath it a dark character. False light. I learned to see when people were telling lies and when they were pure and sincere. I immediately recognized manipulative people who tried to harm others. This talent developed and was an important tool to keep going the path of purity. I became more sensitive, and that also made me more vulnerable, something I was aware of at that moment. During my training I learned a lot about this.

In one lifetime, during the reign of Akhnaton - called Ahnahtah in the spiritual world - I enjoyed the construction of the new city, El-Amarna. The Light that was built there still exists in many conscious souls. In the spiritual world, El-Amarna still exists as a City of Light and Love. It was an age when the Black Priest in Thebes wanted to destroy everything that was based on Light and eventually they managed to infiltrate this Light-based society. They used black magic rituals that led to severe setbacks for the Light. Superstitious as many young souls were at the time, the dark got a hold on them. Like barnacles on a ship, those who came from the lower spiritual spheres would suckle into the energy fields of people of the light, everyone who had a few energetic openings for them. I was aware of these practices.

During a short voyage I was attacked and fell from my chariot. It was a deliberate action of the darkness. I was seriously injured and through my injury an entity was able to squeeze itself within my field of light: a very malignant cunning entity. He and so many others, I know now, have created a lot of misery, a tremendous amount of misery.

Possession

When you are possessed, there's nothing you can do about it yourself. Even when such entity would want to leave, it is often not even possible anymore. The entity usually cannot leave the body into which it has entered on its own strength. The only way is suicide by the one that is possessed. Sometimes, when the entity really wants to leave the body, it can incite the possessed person to commit suicide.

Thanks to my formation in the temple schools during my previous incarnations, I was at times aware of the entity that was taking over my life completely. My soul essence warned me, knowledge that is never lost. It was, you might say, a fight to the death. Unfortunately, the black magic of the priests of Thebes - these so supreme men - was tremendously strong. In spite of being possessed, I was at times aware, and in one of those clear moments I took poison and ended my life.

I was welcomed by my mother who already lived in the spiritual world and by my other guides. I now know that liberating a human being possessed by a low-frequency entity requires very specialized treatment. During the transition I saw a very dark creature, something I will never forget. Light Beings fetched me. The dark entity was brought to another sphere. At that moment, all the lower, darker spheres still existed. That was also where it came from. In earlier lives, this entity had been a powerful man who had caused untold suffering during his reign: a man who had no compassion for the people on his land. And because this man in those lives had such a low, darkness-focused frequency, he needed energetic nourishment and he made sure of that by subjecting his subordinates to his dictatorship and reign of terror. He worshiped Baal and ruled a fear-oriented society.

Fear, poverty, bloodshed, suffering, that was his nourishment. Through his reign he provided for enormous amounts of energetic nourishment for the many who directed him from the darkness. His intentions became clear when we gained insight into this. He tried to satisfy his lusts through me. Usually the attacked person does not notice when another entity intrudes. Thanks to my many lives in the temple schools and my need to learn about these things, I did recognize it. I was terribly cold every time this entity wanted to impose its will on me. Had I been weaker with regard to my soul frequency and without all the lessons learned earlier, I would have been a will-less victim. I would have done exactly what he wanted to experience through my body. I myself was only a moderate drinker, but this entity wanted a lot of drink. Here too I recognized that I was no longer completely myself. My choice of food was, when he pushed me aside, totally different. Where I did everything in moderation, he especially wanted a lot of decadent food.

All in all it was a terrible experience. Still, it taught me a lot that I could use in later lives. Thus I was able to help people who were possessed using black magical rituals. I've been able to do that in many lives. Already in ancient times, when the darkness increased, I recognized possessed people. Many had become possessed with the help of certain forms of violence, often sexual violence as well. In those ancient times there were shamans and spiritual healers who, if the takeover of a body happened not too long ago, knew techniques to remove the entity. They had special care and knowledge for helping victims after such liberation. This knowledge was transferred from healer to healer through the ages. Known by their higher selves there have been many who later used this knowledge again to help people.

Many think that Roman Catholic exorcists are a relic of the past and that possession is something of the imagination: something that is better cured by psychotherapy or medication. Nothing could be further from the truth. Devil exorcism, or rather the exorcism of a dark entity, is something of all times and cultures and light-bearing people in the Roman Catholic Church knew - and know - that their cleansing rituals can work. In Eastern countries they call these dark entities djinns and in Christian traditions demons.

In my last two lives I was a physician-therapist and was able to help many people to become themselves again. Because I worked in what is called the 'alternative circuit', but essentially with old empirical knowledge, I was able to work in a certain silence and in the protective environment of the spiritual world. Fellow therapists and doctors knew where to find me. The space in which I worked was specially created energetically so that the process of liberation could take place. I have had many children and young people in my practice in the last part of my life. Many hundreds have passed me by over the years. Children and young people are easier to set free than older people. That has everything to do with, for example, drinking, drugs and the use of medication. And of course with ingrained mental patterns. The will is then too weakened to resist the intruder's will. Fortunately, there were many fellow doctors and therapists who recognized possession, whether or not clairaudience, and quickly contacted me. I would always and immediately help these children and young people. In my last life I shared my knowledge with people who had sufficient inner strength. Sometimes we helped a patient together and that's how the other person learned from my experiences and my way of doing things. It requires purity and a certain frequency of the soul.

Here in the spiritual world I have the attunement to the Cities of Light and am fully familiar again with the teachers I had in my first period in Egypt. Here are my dear Pleiadic teachers. However, they no longer have the appearance they had in that early period. Because of their own lives in this cycle, they have acquired an earthly, human appearance. In these places in the different Cities of Light there are also Pleiadic and other extraterrestrial teachers with whom we work closely together. One of them is Ohan. He taught me in the spiritual world how to use my knowledge for the benefit of people who are possessed by entities. We gather in a special room where we meet about twenty people who are still living on Earth. Everywhere in the different Cities of Light there are such groups, each attuned to the demographic group they are working with. Each culture has its own traditions and beliefs regarding entities looking for a new body.

In this time of transition, a lot of help is offered from the spiritual world. Light Beings and people from other planets with a lot of empirical experience regarding this spiritual suffering, are committed to transfer their knowledge and expertise. This knowledge can in turn be transferred to the various earthly needs. This knowledge then merges with the earthly experiences of people who do this work: reinforcement, you might say. The entities that are extracted from the bodies are brought to a special area. They are very often souls, people, who in several past lives have descended into deep spiritual darkness; usually with very heavy luggage with regard to people, animals and the planet.

Thoughts

We can't prevent thoughts
circling like black birds
above our heads.

However, we can prevent
them from building nests
in our hair.

Chinese proverb

21. John

Addiction

***Leviahnarah*:** In the collective there is a large group of souls who once had to cope with addiction. Addictions are of all times and take various forms. Basically, they are the same, although for the various types of addictions there are also various therapies and healing chambers. On a free will planet like Earth, darkness and people who serve the darkness have also deliberately introduced addictions and habits to trap large groups of light carriers. Usually they were not trapped in one life, but in many consecutive lives as well. Despite the enormous amount of personal and collective suffering that resulted from this, it has also been a valuable source for individuals and for mankind as a whole to learn very important lessons.

At the end of this cosmic cycle, however, addictions will have to be ended. Souls who choose not to go along with this earthly cycle can hold on to their addictions of their own free will. They will enter a new cycle and move on to another 3D planet, where they can continue their evolutionary path individually and as part of a new collective.

***John*:** Along my lineage of incarnations, you see a number of lives of addiction to mind-altering substances, especially opiates. A certain part of my incarnations was free from this addiction. In fact, in many eras, I warned of the dangers of them. After our transition, we read our "book of life", or blueprint of life. I have had several lives in Asia, several of which in ancient China. I had lives as a doctor, acupuncturist, and teacher in motion and meditation techniques. The common thread through these lives was the preventive health care of the people for whom I was medically responsible, in addition to alleviating people's suffering and helping them heal wherever possible.

As I 'read' my last life, in which I chose suicide, I returned to the point where my addiction began. I was attracted to Leviahnarah's collective to share my story. Every story of every human soul regarding addiction is different. In my story, I want to go to the point where my addiction began, more than 1200 years ago. I was a doctor in ancient China. I had a great intention to alleviate people's suffering. In the many thousands of years of history of China, we see that we were able to do a great deal to help people heal and keep them healthy. Medicine was of very high quality. The energetic medicine, the acupuncture, was used very skilfully, also in operations and for pain relief in people with injuries. With healing hands wounds were closed and healed. At that time we used drugs such as opium to a minimum even though we did have them at our disposal.

I myself was severely injured in an accident. However, at that time I was alone and unable to treat myself, let alone call in my colleagues. I then resorted to using the opiates that I carried in my luggage. It was not my intention at that moment to leave earthly life, I still had so much to do. However, the pain was so intense that the medicines I took brought me great relief at this difficult moment. It took days before I was found and a colleague was able to take care of my injuries. However, I had taken so many opiates that I was half unconscious. Stitching large wounds, not before some days after they were inflicted, is difficult and sometimes even impossible. So I died from my large wounds after all. The last strong thought just before the transition is taken with you to the next life. Because of my infernal pains this thought was my strong desire for more and more pain relief. A yearning for the intoxication and no longer to feel the pain. For this reason, there was an unconscious but strong desire for opiates in several of my next incarnations. I had literally 'taken it with me' from that earlier life.

In one of my lives, also in ancient China, I lived in a big city. As a merchant, I led a simple life and sold my merchandise on the market. As so often happens, it started quite innocently. At a gloomy moment in my life, a friend took me to the opium den. Instead of solving the problems that caused my gloominess, I opted for the temptation of the intoxication of forgetting. So I quickly became addicted to opium and often visited opium dens where dozens of people were using with opium pipes.

So that's how it works: the smells, the intoxication, the disappearing of concerns and the ending of the gloominess acted as triggers. Of course, the problems did not disappear, on the contrary. Attempts of loved ones to keep me away from the opium all failed. I now lived in another world far away from my earthly troubles. When as a result my circumstances in social life became untenable, I deliberately took an overdose.

Another incarnation, again in ancient China, I accepted all the help that came my way. This time I would solve my problems. I tackled what had to change and no longer came into contact with mind-altering substances. This was followed by several incarnations in Asia where I specialized in acupuncture, among other things. My intention was to heal old traumas, reduce pain or, if possible, heal completely.

Vietnam

One life after that, I was a physician in the U.S. Army. I then worked vigorously to fight the pain of wounded soldiers. It was my deep intention to relieve their suffering. Never before in my lineage of incarnation have my disappointments been so great. Within the family in which I grew up, I was told to do everything for God and country. That was the deepest conviction of my parents. My father and uncles had already gone to Europe during the Second World War and their stories coloured our family. From one of them we also heard the stories of the war in Korea. A famous American television series of this war, set in a mobile field hospital, shows its hopelessness. The series is called 'MASH'.

Pictures of the fallen family members stood on the mantelpiece. I saw that they were honoured and adored by everyone. Patriotism was strong in my family. That is how my brothers and I were brought up and all three of us left for Vietnam. My youngest brother stayed at home in the United States. At that time I had already had many lives in Asia, so in a short time I started to love the country, its nature and its people again. But soon I got insights that I had never had at home before. Because what the hell were we doing there? Most American men were struggling with the climate and culture of the country. They were often aggressive and felt pure hatred for the 'enemy'. Many, completely brainwashed, went along with the atrocities of war.

Through a number of hospitals I eventually ended up at the frontline. Apart from a few weeks of leave, I stayed there for three long years. I had literally ended up in hell. A never-ending stream of wounded, mostly young men, passed by, badly damaged both physically and mentally. Their superiors generously supplied them with drugs; drugs that gave them the courage to fight at the front. I now know that during the First World War there was already enormous experimentation with drugs for men who fought in the trenches. From a few people in our collective I know of their experiences with drugs when they were soldiers in World War II. For example, the men who stormed the beaches of Normandy on D-Day were all drugged. Thousands were massacred that day.

Of course, I came into contact with opiates again in Vietnam. In the period of the heaviest fighting, resulting in an enormous stream of often very badly wounded soldiers, I regularly gave an overdose. Knowing that there was nothing we could do for them while they were suffering the most infernal pains, it was a true salvation for them. When one day I myself was wounded during a shelling raid, I was, over-tired and malnourished, sent back to America through a hospital.

In the meantime, more photographs of fallen family members had been added to the mantelpiece at home. Both my brothers had been killed at the front. However, I could no longer listen to the words about their heroism and left for the north, where I stayed with an old friend I knew from the military. We were both heavily traumatized by our experiences in Vietnam. At that time I had terrible nightmares, reliving the horrible experiences of the front. The images of them came to me like a continuous film. A deep depression was the result. It was at this point that I again came into contact with hard drugs. My friend worked for an organisation: the Underground Railroad. That was one of the escape routes for young people who refused to be sent to war. That was very sensible of course, but they were called deserters for that reason and had to be kept out of the hands of the authorities. I joined them then. From my own experience I knew what they had consciously or unconsciously chosen for. I was fully committed to them.
In those last years of the Vietnam War we were able to bring so many young people to safety: young and strong people with a whole life ahead of them. The period in which I worked on the escape route did me a great deal of good.

One more time I went back to my family. They were still doing the same, adoring soldiers leaving for Asia. Although they spoke nice words about the Vietnamese people, I knew at the same time that they were really racist. Because of all my other experiences, I saw that very clearly at that moment. However, my dreams and nightmares became worse and worse. What started with a drink when we took a few people safely to Canada, I was increasingly looking for the intoxication of forgetting. Eventually they became morphine products. Soon I ended up in a very nasty film I couldn't escape from: a film with images of the horrific injuries of the young soldiers who had been burned into my retinas. And even though work on the escape route had become my great passion, the relentless stream of images of the war in my head made me feel the need for an ever-deeper intoxication. It was not so much with the thought of wanting to die, but at one point I deliberately took an overdose.

My personal guide and my two brothers welcomed me. They were with me during my stay in the healing chamber. Every time I thought about them one of them came or both came. Being so quiet together was good and extremely healing. My healing process of the past life, with all its horrible experiences, took a long time. That's how it is with all heavily traumatized soldiers, then and unfortunately it still is. Reading my book of life brought insights that I had not always had during my life. Throughout that period loved ones and Light Beings helped me. With a lot of patience they helped me to 'read' my blueprint of life.

Leviahnarah: In the spiritual world there is no time, but you can compare the healing processes of people like John with one to two years of Earthly time.

John: Later, brought together by our spiritual guides, I met several people who I had helped through euthanasia. In the spiritual world, the Spheres of Light, our subtle bodies are whole. When, for example, you no longer have legs, you are whole again with two legs. You no longer see the physical damages, but the damages on the spiritual level are still there and are often long lasting and sometimes very difficult to heal. Usually they are brought along to the next incarnation. Old physical scars can also come back in the body in a next life. Good regression and reincarnation therapists have extensive experience with this.

I have been working in the spheres for a long time now in a place where wounded soldiers arrive, no matter from which war and from which side. These are highly specialized healing chambers with the right energies these severely traumatized people need. Depending on their spiritual alignment, they can meet there and exchange matters with each other. In this way 'enemies' can talk to each other in the fields and gardens surrounding the healing chambers. It depends on their degree of insight, their spiritual attunement, whether they can see how wars are created, by whom and why.

In this end time, at the end of an Earth cycle, we see an awakening of unprecedented importance. People who have passed over and are interested in this can gain full insight into the Earth divide-and-rule techniques throughout the centuries and of which they have often become victims. And there are now many souls who want to understand how many lies have been sold to mankind through the ages. Studies can be done with regard to, for example, the mineral treasures of the countries where wars were unleashed in order to gain possession of those areas. Or the wars over important energetic places, vortexes, gates and the Ley Lines, terrestrial energy pathways and energy nodes. The deep insights that we were part of immense blood sacrifices of darkness, is what can now be seen and studied by so many people. More and more people visit such a Hall of Knowledge in this end time and their longing for knowledge about all causes and their consequences is huge. In every sphere of Light there are such places. No one is forcing you to do it but it is the growing, collective awakening, which creates this profound interest. Pure Knowledge, stripped of the many layers of lies in which we have lived for many thousands of years. Seeing through these numerous lies also has a profound effect on the Earth's field. It brings mass consciousness and insight.

There are also many doctors, nurses and therapists who have continued and deepened their profession after their transition to the Spheres of Light.

Leviahnarah: One of the things John talks about here is the influence of strong thoughts at the moment of transition. We see this, for example, when people starved to death, which often happened in the concentration camps during the Second World War. How people would talk to each other in the barracks about food; talk about delicacies, the one even tastier than the other. These are strong thoughts in a starving body. Sometimes this manifested itself in a next life in the form of voraciousness, compulsory eating addictions, a feeling of never having enough; having to have cupboards full of food in the house; always immediately replenishing something when it was used; stuff yourself up until you're sick to death. Another aspect is hate; dying with a strong negative thought towards one or more people. That too is often taken to the next life. Usually this goes hand in hand with not being able to see or not wanting to see the cause of that hatred in that next life. Hate is a low vibrating energy. It keeps you in a low frequency and stops spiritual growth.

Experiences of extreme violence, severe injuries, traumas associated with alcohol abuse, addictions in general and the thoughts of 'never again...' also have strong influences on the next life. There are people who are already feeling sick when they get close to drunken people or hear the sound or smell the stench of a crowded pub. The way drunken people speak can trigger old experiences of a previous life.

Imprisonment

Death in captivity is also a strong emotional trigger, captivity in every conceivable form. That could have been an earlier life in a dungeon, lying in dirt and stench: a confinement with many at a time in a small and filthy space. But also imprisonment in a job; we see that with scientists, for example. There is a pigeonholing spirit prevailing in many areas: not being able to be free in your expression and inner possibilities. Not being allowed to express your curiosity for fear of ridicule or worse; when it is prohibited to investigate things that are taboo or lie too far outside the accepted field of research.

And imprisonment within a marriage or relationship, or a family situation you were in as a child. We can think of many forms of incarceration that can be taken with us in the transition to the spiritual world. In this day and age many will feel an extreme need to be able to do things in freedom. Reincarnation and regression therapists have experience with many such processes with their clients.

In our collective and in many others we are busy with people who brought a great sense of guilt with them. At the end of a life, someone's experiences can come by like a film or photo book. Seeing what was created during that life. There can be many reasons and causes for guilt. There is a category of souls who have abused children over and over again in different lives. Sometimes this concerns incest within the family, sometimes abuse of children in religious institutions or in pedophile circles.

We regularly saw that people who abused their own children were also extremely religious at the same time. As if one could erase the other. We often saw that people were convinced that their sins would be forgiven if they went to church every week, prayed a lot or bought indulgences. All of these people will see, feel, and experience whatever they did to others the moment they read their book of life. Their often far-reaching hypocrisy is seen and felt in every detail and in a certain way they end up in a kind of self-created hell. In addition to seeing and feeling the consequences of their own actions, they also see and feel the causes.

When they totally lack empathy and stubbornly cling to the conviction that their actions were not loveless and damaging to the other, they may be given a new life in which they experience for themselves what they have done to others. Where there is empathy, we often see feelings of guilt. Some are then extremely focused on doing good. They will often actually do that, usually with the help of the spiritual guides. They get many gentle nudges to balance old loveless energy.

So there are many different kinds of strong thoughts that people can have at the end of their lives. One I would like to mention at the end of this chapter: the experience of someone smelling the scent of decomposing bodies just before his death, what resulted in extreme mysophobia in the next life. A man who was presumed dead an thrown into a mass grave in a concentration camp but was actually still alive. He died a death in horror. He showered many times in a day and then put on clean clothes. He also washed and scrubbed his hands all day long. With the help of a regression therapist, this man was able to heal a lot by reliving the moment of his death in that previous life. There are many processes like this, although it is no small thing have to relive such an end. Henri de Vidal de St-Germain, since a few years in the spiritual world, has shown us a lot about these things and about the specific help these souls can get.

22. Annemarie

Leviahnarah: Annemarie contacted our group. She responded to the call to collect material for this book. She went beyond the veil a long time ago and chose to stay there. Her story may help people with certain ideas and beliefs about the spheres, or what many call the afterlife.

Annemarie: After my self-chosen transition to the spiritual world, I chose not to incarnate in a new material body, but to use my empirical knowledge and expertise of different lives to help people who chose a self-chosen departure. As Leviahnarah says several times, there are many reasons why people choose to do that. Many do the work I can do in the healing chambers: work that produces results, especially in this period of the end time to the next Earth frequency from 3D to 5D. In this period of Earth's great transition, many souls have been examined and tested for what was energetically unbalanced. Many people are processing the old baggage of many lives that they have never tackled and transformed before. Choices are made before we incarnate and they can be found in the blueprint of life.

However, not everyone will individually be able to balance old negative energy in this Dark Age, a time when so much is happening globally. I realize that many of us are eager to share our experiences in the spiritual realms with everyone who lives on Earth today. This can sometimes lead to repetitions, but I can only impress upon the reader that everything that is said here is so incredibly important and has been hidden from us for centuries. That is why I am telling my story here, if necessary again, so that everyone becomes aware of the positive message that the spiritual spheres want to share with all material souls.

While reading our book of life, we see and feel what has been created by us. We experience the beautiful loving events and what that meant for the world around us. We also experience the loveless events and what impact they had on the world around us. We see and feel the consequences of our actions: hours of truth in which we see what is and see what was. The negative baggage we gathered alongside all the positive things we did.

We see where we grew in frequency and how that positively affected our lives. We also see in all its facets how and where our light strength ended up in lower frequencies and which decisions and impulses formed the basis for this. We see how we climbed up again in our luminosity from such a period and how we preserved it. In doing so we feel what we have done to others: the hour of truth for each of us.

As we read the book of life or blueprint, we can see what our intentions were and to what extent we implemented them. It may very well be that that deep intention did everything possible to balance certain things, but that the environment was uncooperative; each person from their own karmic baggage and blockages. We see how sincere we were or not. How we very cleverly avoided all difficulties or just went straight for it, because we felt that we wanted to solve things or find balance. Many people think that when we read our book of life we are judged and that causes fear for many people when they are in the last phase of their physical lives. Sometimes relatively small things suddenly become big in that person's consciousness. Especially when old imprints from childhood resurface: the teachings of parents, school and church about sin, hell and purgatory. Fortunately there are people who help us through dying guidance to let go of those old imprints. To see the beautiful things we have experienced.

When I chose to leave my mortal body it was seen in my environment as suicide. I asked for help that I didn't get when I became seriously ill. I stored certain medication and chose to go to Switzerland for a month. Friends owned a small chalet where I could retreat for a while. I was in the beautiful nature, without the stimuli of people around me who told me what was good for me. Like for example the conversations with the oncologists and their conviction that chemotherapy was best for me. Or friends who wanted me to prolong my life, while I felt and knew that they themselves carried a great fear of death. Nobody talked about the quality of life during and after those treatments.

I contemplated my life and got the feeling that my guides were helping me with that. It was as if I was browsing through a thick book, sometimes at high speed. There, in those beautiful mountains, I reflected on my life and realized that it had been a full and good life. I had done what I wanted to do and had found deep human satisfaction in doing so. I had worked as a pediatrician in England and had also worked in India and Africa for several periods as a volunteer. When I was in my thirties

I met the love of my life and we got married. We had the same profession and were both attuned to each other with regard to our passion: helping children to heal. So many damaged souls incarnated in this end time to experience and heal. In India we came into contact with physically and mentally severely damaged children, both through incest and abuse in pedophile circles. Later on, in addition to these children, we also met adults with severe damage, both physical and mental deformities. My husband was a surgeon and helped boys and girls to heal wherever he could. From religious circles in India, Africa and England girls came to us who were severely damaged by genital mutilation. Many were scarred for life if they had not already died of blood loss or infections. There were moments in our lives when we couldn't go any further, being exhausted and energetically worn out. Then we would go into the Yorkshire hills for walking for a short period of time and then started our strenuous work again.

There were people around us who exposed child abuse, but who were not listened to or even gagged. This was in the early 1960s. It is only now in the first two decades of the 21st century that we see what was so carefully hidden coming to light. It comes out through books and especially through social media with stories, photos and videos. There are also statements under oath, from people who have had to go through this: everything becomes visible. Even though there are many people who don't want to hear about it, it is now visible in all sorts of ways. Of course you have to want to see it.

Our work on Earth with children with specific injuries was stressful. We were put under pressure not to reveal the many wrongs we could and wanted to expose. My husband fell ill and died of an acute heart attack. I tried to continue our work and left for Africa where I worked with others in the care of child. I did that work for three years. Then I also became ill and appeared to have cancer at an advanced stage. Earlier I attributed my great fatigue to the many hours I worked, the terrible things I had seen and experienced, the stress, the poor food I ate, but it turned out to be the cancer. After returning to England it became clear that the treatment would be a process of intensive chemotherapy. I knew what such heavily toxic treatments did to a body. My immune system was already compromised due to the hard life I had led and as a doctor I knew what was going to happen. No, I wanted to unwind from within and to make up my own mind what I wanted to do.

The weeks in Switzerland were healing and brought me very close to myself. I began to dream and I felt that enough had been enough, I had lived my life the way I had wanted: a full and fulfilled life. I often had to think about my deceased sweetheart and felt that it was good where he was staying, beyond the veil. I often walked past a beautiful place where I would take a rest for a moment and absorb the beautiful scenery. I was aware that if I asked for euthanasia at home in England, it would not be given to me. I did not know any colleague who would want to do that. There had been some scandals and widely reported in the media: some doctor who had given help with a self-chosen departure. It was widely portrayed as a despicable tragedy, while to me it seemed like an act of charity because it was a hopeless situation and the person seeking help suffered a great deal of pain. Even now it is still difficult, if not impossible, to ask for euthanasia in the circles where I was working then.

I decided to take matters into my own hands. I had no children and my parents were no longer alive. In my beloved spot with the beautiful view, I thought about whether it would harm other people, but I couldn't think of anyone. At home in England I had all the documents ready for my funeral. I had taken care of them as soon as I knew I was ill, but at that moment I had no idea how and in what way I was going to leave physical life.

One beautiful day I walked to my beautiful spot in the mountains. I knew hikers would find me there. I was reluctant to depart from the house of my dear friends who had entrusted me with their chalet. I left a letter there for them and wrote to an old friend in England. I described that I did not want to choose the degrading treatments that I knew would come if I opted for chemotherapy. It was the late 1960s. Much has changed since that time, but even now, if I were still living in the physical world, I would not choose that treatment. And I know here that many doctors agree with me.

The medication I took made me fall asleep and not long after that my heart stopped beating. I "saw" myself lying there, peacefully asleep. Next to me was my bag with a letter for those who would find me.

My sweetheart came to welcome me, together with a dear childhood friend. We all stayed with my body until a hiker, who immediately called for help, found it. For this man, Albert, the neighbour of the chalet next to mine, it was not a great shock. During a walk together I had told him of my illness and the choice I wanted to make in the peace and quiet of the mountains. This man had been a general practitioner all his life and seemed to understand my considerations without saying too much. Later I met him in the spheres, after he himself had died at an advanced age, and I thanked him. Sometimes it seems as if certain things are meant to be, especially when we make a well-considered choice.

Spiritual flowers

I went to a healing chamber of which there are an awful lot, all kinds and frequencies. For me there was a special healing chamber for cancer, one with blue and white-golden energy. My loved ones were around me whenever I thought of them. Amazing was the experience of receiving spiritual flowers. Albert, my neighbour in Switzerland, whom I now know had been an anthroposophical general practitioner, carried knowledge of life beyond the veil. He also carried the knowledge that you could visualize spiritual flowers and ask your guide to send them to whomever you want to give them to. It was accompanied by a message: 'white roses for a new beginning, Albert'. I kept them for a long time and took them with me to the places where I continued on my way.

I had to learn again to enjoy the tranquillity of the gardens around the healing rooms. My working life had always been like a rollercoaster. After all, the work was never done, especially in the places where I worked in India and in Africa. The last few years it had been pure madness. What I came across and experienced in my work had a heavy impact on my life as a doctor. Here I now work together in a dimension with many people to take care of children who, after years of incest or pedophilia, decide they can't go on. There are also many adults here who are so badly damaged that they cannot build a normal family life or maintain normal relationships. Here we see how they are as it were veiled by a dark blanket, how they were robbed of their beautiful light energy. When the departed soul needs rest, the healing chambers can be completely private and that is usually the case. But they can also be open so that, and this often concerns young children, they can be going through these processes together. There are children among them who were captive for many years, who were kept hidden and constantly abused. The fields around these specific healing chambers are designed for play and fun.

There are a few cat creatures here that these children like so much. Pure Light and Love that these beautiful creatures share with the damaged children. Receiving and actually feeling pure, true Light and Love is a learning process that is lovingly guided.

There are people here who meet a dog they had a long time ago. A woman in the healing chambers, who had been abused in occult circles, saw a dog walking by. Part of her healing chamber was open and she could look out over the grassy and flowery fields. She saw a little boy with a dog passing by and she got increasingly positive thoughts about the dog she once had as a little girl: a little spaniel. We know that she attracted this soul with her beautiful thoughts about 'when it was still good'. That was before her imprisonment in an order in England. They're back together now, she and the dog. When she was able to leave the healing chamber she walked through the gardens with loved ones who were looking for her and that little spaniel. This young woman had to learn to love and enjoy beauty again. She had spent so long in captivity as a sex slave and, therefore, had seen little nature and beauty.

There are people here who on Earth cared for gardens or were involved in nature conservation. They come to these healing chambers to work with newly arrived people. Just to walk with them through nature, to experience the beauty, through lavender gardens, or through the rose garden with its beautiful light frequencies. Step by step they teach these people to enjoy themselves again and to know that they can be safe in this place, with loved ones visiting them until they can continue by themselves again.

Reading the book of life only happens when someone is fully aware of his or her change and is ready for it. When reading the blueprint of life, which you see holographically, every human being is lovingly guided, without judgment. It is you yourself who sees and feels what is unbalanced. In every next step we look for possibilities to heal that which is unbalanced. There are many ways to do this, which one investigates and then makes choices on how to do it. Now, at this time, many choose to stay in the Spheres of Light until the Transition of the Earth's frequency, the Event, or whatever name they prefer to give it, before making a new beginning in the future 5D Earth world.

People who, during this Earth's cycle, have made karma in their successive lives and thus have caused great damage to the planet, humans, animals and plants, go to areas with a special care where they will be able to peel off their many dark layers until they reach their core.

Considering the deeds we are talking about here, these souls will not be able to go to the 5D World without easily. There are several 3D planets where they can go, however. Here they can experience what they deliberately caused to others, in order to learn their karmic lessons and to try to balance themselves.

Sometimes I hear of such processes and because I have lived in the spiritual world for so long, I have seen so much of what has deliberately been done to people for so many reasons. The bottom line is always that these people sold their souls to the darkness and did what was required of them: they were puppets. Creating pain, fear, poverty, wars, hatred, and violence in all its forms. These are the Archontic energies, entities, parasitic creatures, that long ago invaded our solar system like a virus, attracting beings that need the energy of suffering: evil, egocentric self-serving, life-draining entities. In the Cities of Light, we track the Light Forces that for years have been working to remove everything that is not of the light; soulless parasitic creatures. On the large screens at the boulevards in the Cities of Light and in the higher Light spheres, we all monitor the liberation from this dominating darkness.

The white-gold energy of Lord Kumeka, Chohan of the Eighth Ray of Purification, works with many millions of people on Earth to purify everything that is not based on love: a violent process in which we are helped and advised by peoples from other planets who have lived in a situation of darkness for long periods of time. They each have their own specific stories to tell: their massive liberation makes anyone who is actively connected to this or as a spectator of the world stage, stronger and stronger. It is like a chain; one helps the other with the knowledge and experience they have and share, brought by the people in the Light Spheres together with the light people living on Earth.

Here we take care of the arriving souls who had a hard time and, conscious as they often were, could no longer cope with life as it developed over the last thirty years. Many of the highly sensitive children could not cope with the heavy 3D life, no matter how much they tried. Being clairaudient or clairvoyant and then having to perceive that there is so much darkness around you, not being able to express in word and deed what you experience as a highly sensitive human being. Often, in their attempts to explain it, this was dismissed as ridiculous nonsense. Many were drugged from an early age with all kinds of medication: among others, with antidepressants that cause suicidal thoughts among many sensitive people. Others fled into drugs and alcohol and that certainly didn't bring a solution, on the contrary.

There are all kinds of groups in the spheres for young people who resonate with each other, souls who look for solutions for those who stayed behind on Earth in miserable circumstances. Collectively supporting of each other is tangible for sensitive people. Such collaborations have never before occurred on such a large scale: humanity awakens and, layer by layer, becomes aware of everything that is happening on Earth.

Precisely those who decided not to return to the present 3D Earth in physical form have already been able to do a lot of work in their collectives, thanks to their empirical experiences and training in the Light Spheres. Together with the personal guides of individual people a lot is being accomplished. Empathy and heart love are helping people to change course, no matter how difficult that may be sometimes.

Fear of death

For fear of death is nothing else
than to think one is wise without being wise,
imagining knowing what one doesn't know.

For no one knows death
and no one knows
if it' s not the man's greatest blessing.

They fear it,
as if they're sure it' s our biggest tragedy.

Isn't that the most outrageous stupidity,
to imagine knowing what you don't know?

Socrates (469-399 BC)

23. Theodore

Trapped in stone

Leviahnarah: In this end time, end of this Earth cycle, all things that were carefully hidden come to light. For example, different groups have been formed in the collective that were once trapped in stone. Billions and billions of souls have been imprisoned in the past in Earthly matter, preferably in stone. In this time of transition to a new era, during the Great Reversal, we are working hard to liberate all the souls that are still trapped in stone today. These human souls were trapped by magic to maintain a specific low frequency in a particular place. Many regression therapists and doctors who worked with the spiritual world are familiar with this phenomenon. In the book 'Spectrum of regression and reincarnation' by Henri de Vidal de St. Germain the following experiences are documented:

Abuse of magic

Henri: It will come as no surprise to anyone that magic was abused thousands of years ago. Yet, through regressions to past lives in ancient cultures, facts have come to light that are mostly unknown and extremely shocking. A client who relived a life in Atlantis told the following:

Client: There are people who have developed themselves tremendously through exercises and the like, allowing them to manipulate others. That is not faith. That's an abuse of power. And, of course, people are very sensitive to that. Because such a person can, by the power of his thoughts, inflict anything he wants on others. People are very sensitive to that, and they are cautious to talk about that, and something like that can be called faith, but of course it is not.

Henri: When I asked him what examples there were, he said:

Client: The first thing that comes to mind now, what I see very clearly, is that these people, by the power of thought, I see it happening now, imprison other people in a piece of stone: in marble - a large chunk of stone, in which those people are trapped. Their souls are trapped by the power of thought. As a result, they can't go any further and stay there for years and years. In the courtyard of that city they have even built special pillars for that purpose.

Henri: A participant in one of my regression courses told me about a memory in which he felt trapped in a pillar. There were other similar pillars all around. The participant did not have the feeling of being in a body (people in regression can usually clearly answer the question of whether or not they are in a body). Going back in time the image of someone who had fallen into disfavour with the Atlantic rulers was formed. Therefore he was first brought into a state similar to hypnosis, then tortured and slowly put to death. His soul was, after leaving his body, imprisoned in a pillar as a kind of punishment, to stay there as long as the pillar would last.

Events like this were certainly not a rare occurrence in Atlantis. In later times also the Egyptians - who were strongly influenced culturally, technically and religiously by the Atlanteans - made use of this magical knowledge. Power easily leads to its abuse. It is a saying that has been true throughout history. What we've told here about Atlantis is tragic proof of that. Magic adds another dimension to the use (or abuse) of power.

Leviahnarah: So much for a quote from the work of Henri de Vidal de St. Germain. Since he passed away at an advanced age this special man has an important function in the various groups dealing with traumas from previous lives. He is a true master and teacher to many, a fine example of the life of your passion, of your blueprint of life. It is fantastic to see how, after his transition, he continues his work in the spiritual spheres. In that spiritual world he is so much more now: the joined parts of his greater Self, all healed from previous lives, form the whole of his experiences on Earth.

It is good to know that more and more people are reaching that wholeness and forming powerful fields of consciousness, flowing into the great collective field. The building up of so much light and consciousness cannot be destroyed by regardless any dark intention. The light is multiplying rapidly and that cannot be stopped.

Theodore: I would like to confirm the story, recorded in Henri's book, from my own experience. I lived as a teacher in the temple schools, both in Atlantis and later in Egypt: positive and constructive lives. In the early period of Atlantis people, teachers, who had come from the Pleiades, taught me, like so many others. There were also teachers from Andromeda and from them I learned a lot about non-violent living; about recognizing those who wanted to dominate others. Such people were initially not immediately recognizable because of their false light; often charming and charismatic people, usually very talented. They were able to use their behaviour and charisma to deceive people and groups in a sophisticated way. Few looked through the mask of the false light. Because our work was infiltrated in many different ways, we were glad with the beautiful teaching of the Andromedans. Thanks to their knowledge, we were able to prevent a lot of mischief in different time periods. We recognized the people who were brought forward by those in power to secretly infiltrate among the people who served the Light. Those moles were present in every part of society. It's exactly the same nowadays.

In the third period of the Atlantis era, when darkness dominated, we saw the decline of everything in society that was based on the light. Through lies and deceit, three men, including myself, were imprisoned. Our good names and deeds were completely destroyed ans smeared. The way in which this happened was simply believed by people. It was a form of mind control. Low frequency energies were emitted and kept the masses in a certain state of mind. We were tortured with psychotic drugs as well as physical pain. When I was nearly dead, they trapped my soul in a large stone statue through the power of their mind. I was not aware of my condition but energetically I radiated the suffering that I had experienced so extremely during the torture.

When the tidal waves came at the fall of Atlantis and the area where I was captured in stone was flooded, the statue broke into pieces and I was freed. Millions of souls had been imprisoned in matter during that last period. All were liberated during the downfall of that continent. That was one of the positive things that happened back then.

That the dark power uses light-bearing souls as batteries to drain them of their light is of all times. They steal the light that they couldn't generate themselves. What they did to me then, led to fierce dreams and a lively reliving during my last life on Earth. Once more I met someone who crossed my path in Atlantis in a negative way. This man, with a high position within society, had within his blueprint for life the intention to meet the people he had tortured and imprisoned at the time, in order to balance old, negative energy. This seemed to happen at first; he helped me advance in my career and offered me opportunities to do what I wanted to do in that life. As so often happens in these kinds of situations, one day his mask, his intention of doing good and balancing old energy, fell. Now I know that in this life he had a high position within a lodge, and in addition to the ancient magical knowledge of all his past lives, he now also carried within him the occult knowledge he had learned within that lodge.

When the mask fell I had a shocking experience and had dreams about that time in Atlantis. Now, in the spiritual world, I know that this man had the choice to realize what he had intended to do in his life's blueprint. But here, I also know that if someone has frequently engaged in black magic on Earth, it is extremely difficult to let go of. That is only possible when someone has become so strong that he can detach himself from it on his own strength. Black magic gives someone an incredible amount of power and that is very addictive.

This man then again took control of my mind, using his knowledge to control the minds of others by thought. I looked for help, but I couldn't get rid of his control over me. Gruesome images and dreams made my life a real hell. I sought the peace of nature and went into the mountains. The long walks seemed to do me good at first. His influence came and went like the waves of the surf. For a moment I things went better, but then fearful dreams flooded my mind.

I didn't intend to end my life at all. I was full of plans but still, one evening it happened again. I left my tent in the mountains and tried to relax a bit in the open air. As if I was hypnotized I stepped off the edge and ended up at the bottom of the ravine. I died instantly and didn't feel any pain. The jump ruptured the encapsulation the old magician had made. I was standing next to my body, together with two Light Beings whom I later recognized as old loved ones. Around my soulless body I saw another twelve Light Beings making a circle of light. I saw how they transformed the energy of that dark encapsulation. A lot of the specialists in transforming such energy are at work right now. I was brought to the healing chamber completely unconsciously. While reading my book of life, I later discovered that my body had been found by mountain hikers. The police concluded that I had made a fatal fall.

I know that with the increase of the Light there are now people who can help others to get away from such encapsulations while on Earth. At the same time, we can see how this dark energy is now being sent back to those who once sent it. This has to do with the reversal that is going on; in fact, that's what is called the Law of Attraction.

"Be aware of what you think," is a great truth. Within the collective in which I now work, there are examples that such dark energy that was sent to someone in this life, for example, comes back like a boomerang to the one who sent it, twice or even tenfold.

I know that no one can alleviate the pain and sorrow of a loved one who suddenly departed from life. Each person goes through his own mourning process in his own unique way. For us as a collective, that is so intensely concerned with those who arrive in the spiritual world by suicide, it is important to tell them that there is no such thing as hell, if that is what they believe based on their earthly programming, their earthly beliefs. Many such beliefs originate within religious and cultural traditions and behaviours.

These thought forms, often many centuries old, materialized into elementals that, up to the present day, influence whole groups of people. Every human being is welcomed after his or her self-chosen departure from the material world and brought to the healing chamber that suits the frequency of that soul: every soul is welcomed by loved ones, always. That may be family members or friends who are in the afterlife. When there was an encapsulation due to black magic, such energy is first removed by a team of Light Beings and then taken away for transformation. Specialists in the field of black magic and encapsulation do this in another dimension. Everyone can look back on those events at any time when there is a need to do so. My own experience with such an evaluation has brought me a lot of good.

Because an accident was indicated as the official cause of death, there were no negative thoughts at the memorial service about a possible suicide among those present. I know that thoughts about suicide can be very negative and can linger for a long time in the mourning process of a group of family members and friends. People influence each other with negative thoughts about such things.

My favourite music was played; my favourite flowers were there. There were loving thoughts. If only more people knew that we could see and hear every detail of such a gathering if we so wished. Thoughts are open when you are in the spiritual world. There were two people, both sisters of mine, who sent me spiritual flowers when I was in the healing chamber. I kept them; they're dear to me. It showed me that they knew that the soul does not die but lives on. A piece of acceptance of What Is, despite the great sorrow they felt.

Many people have dreams about the people who chose to leave. There is a place that many call Summerland, where the departed soul and those still living in an earthly body can meet. A great place, a green hilly area in the spiritual world with trees and many blossoming flowers; fields with identical flowers everywhere that provide a certain frequency for those who visit this place. For example the lavender and rose gardens that have an extremely soothing appearance. Here, where their spiritual guides bring people, a lot of 'old pain' is processed with each other. It has a healing effect on either side. The stragglers are often helped in their mourning process to continue with life on Earth. Everything needs time and how much is different for everyone. No one can tell you how to do that.

At a certain point I continued my way and at the same time the feeling with my family and friends that I was close from time to time disappeared. Every now and then I did visit them again. Sometimes I stand in front of my sister. I know she can't see me in my subtle body. But then she will often looks at my portrait on the cabinet and telepathically sends me the thought 'you're doing well, dear little brother of mine'. So she definitely feels my brief visit and my loving thoughts towards her. We had a powerful and loving connection. I know that many people have such experiences. A love connection is eternal and is not broken by a temporal transition.

Sometimes there is my sister's son who can see me, a little boy of four. With shining eyes he looks at me, like he did when he was a baby. He 'sees' me and then follows me with his eyes. He then mentions this to my sister and repeats my words, that I am ok.

Please know that many of us are visiting loved ones and that sometimes children can actually see us. Young children are still very open to the spiritual world and often remember bits and pieces from past lives as if it were yesterday. This is not a fantasy. We are still here.

24. Eliza

Eliza: I ended my life when I was eighteen years old. I was the youngest in the family with two brothers and two sisters. I was a quiet and introvert child. However, within the warmth of the family, I developed well. For the first eight years of my life, the family was a cosy and safe nest. Being busy with paint and clay were my favourite pastimes; I loved being creative that way. As soon as I was in a group I became insecure and sometimes even downright scared. I was sensitive, clairvoyant and when people weren't sincere I could sense that flawlessly. I intuitively 'saw' lies and vague truths and how people often believed them themselves. I drew to children who were 'real'. As I got older I experienced the world outside the family more and more as negative and unreal. So many people say one thing but they mean the other.

My grandmother supported me. With her I spoke openly about all these things and she understood me. High school was a real hell for me and I got depressed. Retreating into the safety of the family unfortunately became more and more a thing of the past as I got older. The years of playing were over; schooling became more and more serious. My parents and the teachers to study more and to get high grades put pressure on me. My parents were both academics and had high positions in the medical world. My eldest sister and brother also studied medicine. I was still highly sensitive. Strong stimuli and crowds were difficult for me. I picked up so much of my environment because of my clairsentience. I was very sensitive to the radiation of wifi with which I was completely surrounded both at school and at home. All kinds of complaints arose, including extreme fatigue. No matter how caring the family was, they shrugged their shoulders over it. It was dismissed as nonsense.

My mother, who worked in the medical field herself, took me to see a friend psychiatrist. The result, of course, was that I was given medication. One of the drugs I was given was to make sure I would do better at school. It worked like speed, but it also gave me strong suicidal thoughts so other medications were immediately added. Sometimes I stopped the medication, hid it or threw it away. Mother didn't listen to my objections and my father was travelling too much for his work. Here in the spiritual world I realized that many young people are treated this way and even from an increasingly younger age.

My lucid faculties that had been such a natural part of myself had disappeared over time. I could no longer see the beautiful colours and radiance of people, animals and nature. I ended up in a dark and colourless world that made me very gloomy. In the family in which I grew up it was quite normal to study hard and where necessary there were tutoring lessons. My big dream, however, was to go to the academy for visual arts. A few older friends sometimes took me to exhibitions and graduation ceremonies. I enjoyed the different expressions of creativity.

My last years in high school were hellish. My mother was clear and very compelling in what was expected of me. When my father was home every now and then, I was gently pushed also by him to study hard. Both mother and father wanted me, just like them and my brothers and sisters, to study medicine. My grandfather on my mother's side and his father were brought up time and again as examples: one had been a family doctor, the other a neurologist. Why didn't they see that this didn't suit me at all? Later after my transition I saw clearly how I was deformed this way, already from my earliest childhood. Why didn't I make a resolute decision myself to go to the academy and develop my creative side?

My parents acted from their own awareness and beliefs of what was good for their children, and the academy of fine arts was, in their opinion, far below their standards. When I brought friends home who attended the first year of that academy, my parents clearly showed their disapproval. Unpleasant remarks were made about clothing and hairstyles. Not a word of appreciation for a friend who made a beautiful painting of our dog, which led to an extremely painful moment for all of us.

I had started keeping a diary at a young age. I this way could at least express my thoughts about the things in my life that I didn't feel good about. Only with my youngest brother did I have some sort of emotional contact. I wrote in my diary about the few conversations we had together. His love for nature and animals was great. He taught me a lot in that area. I drew and painted the birds, plants and flowers he told me about. I had written about his concerns about the poisoning of our farmland in my diary. His words impressed me. At the dinner table, however, he was not allowed to speak about it. That subject, like my clairvoyance and clairsentience, was dismissed as nonsense. After all, Father worked in a company that developed medicines.

My drawings and paintings on thick paper were in a folder. Mother told me over the years to put everything away, hanging it on the wall was not an option. Clairvoyantly I observed a lot, especially in my younger years, before I had been prescribed so much medication. I drew and painted the negative aura's I saw in people and added my notes to it. Angry people, an outburst of anger, compelling energy, hate. The drawings in which I had painted beautiful positive and loving energy were kept in a separate folder, as if they were not allowed to touch each other when stored. Our dog with her beautiful charisma, that animal was pure love. Unconditional.

The love of my parents was not unconditional. They were only sweet and caring if I met their conditions. And so I agreed to their wishes and often thought that it was all my fault, that my deepest desires just weren't real. In a family with only academics, I was and remained a kind of outsider. I sat there and watched them, their great ideals and deep convictions that were not mine. No, their expectations were clear to their youngest daughter: she had to become an academic.

What about me? I never really disagreed with their plans, it was like I was trapped in a spider's web. I failed my final exams, despite all the tutoring my parents had paid for me. Their reactions were downright negative. The plans for the next school year were widely discussed with me. I felt guilt and shame and felt like I was a failure. It was pure negative energy that my parents sent to me. The atmosphere in the house was awful. Their words about my 'failure' were constantly going through my head. New medication was proposed that should provide better results. The fact that I would have to go back to the psychiatrist hung like a dark cloud over my future. I wasn't good enough, that continued to go through my mind. Also, the new medication I was given had the side effect of getting suicidal thoughts.

My parents cancelled the holiday with friends I had been looking forward to because they wanted me to prepare for the new school year. I wrote about my deep disappointment in my diary. I was also not allowed to go to the graduation parties of my classmates who had passed their final exams. My friends didn't mind, they understood and accepted. Some of them knew about the situation at home, the coercion, the stress, and the medication. I nevertheless slipped out of the house and went to a graduation party. It was wonderful; I enjoyed it to the fullest.

On the bike on the way home the suicidal thoughts came over me like waves again. This time, however, the thoughts were overwhelming. On the railway crossing on my way home I jumped in front of the train. My bike was lying in front of the railroad trees with my bag. I didn't experience anything consciously as the destructive blow was too hard.

I woke up in a blue-green environment in a healing chamber. My grandmother, the only one who always had an understanding for my sensitivity and experiences, was standing next to me. She was wearing a soft blue-green tunic and looked like in an old photograph I had seen, taken at the time when my father was still a child. She herself had passed away at an advanced age. Patiently she stroked my hair. My body was intact. I didn't have a badly injured body. She later explained to me that I had jumped on a whim and that the blow had been so hard and that it all went so fast that I had no conscious memory of it. Grandma always stayed close to me. First in the healing chamber and later when I went for a walk in the rose garden. Nowhere was there any reproach. She was neutral and loving.

On different levels there are special healing chambers for medication-related suicides, such as antidepressants. I discovered that many hypersensitive children around the world commit suicide. I got the idea that the many Light children who incarnate in this end time - the transition to an age of light - were being eliminated in this way by the still prevailing darkness. A whole stream of 'children' who would be able to create a society based on love and empathy.

In my early days in the spiritual world, I met many people in the large rose garden with similar stories and backgrounds to mine: sensitives that got stuck in the hard materialistic world - often a very loveless world. Grandma guided me through these early days. Reading my book of life gave me a lot of insight and answers. I saw and relived that my mother did exactly the same things in previous lives as in this life. She had often been extremely successful as a male physician. Sometimes as a man of great scientific prestige, who brought out his 'truths' with great authority, unable to accept 'truths' of others. His rigidity lacked any openness to see (or want to see) that many theories were completely based on nothing more than temporary assumptions. Once he had established his "truth", he remained stuck to it, unable to consider truths of others or to accept or investigate new developments.

This rigidity caused a lot of misery. I also 'saw' in that book of life how this man belittled other people when they came up with new ideas in and around his area of expertise. Everyone in our family had been incarnated with this soul before and each of us now, in this life, had lessons to learn and free choices to make. I saw how I had been deformed and trapped again in my last life. I was energetically unable to stand up for myself. In my incarnation there was a possibility and an intention that as a creative and sensitive girl, as an outsider in that family, I could break through that old rigidity with both the compelling mother and the uncritical father.

The news of my death shocked the family. Grandma and one of my spiritual guides brought me to them several times. The grief was great with my brothers, sisters and father. Outside the body you see and feel everything. Thoughts lie open. Mother was ashamed and did not dare to say that in her surroundings. My father and my youngest brother found my diary. Both of them discovered a world of thought that could never have come out in that family. Both became aware of what I really wanted with my life. They also found the drawings and paintings in the folders.

A world opened up for my father. For him, the contents of the diary and seeing the paintings was like throwing open a previously closed door. Hidden away in my room they found the medication of years and years. They read in the diary that it made me so sick and also made me think of suicide. And that I didn't want something like that, I wanted to live, make beautiful things and have an education that fitted in with that. Father who had worked so much time abroad felt guilty that his youngest daughter had not been able to reach him with her deepest wishes. He was usually only at home for a few days before he had to travel again. He blamed himself for not seeing all this and blindly trusting his wife and her 'good care' completely.

He confronted my mother with the remains of the prescribed medication that I had been saved up over the years. She tried to explain to him with what she thought were convincing arguments, that this had been necessary. Father also visited my psychiatrist together with my youngest brother and had a long and heated conversation with this man. With a shock father had realized what such medication did to people. My youngest brother immediately stopped studying medicine. He went to study in another city and became an agricultural engineer. In one fell swoop; he got rid of his mother's compulsive choices.

Father then divorced my mother and moved elsewhere. Aware of his own uncritical behaviour, he realized that he had been so little at home with his family assuming that my mother was such a good mother. The true extent of the damage they had done gradually dawned on him. My youngest brother found a job in Australia where he was engaged in what was his passion, organic farming methods. He married a very sensitive woman. I now prepare to incarnate with them as his daughter.

Consolation from the other side

Don't worry now, I'm free.
Despite your grief, think of me
And know that now without pain
Without sorrow in light, I will be

And what you see of me now
Is what you know, but is no longer me,
It carried my life through time
And brought me to infinity.

I give it back to Mother Earth
Who retakes it and saves it
And I myself am going to my Source
Where all life began.

Dry your tears, you'll be all right,
I've always suspected it:
My best dreams were true
So now dream on for each other.

Keep thinking about me, the way I was
Especially when I was happy.
Grow on that memory,
Take courage from that for a new beginning.

From 'Zaaien in Tranen - woorden van verder dan de dood',
Yvonne van Emmerik
Published in Dutch by Ten Have (no longer in print)

25. Lucille

Leviahnarah: Suicide has so many different causes that it's impossible to cover them all. We can discuss the most common ones. Lucille's history has to do with a series of previous lives in which she felt unworthy of herself. We usually learn from such lives, and most of the time we don't make the same negative choices.

In a life in 16th century Spain, Lucille was a beautiful and wealthy woman, wife of a high-ranking man in royal circles. She was aware of the manipulations, the gossip, the keeping up appearances in royal circles. However, the exterior of beautiful clothes, houses, country estates was less important to her than her inner life. She became deeply aware of the hypocrisy within the Roman Catholic Church and its rulers. Therefore she longed for children and a family life outside the walls of the palaces, but to her great sorrow she did not have children.

Her husband blamed her for their childlessness. Only now we know so much more about sexually transmitted diseases. This man had syphilis himself and was therefore infertile. He was unpredictable and sometimes suddenly violent. Lucille, unfamiliar with such diseases, was reduced from an eloquent and self-assured woman to a shadow of herself. In an unrelenting stream of words she heard for years that she was nothing and was insignificant. Like energetic venom, she was poisoned by it, it formed dark particles in her energy field.   When her husband, now completely insane, died she went to a monastery where the dominant nuns 'belittled' her even more. She would die of the contagion that had been transmitted to her by her husband. Those who nursed her in the convent hospital until her death were very judgmental about her illness. She was in an unloving way cared for in her last days. She was treated as a 'fallen woman', while the only person she had ever had sexual contact with had been her own husband. Her loneliness was great in the realization that no one loved her. When we incarnate, we often take with us the intentions of an earlier life. We can also take energetic traumas with us to the next life. Lucille longed for warmth, love, children and authenticity.

In a next life she incarnated in Southern Italy, in a simple peasant family. She married young and had seven children. Lucille enjoyed that life. She got to know love on many levels with her husband, her children and later her grandchildren. Yet the feeling in her that she was unworthy had not completely disappeared. What had been put into her energetically in her life in Spain through negative words and physical abuse, was like a dark poison that was not entirely gone yet. In spite of the fact that she tried so terribly hard to take care of her family, to show them her worth, she herself struggled to receive the love she got from her family unconditionally. Lucille was therefore overzealous in her service and care; as if it was never enough to show others what she was worth.

In a subsequent life, she incarnated in 18th-century France. The husband from the life in Spain had the intention to balance the negative energy of that Spanish life. So their paths crossed again and they married. Lucille was a gifted potter, born into an artistic family of artisans with their own business. Their start was extremely positive, as is often the case when the new persona is linked to the intentions of the blueprint for life. He was a man who had a boring administrative job, without any prestige. To the outside world, however, he was a complacent man, ambitious, eloquent and full of promises. Lucille worked for the family business and enjoyed her creative profession. She painted tableware and pottery.

Her family had their doubts about Lucille's husband. Intuitively they felt that there was something dark behind that beautiful friendly mask. When she had had two miscarriages, it triggered something old. Slowly old energy emerged. While in that life he had planned to balance old energy, his behaviour began to resemble that of the Spanish life more and more. Both verbally and physically he became violent and poisonous with words. This triggered Lucille's memories of the drama in Spain and thus what needed to be balanced again ended up in a downward energetic spiral. In her work she felt worthy and a valued craftswoman, but in her marriage again an unworthy wife.

When Lucille had another miscarriage it escalated to such an extent that she ended her life. After a heated argument in their bedroom with the necessary physical and verbal violence, Lucille ran away. Deeply feeling not being able to go any further, she let herself fall from the high stairs on a whim. She broke her neck in the process. Because her body was so bruised and swollen, and also full of old scars, her husband was suspected of murder. For a long time there were rumours that he had pushed her down the high stairs, which technically was not the case.

Of course, suicide solves nothing. In the eighteenth century, however, running away from a marriage, which most people at that time saw as sacred - a union created by God - was also impossible. So, few people did. Marriage could thus become a true prison. The intention in the man's blueprint was not realized and even new negative baggage was added. This man would continue to repeat himself in new incarnations. The power aspect was very addictive to him, as was his violent behaviour, both physical and verbal.

Lucille then incarnated in the Netherlands, in a strictly reformed family. Her husband from previous lives was now her father. With a roaring voice he would read from their family bible every day: words of charity, purity, but also words of sin and guilt, of obedience of women to men. Lucille, however, was a girl who did not take everything for granted; she was someone who thought for herself. She did not allow herself to be forced into doing things that seemed wrong to her. But every time she made herself heard, she was punished. Sometimes the little girl had to rinse her mouth with soapy water and at other times she got a beating. The energy in the family, which specifically came from the father, was like a dark cloak hanging around her. It got worse from the age of eight when her father started sexually abusing her. He abused both of his daughters, Lucille from the age of eight and her sister from the age of ten. His power was great.

Their mother did everything her husband demanded of her and increasingly led a secluded life. She, too, could never do anything good. She felt unworthy and she behaved the same way. Even though she knew about the sexual abuse, she never lifted a finger to protect both her daughters. When her eldest daughter got pregnant and had a child from her father, she was fifteen years old. The mother, who was in fact the grandmother, raised the child as a daughter.

So history repeated itself and Lucille was terrified of her father. When she also turned out to be pregnant of him, she became completely hysterical. Triggers to past experiences with the soul that was her father in this life caused that. His triumph was great and he showed it to her. At the dinner table and on Sundays in the church it became clear how hypocritical he was: a man of great esteem in the religious community. On the surface a model family, but it turned out to be a loveless family and a loveless faith. It was the early twenties of the 20th century, in a fairly large city.

Lucille miscarried and everything was swept under the rug. Lucille wandered around feeling desperate, her grief, a feeling of not being able to move on. The loss of her baby, the hormonal disruption of her body due to an aborted pregnancy, the eerie silence all around her and again the feeling that she was worth nothing. As she walked along the thick frozen ice of the canal with all these thoughts and emotions, she walked up the ice and deliberately stepped into a hole.

She would later reincarnate in the Netherlands, with very specific wishes regarding the karmic aspects with the man from Spain, France, Germany and the Netherlands. She told her that his 'karmic baggage' had become very heavy and that his experiences in different lives had not led to insight and change. She knew he would cross her path again and made conscious choices to do things differently. Her current parents raised Lucille very self-confident. All possibilities for self-realization were offered to her. Choices were respected. She would physically and mentally find out where the symptoms came from, identify causes and learn how to deal with them. Her creativity was encouraged. She received drawing and painting lessons at an early age, she modelled and spun pots. The open school offered her many opportunities to do this. She followed an intuitive developmental course, experienced regression sessions to past lives in which she discovered much of herself and that man. She played the violin, sang in a choir and later in a student band. Her younger sister was her older sister from the previous life, who became a midwife this time, inspired by good care for mother and child. Lucille herself became a nurse and specialized in paediatrics.

When the man in question came back on her path, she had grown into a strong and self-assured woman. In her circle of friends he was popular, a charismatic pretty boy, a tough drinker with a smooth talk. However, it was as if she looked right through him and saw what really lay behind that beautiful face. He stalked her for a while, waited for her after her shifts. Occasionally the old feeling of fear came to her when she unconsciously recognized his energy. When he was bothering Lucille at a party, she reacted by making a lot of noise.

He also harassed her younger sister and he even attempted to rape her. They reported him to the police, who had already received several complaints about him. Lucille saw that he could no longer get away with his behaviour; it seemed to pile up as if this was the endgame of many experiences in many lives. He dropped energetically to a very low level. In the end, he became an addicted sex offender, partly living a wandering life and partly in jail because of his crimes.

The openness of our time, a totally different consciousness of people, makes certain behaviours come into the spotlight. The prison of an education in a restrictive religion, the absence of sex education, closed-mindedness about sexually transmitted diseases, etc.. The tolerance and hypocrisy are over. Conscious people see the many examples.

Lucille has recently arrived in the Spheres of Light and joined our group. She had a full life with a job that really suited her. She had a positive and compassionate husband as a partner and they had two beautiful children. Through regression therapy with a gifted therapist she was able to make many things conscious. She sought and found her way in natural medicine, including blossom therapy, which helped her soul on its way to healing. In the Light sphere of her attunement she now accompanies children who had to deal with incest and paedophilia during their lives. Many of them committed suicide out of pure despair. Very specific healing chambers have been created for this category of souls.

During the day, many people will experience a certain strength when there are tempted again to consume alcohol or drugs. It is also often a wonderful opportunity for those who help with guidance work to balance old energies of their own. The areas where these healing chambers are located offer great beauty. There are people who, after leaving the healing chambers, have to learn again to enjoy nature, peace, loving togetherness and care from the heart. There are always loved ones who have preceded them, who come from their own sphere, to guide them toward their new subtle life. They help them to show themselves to children and clairvoyant people on Earth with the message that they are doing well now. Stories of this are numerous.

It is important to know that they are doing well. The problems they wanted to escape from, especially the addictions in various forms, will be dealt with in the next incarnation. Most of them will succeed, is our experience. Lucille overcame the traumas in her last life on her own.

Lucille was a gifted pediatrician during her last life and has seen a lot in this field. Heavily damaged children and although the years of incest and paedophilia were physically invisible, Lucille had learned in her intuitive development training, to see the traumas on the inside. In the healing chambers where she now works she is a professional nurse but at the same time also an expert by experience. She knows what she is worth at the place where she works. For example, many people work in the healing chambers where people go immediately after their transition.

For young people who left material life in desperation, specially adapted healing chambers are available where they can rest, loving guidance with the right energetic care. There are healing chambers where there is a soft pink-gold energy that permeates everything. There are also healing rooms with blue-white-golden and soft silvery energy: specific energies are available for each trauma. There are always loved ones in their immediate surroundings who have come here to assist these young people during their processes. Such a process is different for everyone. This depends on the underlying causes, old karmic baggage, etc. In this end time, when we move to a higher frequency, a lot can be worked out, even after a self-chosen departure.

There is a group of people who chose to commit suicide who were addicted to drugs and alcohol. After their period in the healing chamber and reading their book of life, they continue on their way, when it suits them, by learning to become guides themselves. This study cannot be compared to any kind of education on the physical 3D-Earth. The duration of the course is different for everyone, depending on what they are looking for. There are many counsellors who do excellent work together with the guides of the individual in question. One of those people, a woman, showed us how she guided a dear friend who was still in his body on Earth to help him drink less and stop taking pills. At night, they meet in what many people call Summerland. Many afterwards believe they've dreamt about their loved one in the spheres. Unconsciously they take the insights from the in-depth conversations into their daily lives, important lessons learned and at the same time a feeling of being able to cope with things.

26. Euthanasia

It remains taboo: suicide and euthanasia

Margaret: My research showed that there are still many taboos around the complicated topic of suicide. Many people don't even want to talk about it. As the inner urge to end life gets stronger, it often becomes even more difficult to share it with others. People are afraid of disapproving reactions.

I visited the part in the spheres where people go who killed themselves. On my first visit I met people there who in the meantime have reincarnated into a body on Earth. I met two people this time and clearly saw that suicide does not offer real solutions. The lessons that our Higher Self wants to offer us always come to us at a certain moment. Once in the spheres and looking at our own book of life under loving guidance, people see very clearly the meaning of certain aspects of life, of negative events in previous lives. However, there is no judging god who will bring hell and damnation, as many people assume, it is you yourself who contemplates processes of the soul.

I know that counsellors like Thea who receives this book are asked many questions about suicide and euthanasia, which can also be seen as a kind of suicide. There are many people in this day and age who are considering ending their lives if they have cancer or another life-threatening disease. Sometimes the first thought in confronting such a disease is to end life, to anticipate any suffering that may lie ahead. Yet it is precisely the period of illness that offers people so many opportunities for change. Things that used to be so self-evident are suddenly no longer so. Other values emerge. For every human being things are different, but almost always there are great lessons to be learned. It is a choice of the soul.

I have seen that precisely those periods of illness of people have led to great transformations. How in such circumstances great love can blossom between people, how people were allowed to experience friendship that comes straight from the heart from their surroundings. How the masks fell, how unexpected miracles can happen in the field of human relationships. How sides of life that usually remained superficial suddenly acquired new depth and a completely different meaning. How people in such a period learned lessons that would otherwise have taken four or five lives. How people who were stuck in certain aspects of life now managed to tear down the self-built walls. Old negative beliefs can then be transformed by one's own insight and a new beauty is discovered that changes one's whole radiance. How dark colours and veiling in a person's energy field are transformed into beautiful, bright colours by such a transformation. It may be that the material body loses all strength and people in the environment only perceive a sick man or woman, but from another perspective the energy field becomes lighter and lighter. Then the most beautiful colours are created, which can sometimes also be perceived by the dying self, even though the person dying is often not aware that it is his own brilliant energy.

A human being who knows that he has nothing more to lose, stands differently in life, which is for sure. Then one can enjoy things that were not noticed before, all those little things one does not see in a hectic existence. On an energetic level I have been able to see how people changed, dark parts in them transformed and how they enjoyed every particle of light that entered their existence. People who have gone through a process of euthanasia themselves, I can let them speak here, happy if they are that their story can also be heard in this way. Often the stragglers on Earth have feelings of guilt and doubt and that is not necessary at all. Maybe these stories contribute to some insight into what goes on behind the veil of our material existence.

Euthanasia group in the spheres

Margaret: Elise put me in contact with an euthanasia group in the spheres and I spoke there with some people who chose the 'soft death' to leave earthly life. There are several of those groups here. It seems that there is greater tolerance for euthanasia in the Netherlands than in many other societies. There are still many taboos surrounding this subject. I think it is right that euthanasia is dealt with great care and it is quite understandable that many people have their objections to it; all the more reason to explore this topic. I can't create a complete picture, but perhaps give a small peek behind the scenes.

Ohan, one of my spiritual teachers of the recent period, joins us. We go to a place close to the healing chambers. Fifteen people have gathered. They form a study group and offer support and a listening ear to people who have just arrived. We are in a garden with a large round wrought iron arbour. There are easy wicker chairs everywhere. The whole looks pleasant and welcoming. There is a warm, friendly atmosphere. Around the arbour, champagne-coloured roses grow together in small groups. Along the fence grow soft pink climbing roses. I looked around with amazement; the peace, the harmony and above all the great beauty of these places keep touching me. A master hand has been at work here, like in the rose garden in Summerland.

Ohan: Such places can be found in every sphere of light. Everywhere in the spiritual world people arrive who feel the need to occupy themselves with flowers and gardens. For many people, caring for a garden is a healing on a high level. This also brings benefits to others, because those who are concerned with such a place enjoy and heal old aspects of life on Earth, while others can enjoy it at the same time. They can wander around and find their place of silence. Such a place of great beauty also offers a great opportunity to meet each other, as is the case with this euthanasia group. These places are especially suitable because many of them were sick for long periods of time, and were cut off from the outdoors. During their illness, many have longed for nature, for a garden to be in. That is why bringing a beautiful bunch of flowers can be so important for a long-term sick person. Flowers have a certain energy that can be important in a patient's room.

Three men and a woman join the group; they were all doctors in their last lives. The meeting begins. Two new people are welcomed, a man and a woman. They recently came from the healing rooms. Both are from Holland. Everyone seems to understand the reason for my presence. Because there is so much uncertainty and guilt, there was a collective desire to share their experiences with the readers of this book. Information is exchanged between them. New people can ask their questions and anyone who has something meaningful to say will respond. I want to start with the story of Ed, one of the men.

27. Ed

Free choice in love

Leviahnarah: Ed was thirty-five years old when he was diagnosed with AIDS. Together with his friend and partner he had lived in a large city in the Netherlands since he was thirty years old. He had become familiar with the disease as a phenomenon, because in his circles many were infected with the HIV virus. He had also regularly witnessed the disease process and the death of good friends, both men and women. His life partner was more than fifteen years older. Ed had transmitted the virus to his partner and they were aware of that. Later, on the other side, he discovered when and how it had happened and he got complete clarity about his process, about the how and why of his illness and the transformation process he had consciously chosen.

Ed: I felt more for men than for women at a young age. Yet I loved women in my own way. I have always loved my mother and my sisters intensely. There was no misogyny, I'm sure of that now, even though people suggested that at times during my life on Earth. I'd be afraid of women; that's what it came down to. I was incarnated in a family with a lot of feminine energy, with a dear mother and four dear sisters. That was mainly intended to experience a process of healing together. In a previous life I was severely damaged.

In 19th century England I lived a life with a dominant, controlling mother, in which I was given no space to develop myself or to make my own choices. She determined what I did, what I wore and what I ate. My parents were very wealthy. My mother's meddling was oppressive and suffocating. I had three sisters and a brother. My father died young and my mother ran the estate together with my older brother. He was completely controlled by her. She chose his wife and determined just about everything in his life. I fiercely resisted all this. Somewhere inside me there was always a warning light flashing, although my life and upbringing were an outright brainwashing.

I fell in love with a girl from a lower class than me. We met secretly on my horseback rides through the hills; all very innocent. We held hands and spent many hours together in nature. We looked for solutions for the future, but we didn't find them. Yet we kept seeing each other, we didn't give up. I decided to take the bull by the horns and go talk to her father. He rented a large farm on my family's land and I thought there might be a job for me there. I was very good with the horses and willing to work in the fields as long as I could be with my lover.

From that moment on, everything went completely wrong. My family had finally figured out where I was always going and with whom I was always together. At home I was usually an introverted young man, but when I came home from my rides I was shining all over. Love made me a different person. I spoke to her father, who in the meantime had been approached by my mother and brother. Threatening to lose his farm, he told me that I was no longer allowed to see his daughter.

My mother arranged for my loved one to be sent away to a place far away, somewhere with relatives of hers close to the Scottish border. Mother manipulated everyone and was awfully good at frightening people. She enjoyed her power, which she abused to a great extent. I was disgusted with her; I hated her. In vain, I went to my beloved's farm and heard the story. The man was deeply saddened. He had sent his daughter away under great pressure from my mother.

After that everything went fast. My mother forced me to marry a young woman from her circles. The first meeting was very much like a meat inspection. This woman was not impecunious and brought land, farmland and a lot of money with her. I was so paralyzed by all this and influenced by the brainwashing of my upbringing, that in that stressful time I let myself be dragged into everything my mother had prepared for me. The resistance hidden deep within me had disappeared. I was trapped in mother's energy, like a fly in a spider's web. I now see that this was indeed the case. Her controlling energy wrapped itself around me and deprived me of my own free will. I let the possibility pass me by when I in the years of my deep inner resistance could still have gone away. If only I had taken my beloved to another place and done what we had so often talked about when we were still together. Undoubtedly, we would have managed quite well, because we were willing to work hard for a free life of our own, independent of the rule of my family. At that time, I was even offered a job by an old school friend who knew about my secret love. A job in faraway India. My beloved had a hard time leaving her father behind. Only later one see the choices that passed you by. I only saw my beloved again in the spiritual world. So I married my family's choice. I began to hate the suffocating women in my life more and more. I gave this woman four children. I did not love her, but I was expected to provide for offspring. She was also dominant, controlling in everything, leaving me no space for my own personal interests. She controlled every action and if things didn't suit her, all hell broke loose. And in all things she allied with my mother and my sisters. All these women tremendously indoctrinated our children.

Now I know that we had to experience what we had done to others before, in another life. That whole bunch disgusted me, but once I was like my mother and my wife in that life. I had to learn to turn my hatred into compassion. The more they restrained me, the more I withdrew into myself. Even riding a horse didn't give me pleasure anymore. My wife always would always arrange for a male relative - her brothers and cousins - would come along to keep an eye on me. I became more and more unbalanced and had a serious accident with an open carriage. The carriage got off the road and toppled over. I was severely wounded and became paralysed on my lower body.

In the time before that I had often longed for a kind of 'nothing', also for exemption from my conjugal duties. And so there I was, in a wheelchair and spending my days in the conservatory or the downstairs room that had been set up especially for me. I got a nurse. She was just like my mother and although she looked after me very well, she choked me even further. I was controlled in everything now, worse than ever before. I was given a lot of time to read and I had a wide interest. An old school friend regularly brought me some good books. But if my wife or my mother didn't find those books suitable for me, they disappeared from the house just as quickly. They decided what I was allowed to read and that was certainly not of my own choosing. I had found a secret place for the books my friend took with him and for a long time I could read what I wanted; until that too was discovered.

My wife decided that I had become a pain in the ass and wanted to get rid of me. My old school friend told me that she had her eye on a widower and he had his eye on her. I had become redundant. This old school friend has been my life partner now, in my last life. Old connected souls. In that English life, we were very good friends. My wife got her way. She was always the one who brought me my food when I ate in my room, sometimes she even kept me company and encouraged me to finish my plate. The family praised her caring, but I died of a carefully planned poisoning. It took her over a year to help me to the other world.

Gloomy as I was and full of resentment towards the women who had controlled me so much, I went to a twilight sphere to which I was spiritually attuned. There I was visited by a sweet appearance, I recognised her vaguely. She continued to appear, but my being was so darkened by that life, that I was unable to perceive her light. My resentment towards the women in that life lasted quite a long time, probably because the feeling was close to hatred. Thank God it wasn't, because the sphere of hate is a terrible place. The vague recognition was always there. Finally, after a long time, her light could reach me. I started to seek her help and that was quite something for me after all those suffocating experiences with women. I could go to a brighter place and thus began my way up to more light. When I finally recognized my old lover in the apparition, my joy was incredible. She had been in the spiritual world for much longer. Shortly after leaving our region, she had become pregnant with her new master, that distant relative. However, neither the mother nor the child had survived the birth. We had so much to tell to each other. I trusted her completely and in spite of my bad experiences with women, that never changed. But if I thought of that controlling family and my nurse, deep darkness came into my energy field. They showed me how that worked and how they were looking for ways to cure.

Reading a book of life is sometimes an enlightening experience. When I read my book of life, I discovered that I too once eliminated a wife by administering her poison in very small doses. That was in ancient Egypt and I did it because I wanted to marry the woman of my choice.

In yet another life, I had used poison to manage a situation according to my will. I had poisoned my older brother to get hold of his heritage. After all, he would inherit the manor and the lands, as my father had decided in his will. I only got a farmhouse to live in and a piece of land to farm. The hated the fact that my older brother was my father's favourite. The poison did its job and I came into possession of the entire inheritance and thought I would be happy with it. That turned out not to be the case, on the contrary, my greed grew, as did the remorse for my deed. I had a lot to balance. And, that is the essence of karma; I had to suffer the suffering I had caused to others. Especially my arrogance was a difficult aspect to balance and I had to gain a lot of life experience in this area. Getting such an all-dominating mother in England was definitely part of that.

My life as Ed in Amsterdam was a happy one. The women who surrounded me there were lovely: they would let me go free. I had a happy childhood with them. That I turned out to be a homosexual was fully accepted by them. I could always receive my friends at home and when I finally found the love of my life they closed it in their hearts. My English mother was my mother again in that life, but in between we both had had several other lives.

So life lessons, if we want to learn them, can make big changes. My eldest sister in Amsterdam was my wife from England. She too had learned important lessons. For example, she had been a nurse in a previous life during the Second World War and had learned to turn negative aspects into positive ones. Also in the life that followed she became a nurse, she was caring, but still a bit dominant. In that profession, this characteristic is certainly not always considered bad. She does not allow herself to be commandeered around by the patients. Her way back to a balanced life in the Light was difficult. She chose to help others and that suits her.

When I got sick as the youngest in the family and only boy, she took care of me like a mother. Much later, when I was diagnosed with AIDS, she stood by me when I was scared or sad. Together with this sister and my boyfriend, we went to doctors to be educated about possible medications. My boyfriend was not open to experimental medication, I was. Sometimes I was very sick and then I couldn't go to work. My mother and sister would then take care of me. My partner dealt with his illness very differently than I did. He couldn't accept that he might die. He closed himself off to alternatives and was certainly not willing to investigate them. At that point I was able to be an example for him.

Amsterdam is a city that has a lot to offer. I went to take special cooking classes. I learned about nutrition and how to work with healthy food. I found an orthomolecular physician from whom I learned a lot. I read everything about vitamins and minerals and was almost an expert at one point. In turn, I taught people in our circle of friends about this. It was clear to me that I felt better and more energetic with my new diet. My resilience increased and that was measurable in the hospital. We went on holiday and enjoyed nature, the peace and quiet. We travelled a lot and saw beautiful places. For me it was mainly a period in which I learned to enjoy the very ordinary things in life; aspects of life that I had never noticed before. Like my boyfriend, I was someone who didn't necessarily have to go out, but we had a large circle of friends. Eating with close friends was a favourite pastime. I read a lot and was now completely free to do so. Nobody decided what was good for me anymore.

My attending physician and my sister explained the possibilities to me again. And I really couldn't go any further. I prayed for help and asked for insight, for a clear dream or a sign. When that insight came, things moved quickly and I asked for the help I was offered. My friend stuck his head in the sand and didn't want to know anything about it. My mother and sister promised to stay with me until the last moment. I was given an injection and I drifted away out of life.

Once released from my body the pain and weight of my illness fell away. I remained attached to my body for several more hours. I saw my boyfriend, my mother and sister next to my dead body. Finally there was some relief for my boyfriend; he had not been able to witness my suffering. It was all right. I could see their thoughts. My mother and sister prayed for my soul's salvation and their intention was pure, I could see that.

After that I could no longer perceive anything and after the silver cord was broken, I went to a healing chamber in the next dimension. It was accomplished. I had again experienced the action of poison in my body, a karmic process. But this time I felt the redemptive and positive effect of that poison, the gentle death. Nobody waited for me with a raised finger. There was a lot of love and care around me in the whole room.

I was in a Light sphere. I was in a place where only AIDS patients were healed, where there were separate wards for men, women and children. I learned my lessons. The process of my illness had shown me the great value of life. I learned to enjoy the little things in life that can be so great. In my youth I had already learned to enjoy life in this way and also later, when I became an adult, but it deepened especially in the years of my illness. Especially when I was diagnosed with AIDS. I was not afraid of death, read many esoteric books and channelled information in those years. The books about near-death experiences also taught me a lot. I had no fear of death. Yet at first I did not choose euthanasia, because I loved life so much.

This whole process of daring to let go and accepting a merciful death taught me a lot. I learned how healing love is, how important mental and physical freedom is. Especially as a homosexual, experiencing freedom was very special. I recovered from the fear of women and the most beautiful thing is that I completely transformed that old pride. That had caused me a lot of misery. My old fear of scarcity had also been transformed.

I met my mother, my sister and my boyfriend for life in Summerland. My friend received a certain degree of acceptance through our in-depth conversations in Summerland. He thinks he has dreamt about me when he has been in there at night. He carries with him the memory of our encounters as an inner light. My sister and mother have both transformed many old negative beliefs. They have also become more aware of the great value of life. Precisely our deep conversations about the possibility of euthanasia have made us realize this value. That was important to us, because we once handled life very lightly. I joined this group in the spheres because I felt the need for exchange. I learn from the stories of the others. Each has his or her specific background.

I insist that we should not take euthanasia lightly. Life is a gift, no matter how hard it is sometimes. I know that euthanasia is generally handled very ethically in the Netherlands, no matter how people in other countries can speak ill of it. It is also quite a step for a doctor to participate in such a decision. It can be a learning experience for everyone. Everything has to be carefully weighed up and even if it sometimes seems that way, it is not a decision you make lightly. It is and remains a difficult subject and maybe that is a good thing, because if every person who goes through a deep depression and has lost the will to go on, could just get a syringe, we would be heading in the wrong direction.

Margaret: One of the doctors agrees with Ed.

28. The Doctor

Doctor and euthanasia

Doctor: 'In my last life as a doctor I worked in a large hospital in Boston. I was an oncologist there. I arrived here not so long ago, in the late nineties. I have always worked hard in various hospitals in the United States. I was fifty-nine when I was killed in a car accident. I was tired, say exhausted, due to long working hours, a very high workload and also due to great stress in my personal life. Nevertheless, I could not relax my attention and responsibility for the patients entrusted to my care. In my career I have seen many cancer patients and many forms of therapy. I have seen how regular medicine became more and more sophisticated and how methods developed that were softer and kinder than those in previous years, the radiotherapy, chemotherapy, complicated operations. I have seen so many technological tours de force and felt admiration for it. I applied them myself.

But now that I'm here, I realize how I haven't seen the profound human side of the whole process. I was dealing with cancer, with a sick part of the body, and that's what my work focused on. I've always struggled with people's emotions and I can now say that I didn't have much affinity with them. Hundreds of times I had to tell people that they had cancer and that there could be little hope of a cure, that they had to prepare themselves for their departure from Earth. I myself did not believe in anything like an afterlife. I was a rational, down-to-earth person with both feet on the ground, at least that's how I saw myself and was proud of that.

I was a scientist. Among colleagues, also specialists, we sometimes made jokes about people's stories about an afterlife, about people who claimed to have had a near-death experience. For me and most of my colleagues everything ended with death.

So that's how I spent a lifetime working and that's how I treated my patients. I closely kept track of every new medical development and constantly added new technology to my treatments. I went to extremes in terms of medical action. I saw the loss of a patient as a personal failure. I often managed to persuade people to try a new therapy. The fact that the chance of success was sometimes only three percent did not bother most people. Usually the fear of death was so great that people were prepared to go to the limit. The fact that such an experiment involves the loss of every quality of life never really got through to me. That's the way it was, go for it. The last phase of the disease was then often terribly hard, an agony. Also family members often insisted on yet another treatment and one more, if only their beloved family member could stay a little longer.

Everyone was afraid of death, including me. In the last five years of my life I was confronted in different ways with very strong people, people who refused my advice. An increasing amount of people came by who chose to be treated only to a certain extent and were looking for alternative therapies, alternative food, spiritual healing, Simonton therapy, CBD and so on. I was absolutely not open to that and I thought it was pure nonsense.

One of my patients had breast cancer and I suggested she have both breasts amputated. According to my diagnosis, that was absolutely necessary. Such advice is given on good grounds, but she pertinently refused. She didn't want to change her mind. I gave her a week to reconsider, but she was determined. I thought her decision was extremely unwise. I called in a colleague, we talked to her for a long time, but her mind was made up. I couldn't let go of her and suggested that she come and see me regularly for examination.

In those days I saw a growing number of these 'unwise' patients. A man with a very aggressive form of cancer refused the proposed surgery and therapy. I estimated he only had a months or two left to live. The man looked at his scan for a very long time while I gave him the requested explanation. He wanted to think about it and left without agreeing to the treatment. I would have preferred to have him hospitalized right away. He only came back after two weeks., when he said that he had accepted his illness and was well aware that the cancer was spreading rapidly. He wished to spend his last days together with his only daughter - who was a nurse - in the best possible quality of life. He came to me for a check up from time to time and I couldn't understand that. At one point he sold his big house and property and gave the money to his daughter. She would take care of him in the last days of his life and she quit her job in the hospital. The man spent his last days in the countryside, far away from the city. Through his doctor there he kept in touch with me. All he wanted from me were painkillers, just in case.

I was flabbergasted by his decisions. I had a strong urge for material possessions and couldn't understand at all that he had sold all his possessions. Some time later, his daughter came to me and told me that her father had had a wonderful summer and autumn. He had fished on the big lake, walked with the dogs, worked in the vegetable garden. He had done everything he felt like doing. I had given him another eight weeks or so in my file. After his last visit to me he had lived for more than ten months. I was pleased to hear that the man had enjoyed his last months of his life and had lived so much longer than I had statistically thought possible. In consultation with the attending family doctor and at a well-prepared moment she gave her father an overdose of morphine. His daughter was very honest and she took quite a risk, because in America people still think very conservatively about euthanasia.

They had done a lot of talking, taken care of unfinished business, things from the past. The father was very aware of the value of life. He had lived life to the fullest and, when the value of his life had diminished to an unacceptable degree, had said goodbye to it with dignity and in his own way. With his daughter and his dogs nearby, he determined the moment to let go of life. Before he died, he and his daughter thanked God for the wonderful months he had had. He was very aware of the quality of that period. He had lost his own wife to breast cancer and experienced her difficult process in the hospital. He felt no fear of death, but wished to be at home at that moment and not die in a big, cold hospital. That decision also had to do with previous experiences in previous lives. His last period was characterized by love.

In the last five years of my own life I had several such experiences. It made me think, it worked like a crowbar to my old beliefs. The woman with the breast cancer visited me again after one year and asked for a scan. She looked good and I thought she might have been treated elsewhere. She handed me some documentation from attending physicians at a clinic for alternative medicine in New Mexico. I had heard of these kinds of clinics, but didn't believe it had any value. I read about the therapies she had had there. Apparently the focus was on healing and self-healing, supplemented with high quality food and vitamin-mineral supplements, applying art as healing, from certain dances to drawing mandala's.

My client had resisted chemical treatments, based purely on her intuition. She was stuck in a hectic life in the big city, always busy and rarely having time for herself. She knew that she usually ate badly and took too little exercise. Emotionally she felt resentful about her parents and her bad childhood, and later her husband who had treated her very badly. With great dedication she did everything for others, but rarely anything for herself.

In New Mexico she had found a new way in life. She had processed and transformed all those old things. She learned to use the energy of the Source in light exercises and self-healing. Every day there was a group healing and personal sessions; she did yoga and Qi Gong. Her whole life had changed. In a hospital in Phoenix she had a scan done and discovered that her cancer was getting smaller. Every day she did her light exercises and Simonton therapy. And there she was, a confident woman who knew what she wanted.

The scan I had done showed that she was cured. She wasn't surprised. She had already seen that in her meditations, she told me. I had to make an effort to avoid a certain mockery in my words, because in my mind I could only laugh at this. I called them New Agers, but this woman had apparently been put on my path to transform my thinking. She spoke very openly about all the old emotions, the period of incest in her youth, the misery and violence in her marriage. I had never paid attention to that, I looked at people in small pieces, in sick body parts that could be cut away or treated, but holistic thinking was completely alien to me. I would send people with problems I couldn't cut away to the psychiatrist and that are what I believed to be the right way. I was only dealing with sick body parts, nothing else.

I saw her again, about a year later. She was checked and on the scan the cancer was no longer detectable. I talked to colleagues very carefully about it. Certain things you can't say without becoming an outsider. I studied the alternative treatments for such patients, followed patients who opted for a combination of regular and alternative medicine. Others came up with their stories and we carefully examined what seemed to be going on before our eyes. After all, we were and remain people of science. I was taken to an organization involved in near-death experiences. One of my colleagues had told a few stories about patients with such experiences. With some reluctance, I went with her. A paediatrician spoke, a man who had always thought like me, but because of his experiences with children could no longer avoid that other reality. This dr. Melvin Morse has written several books and medical journal articles about the phenomenon. Very carefully a new world opened up for me. Would these stories of my patients really have meaning? I had always considered them to be nonsense and religious fantasies and believed that these people only saw what they wanted to see. Doubts were beginning to enter my mind.

I started reading more on the subject and from one came the other, a whole new territory unfolded before me. Cases like the ones described above, dozens of them in recent years, were my proof. It was as if a big, messy puzzle fell into place piece by piece. I started to become a different kind of doctor and I began to understand why people could choose a different kind of treatment. Only I didn't believe in reincarnation, which seemed ridiculous.

One Sunday my youngest daughter came to our weekend home at the lake. My four daughters didn't visit very often, they had each built up their own families and lives. My youngest daughter had to travel far, she came from the other side of the country. She lived with her husband in Southern California where she was a primary school teacher. She was alone and that, in itself, was unusual. She wanted to talk to both her parents and so I sat with my wife and daughter in front of the big fireplace; a homely scene but one with a bitter ending.

My daughter told me that she had uterus cancer in an advanced stage and that there were already metastases. I knew of her wish for a child that had still not been fulfilled. We sat very quietly together for a while. There I was with my overwhelming emotions, with my youngest, our dear child. She told it so calmly as if it were about a completely different topic. But my whole world was turned upside down. Nothing was the same after that, not at home, not at work, nowhere. I kept thinking about it, I couldn't let go of it. I realized that this is how it must have been with all my patients and their families. My daughter told me that she would go to a special hospital where they would be offered complementary health care. I went with her, immediately cancelling all my appointments.

In that following period, I learned a lot. Her cancer turned out to be of a very malignant, fast-growing kind and was no longer operable. She rejected chemotherapy and radiation, she thought they were just attempts to prolong life for just a little bit. It was impossible to heal. We both knew that chemotherapy would take its toll and my own daughter wanted to live with the highest possible quality of life.

After a few weeks she came to our family home at the lake. My wife took care of her. She went to the hospital once more and one of my colleagues became her attending physician. The scan showed that the disease was rapidly spreading.

My son-in-law settled himself in my study to work on his computer. I myself travelled back and forth between my work and the house at the lake. A miraculous time arrived. I saw how my daughter enjoyed herself intensely, sometimes close to the water on a rest bed. She walked with her husband, for as long as she could. Our evenings together were unforgettable. Nice and less nice matters were discussed. When I saw all four of my daughters together one weekend, I realized how little time I had spent with this wonderful family. We were talking of the past and I honestly acknowledged that I had neglected them in my great urge to make a career. We laughed and cried together. Never before in that life had I shown and felt emotions and now it was like floodgates opened.

Now that I'm here, I know this has also happened in a number of previous lives and where it started. It is only in this place that you can oversee multiple lives and perceive the wonderful game of life and death in all its facets. It was fascinating to see how I had become like this and the holographic images did not lie.

My daughter asked me if I would be willing to help her die if she could no longer bear the pain. That was the most difficult question I had ever had and I struggled tremendously with it. I couldn't give her an immediate answer at the time, and afterwards I considered that very cowardly of myself. For days I had to think about it, but at a moment when she was having a really hard time, suddenly there was this inner decision that I would do it if there was no other way. That's what I told her then.

I also had other objections that I had to overcome. My daughter used cannabis and told me that it helped her to sleep better, something that I could observe myself. I had always rejected the use of soft drugs and had always been very explicit about it. But in her good moments she put me on the spot and said, 'Daddy, you prescribe people the most horrible chemical drugs, heavy sleeping pills. Cannabis is a natural drug, it helps me in this period, will you please accept that? She gave me a book on soft drugs that I started reading by her bedside. Little by little I let new ideas into my world and realized how we as doctors are brainwashed during our education.

My daughter believed in an afterlife and told me about it as quietly as if she was describing another city or village. She told about other dimensions, how we possess material and subtle bodies. She also had books about this, and I read them sitting next to her bed. She organized a small family meeting and asked me to buy champagne and delicious treats. I had trouble with that, but gave in to her wishes. So we were all together, a whole afternoon. Both her grandparents had come and her three sisters with husbands and children. In the morning she wanted to sleep longer to be prepared for the visit.

My wife was busy and struggled with her emotions. She was troubled by the wishes of her youngest. When the visitors arrived my daughter was lying in front of the window, wearing her most beautiful pyjamas and her long, blond hair braided in a beautiful tail. She was the most powerful presence in that full room, between her nieces and nephews. Children actually deal with death very naturally. My eldest grandson asked her if she was 'becoming an angel' and my daughter simply said 'yes'. To me she was already a little angel, as fragile and emaciated as she lay there in her silk pyjamas. We drank champagne and ate snacks. The room of the cottage was full, it looked like an intimate family celebration, a birth or engagement.

Only later could I understand that it was indeed a party and that together we wanted to celebrate the inevitable. Her party went according to her wishes: all of us were together for a moment. That hadn't happened for a long time, because we lived so far apart, after all, America is a big country.

When everyone had left, she lay tired, with blushing cheeks, looking at us with a broad smile. The day after the family celebration things quickly worsened. She couldn't get out of bed, so I sat next to her and held her hand. My wife would take my place from time to time. On the other side sat her husband. In between, he slept on a camp bed, next to her. For the first time I really experienced the whole process of a dying person. Up until then I had always walked in and out of the ward, I had never been with a dying patient for more than a moment. After all, a patient dying was a failure on my part and I had always struggled with that. In everything I felt that my daughter had now decided to leave. The family celebration had been the well-chosen turning point.

In those last days I thought a lot about euthanasia. I thought about the fact that I would easily administer morphine to my patients if the pain had become too severe in the final stage of this disease and that was widely accepted. When would I do that? The thought stuck in my mind. I also thought about what she had told me about the 'afterlife' and hoped with all my heart that it really would be like this. I wanted nothing more than to see this sweet girl again if I would leave later myself. There was hope in my heart, I thought of nothing else. In the end she didn't need my help to die. She died by morning, five days after the party. "I see angels," she said, and she looked so happy. I hoped it was so. Shortly before her transition, she said something else: "See you soon, Dad."

She died very quietly, in full acceptance. She looked so happy. I don't know how many times I looked at her, giving her a kiss like before she went to sleep; a stroke on her head. On the day of the funeral, I snapped. Totally exhausted that day, without much awareness everything passed me by.

My other daughters and their husbands were a great help. My grandson didn't leave my side. In the evening, when all the guests had left, I walked along the lake. Her funeral had taken place in the small cemetery of the village. That was her express wish. Also the older graves of our family were there, like the ones of my grandparents. Our house by the lake had once been their home. The lake gave me a certain amount of peace, but I couldn't think properly anymore. Never before had I felt so many emotions; there was no escape, every molecule of my being had been touched. Suddenly I heard in the silence of my inner her "see you soon, Dad". What did she mean by that? I was fifty-nine, healthy and planning on working for a long time to come. Still, she was right, but don't ask me how she knew that at the time.

I stayed home for a week to rest and then went back to work. I threw myself into my work like never before. There was a lot of work; my presence in the hospital was much needed. I thought work would help me get over my grief, but I couldn't hide it away as I had hoped. I tried to return to my role as a specialist without emotions, but without success. My skill had to serve as a shield, especially towards colleagues I tried to act as 'normal' as possible.

But everything felt strange and unreal: I had changed, my whole life had changed. Emotions couldn't be suppressed anymore. Death was no longer just death. Constantly I had to think about her and wondered what it would be like for my dear girl. Would she live on in the way she had described? My wife had her own great sadness and was worried about me, because more than ever before I started to behave like a workaholic. More than three months after my daughter's death, her words came true.

I drove to our house at the lake, it was dark and it was raining hard. I was exhausted and hoped that the weekend would do me good. A deer that crossed the road made me brake and forced me to swerve. My car went off the road and overturned. I died instantly. I was floating above the car and saw the wheels still spinning. I saw my wounded body leaning against the window. It was a very strange experience to see myself there like that. I didn't feel any pain, which was strange. I moved closer to my body and realized that I wasn't my body. So my daughter and all the others were right after all. I lived on. It was a short overwhelming experience, and then I became unconscious and only came to my senses again in the healing chamber. In a special ward where people go who are suddenly being smashed out of their bodies, like in a car accident. Such a very specific trauma requires special treatment.

I woke up in a soft pink and green room. I felt great and thought for a moment that I was on Earth, in an ordinary hospital. Next to me sat my youngest. No longer emaciated and sick. She radiated and stroked my head. She had a long blond braid on her back, which I always liked so much. And then I realized immediately that this was 'death'. My daughter and I enjoyed our reunion.

Thus began a new life for me in my subtle body: a journey to discover that things were very different from what I had thought in a whole series of lives as a doctor. My daughter became my guide, just as she had been on Earth in her final months. She introduced me to another world. So began a path of renewal, of lessons in the Hall of Wisdom. There I often met dear colleagues, who once believed the same as I did. They formed a strong group, in which they welcomed people like me and taught them little by little.

The euthanasia issue came up and I realized that my own experience with my daughter had brought about an inner change. It wasn't so black and white anymore. I met people here who had committed euthanasia and I was allowed to see their books of life. Sometimes we did that with a few doctors and learned a lot, together with the people from that particular book of life. I discovered that people who had thoughtfully ended their lives had a deep respect for the value of it. I saw karmic aspects and what was once black and white for me became a complex pattern, with countless nuances. And now I'm only talking about aspects of AIDS and cancer.

I don't concern myself with psychiatric aspects; that's an area I know almost nothing about. That may come later. I think that people are too often kept alive because advanced techniques are available to them. Also, many doctors are simply afraid of death. People will certainly grow to a new consciousness, in which doctors learn to accept that sometimes the body can no longer be healed. A consciousness in which there is full awareness that man is not just a body, but so infinitely more.

The rapidly developing palliative care will become more and more important. Preferably in places that feel almost like 'home', but where the necessary care is available. Where, together with family and friends, one can consciously grow towards the completion of life. This can only happen if the fear of death slowly disappears. Also a deep inner knowing that life will go on in another place will contribute greatly to this. I felt obliged to contribute to this collection of stories on all sorts of levels. Although I am now thinking differently about euthanasia, I am not in favour of giving everyone a pill to end life at any moment. Doctors should first overcome the fear of death within themselves and learn to accept that helping people to die can sometimes be an accepted option. This help could then best be provided within a framework of trust and after consulting a second physician. I am studying patient files of doctors in the Netherlands. That's just a small country on the map, but with a great awareness of things sometimes. Perhaps the Dutch are less dogmatic, have little or no concern for the laws of the Church and take individual responsibility. These developments are worth studying. Above all, let people continue to deal with life in the most ethical way possible.

On the holographic screens I have seen many cases where it was an act of grace to help a sick person die. Where a life was ended with respect for the suffering person. And everything here revolves around the relationship of love within which this act is performed. And love is what it's all about.

I've attended several lectures on suicide. There many questions were addressed about the many different facets of suicide and as always, one situation can never be compared to another. I decided to explore this area as part of the book. Ohan has guided me in this process. I deliberately did not talk to people who had committed suicide, but I did talk to their spiritual guides. A number of these people have reincarnated, sometimes quite soon after their self-chosen transition. I was especially curious about the most important aspects of their choices.

29. Ellen

Everything under control?

Leviahnarah: Ellen is a woman who chose the time of her death herself. When I met her, she already had left the healing chamber behind her and was reflecting on the future by first reading her book of life. She was almost thirty when she was diagnosed with MS, multiple sclerosis. She had grown up in a loving family and had a pleasant childhood in a small rural town. Her life was focused on a career with a family in the big city. Step by step she had planned her life and sometimes she got confused if things turned out different. She couldn't cope with that from a very early age. She wanted to be able to oversee and control things and preferably force and shape them according to the image she had in mind. In her early years, her parents and family did everything they could to manage that ultimate urge to control. Especially father tried to show his daughter time and again that life is not controllable and also her grandparents put a lot of energy into that.

Something like that can be found in the blueprint for life and so the right people will meet and help each other. In this case it concerned related souls who had been together in different family relationships throughout the ages. Her parents encouraged her to do things that could heal her insecurity and help her to let go of that need for control. They did everything they could to teach her to trust. The foundation of Ellen's life was love and the understanding of her parents and family, and later of her husband. It could hardly be better.

When she was diagnosed with MS, she had a job, two lovely children and a husband. The young family lived in a big city, in a beautiful house. She was a nurse and went back to work a little while after her children were born. Her husband was an architect and worked mainly in his office at their home. That worked very well for both of them, because it also enabled Ellen to devote herself to the work she did with so much love.

Her work as a nurse came straight from the heart and she relieved a lot of karma. For years she nursed people with ALS, MS or Parkinson's disease. She paid a lot of attention to the people she sometimes nursed for longer periods of time. Sometimes people in the hospital would joke about her need to oversee and control every step of life, her dominant behaviour, her need to manage everything. But those jokes made her think and because she had learned to look at typical characteristics of disorders, she could also look at herself and thus she tried to change her dominant behaviour towards patients and housemates. But that didn't really work out.

Ever since she was a child, she had planned her life meticulously. It was even distressing for those around her. She believed that she had to insure herself against all possible accidents. And so Ellen not only planned her own life, but also that of her husband and children, cradle to grave. And once those plans went off the rails, she immediately got out of balance and tried to get the things back on her track in all sorts of ways. At that point her behaviour became compulsive neurotic and difficult to bear for those around her. In the hospital where she worked this also caused tension, both among her superiors and among the staff under her supervision. Sometimes people saw crying apprentice nurses running away from work. Sometimes this led to panic at work and then to disharmony at home. Her urge for control became worse rather than better, despite all her positive intentions to change that. I will let Ellen speak for herself.

Ellen: I left everything that was given to me from the spiritual world untouched. I didn't see it at all. I felt that people shouldn't whine whenever I was struggling with my tendency to control and my neurotic behaviour. Here in the spiritual world I can fully oversee and understand my behaviour. If I had realized that better in that life, I would have been able to change in a gentle way, without the need for that disease.

Leviahnarah: Her husband Peter tried to show her that it is impossible to control life in all its facets. He loved her very much, but her behavior suffocated him. Above all, he had helped to enable her to do get a part time job, creating some space in their marriage. He was a man who could play with the things that came his way and he loved new challenges. He was creative in his job and in everyday life. They were clearly each other's opposites in this.

When Ellen got MS she was in her late twenties and her children were only four and six years old. Although symptoms had already shown themselves, the diagnosis came rather unexpectedly. She was admitted to a large hospital and suddenly, her regulated and organised life was determined by others. The roles were suddenly reversed. A deep depression resulted. Her illness made it impossible for her to continue working and her 'making her own money' was no longer an option. Her fairly independent job had been so important to her, just like being of service to others. However, she did not feel the need 'to be of service' to her husband and her children; at least, not as self-evident as the patients in the hospital who had been entrusted to her care. Apparently it was much more difficult to deal with the things that were so close, the care of her husband and children.

Her smile was a bit grim when she told this to me. After all, she was now reading her book of life, together with her spiritual guide, and she began to understand certain aspects of her life. Seeing What Is, without judgments. She began to discover how many loving opportunities there had been to gently translate her soul level intentions into action. That the gentle way is always the first option and that, only when it really doesn't work out, stronger measures are taken. She studied the blueprint of her life and saw the point at which she had drawn the disease to herself in order to learn a certain life lesson in a much more drastic way.

She also saw that many people incarnate with a predisposition to develop a certain disease, but have often already transformed that predisposition in youth. As a result, such a disease does not have to manifest itself in that life. There are also people who are determined to use a disease for the transformation of their old negative experiences. Her guides have shown us how people often easily get through that first phase and transform their issues, for it is precisely the childhood years that are predestined to transform the negative, in the right environment and with the right people. When you are young there is still a certain connection with the place where you came from, and you are more open to the help of both the material and the spiritual world.

But let it be clear, many people at the soul level choose to go through a certain disease process, and such a decision may also have to do with the learning processes of the people around them. There are often more souls involved in such a plan. For example, it is dangerous to judge certain types of illnesses, or to put them in a (spiritual) box. In the course of my journey on this side of existence it has become very clear to me that there are countless ways to work out certain karmic aspects. They are not judged here, and sadly that is still often done on Earth. That needs to change. Fortunately, this message is repeated time and again from the spiritual world and luckily many people are already willing not to 'judge' and no longer put everything in boxes. Every human being is unique and will search for his or her own way to the Light. Not everyone learns quickly and some literally need a slap in the face to wake up from a certain condition. Look around you, how often doesn't a violent event set big positive changes in motion.

Ellen now saw how she had missed out on everything beautiful that had been given to her and how she therefore got herself a more difficult assignment. Yet people who showed a big heart full of love surrounded her, people with a lot of compassion and patience.

Her husband Peter, started to adjust the house for her handicap. Little by little he rebuilt the house. An elevator was built on a sidewall of the house. He saw challenges in the problems he encountered and creatively sought and found comfortable solutions. In the kitchen there was a fine countertop that was adjustable in height. On the garden side, a spacious conservatory was built in which Ellen could indulge her love of flowers and plants. At wheelchair height she could take care of the flowers and plants.

From this dimension she saw how Peter had been constantly trying to make her as comfortable as possible and that he only did this out of love and respect for her and not to 'patronize her', as she expressed to him. Ellen had assessed everything by her own standard, she believed that Peter wanted to control and dominate her life but it wasn't like that. Sometimes there were great tensions because she could not accept her illness. She kept resisting it for a long time.

Ellen: Something like that happened to someone else and not me, my job in life was to nurse and care for such patients. I couldn't change myself and accept the opportunities that were offered to me. I felt very pathetic; I was the victim. And I had seen so many people who were infinitely worse off than I had ever been: people who, despite their condition, were positive in their expressions and their actions. People who did not give up courage and did everything they could to get as much quality out of life as possible. For years I witnessed this with others. They lived on, developed new interests and got to know new people, created an alternative life. I closed myself off for that. You can say that as soon as the diagnosis was made, I declared myself 'dead'.

My life was over and I didn't want to exist for the people around me, for my family, for the doctors and nurses. When I met such a patient as a nurse, I did everything I could to encourage that person and bring them into contact with people who were positive in life, some of whom had been dealing in a positive way with their illness for years. People who were full of life and who, despite their illness, developed a high quality of life.

Leviahnarah: Ellen was not always in a wheelchair, that wasn't necessary. But the process went fast and when she was thirty-five she became really dependent on help and that made her furious. Sometimes former colleagues came by and talked to her. One of them offered to help her, but she refused.

Ellen: My manipulative behaviour got worse and my inability to control and manipulate everything made me furious over and over again. I also had absolutely no regard for the loving intentions of my colleagues. I hurt them deeply. My dearest friend and oldest colleague could no longer work because of her back. But in spite of that she wanted to take care of me together with Peter. She came by to present it to me, but I spoke extremely hurtful words and chased her away. In tears she left my house and I didn't see her anymore. I know now that she prayed for me every day and many people did that in those days. She came to my funeral, in spite of everything I had said.

During the periods I was in the hospital, I was a very difficult patient. With a lot of patience I was nursed, I see that very clearly here in my life hologram. But again and again I sabotaged my treatment.

At a certain point I only wanted to die. I even started to say that to Peter and the children. That death wish has actually been there ever since the diagnosis was made: sometimes strong, sometimes less strong. The main thing was that I couldn't accept anything from others that I hadn't overseen, controlled and arranged myself. And that was simply impossible. I refused to adapt and take a new direction in my new situation. I could only think and act from a negative perspective, which made it very difficult for me as well. As I became more attached to the wheelchair, the death wish became stronger and stronger. I started hoarding medication; after all I knew everything about pills. I knew exactly what I needed.

For my husband and children, the situation became more and more difficult. When they reached puberty, I could not accept the changing behaviour of my daughters. Peter tried to show me that certain behaviours are part of adolescence and that I had to accept that my daughters were no longer obeying all my instructions and wishes. They clearly went their own way, while I had mapped out their way and demanded that they did what I thought was 'good' for them.

First the eldest left home at the age of fifteen. She could no longer cope with the situation and went to live with my mother. Her studies suffered greatly from domestic tensions and quarrels, she wanted to move on with her life and she felt she had done her bit to help and assist me. I know now that she was right, it was over, totally over. I took a lot of energy away from everyone. On the advice of our family doctor she left the parental home, our eldest, who loved her mother very much, but almost collapsed herself. Two years later our other daughter left home as well. In the meantime she was quite damaged by my whims. All the time she felt the presence of a very angry mother: angry at her body, angry at the world and the people who didn't 'understand' her. In my anger I often threw stuff, even at my youngest. I regretted that later on, but by then the evil had already been done. Both children stayed with grandmother until my self-chosen death.

My mother was very understanding and took care of the girls well and lovingly, without ever saying negative things about me, her daughter. After my death, meeting my mother in Summerland I was able to talk to her. Luckily she has no feelings of guilt, she knows she has done everything possible. I have been able to talk to my mother several times and tell her of my regrets about how everything went. I now know that she is a beautiful, strong person.

A year after my youngest daughter had left, I decided to take action. With carefully saved sleeping pills, I ended my life. When I now look back at myself, and the way I did it, I feel compassion. I didn't choose a quiet place like my bedroom, but chose to do it in the middle of the living room. In a handwritten letter I let Peter and the girls know that I didn't want to live on. I had lit a big candle and prayed, hoping to get rid of that body and all my problems. I imagined a tunnel of Light and Love because I believed in an 'afterlife'. That was because of several near-death experiences of patients from my time as a nurse and because of the many stories I had read about it. I didn't feel fear or resistance, but I did feel a sense of relief when I took the pills, together with some custard. With every bite I felt relief that I had finally taken the step I had taken so many times in my head. A CD with Mozart's Requiem was on, which I had always loved so much. It was as if the music took me by the hand on my way to another life, away from this one. Our cat came to sit next to me. Now I know he was lying there until I was dead. What love and devotion!

I experienced my transition partly consciously. For a moment I saw a tall man standing there with a blue tunic and long hair that reached his shoulders. He radiated peace and great love. He reached out his hand to me and I went to him. After that there was nothing, no tunnel and no light.

I was brought to my place of attunement in an unconscious state. I remained connected with my material body for a few more days, but I did not experience anything of what was going on around it. Time does not exist on the other side. I did go through some kind of tunnel of life experiences and it was the negative things that came to my mind. That went very fast. I fell into a state of 'nothing'.

When my body was to be cremated I was brought to my own ceremony by the kind man in the blue tunic, together with a woman with a soft appearance. I wanted to run into the auditorium and tell everyone that I was sorry, but my guide said they couldn't see or hear me. I saw my husband and daughters, my parents and grandparents, colleagues and friends. All the people I had chased away were sitting there. There were a lot of flowers; there were candles. I could see and feel their feelings; their thoughts were open to me. I learned so much in those moments of the ceremony. Without false self-pity I could 'See What Was' and there was so much love in that room. My youngest daughter and a friend played a piece for violin, the beautiful sounds filled the auditorium. My eldest, a very spiritual girl, turned her attention to the coffin where my body lay. Then she focused her energy on the roses, which have always been my favourite flowers. There was a white rose among the many red roses. I caught her prayer for me, beautiful in its simplicity. That white rose was hers, for the new beginning.

It all touched me very deeply. In those few short moments I received more really deep insights than I had had in my whole life. I realized that these people had done so much for me. My guide pointed to the energy you could see flowing from the hearts of the people in the auditorium. I now know that I was lifted up in that energy for a moment, that's why I was able to perceive those flows of energy so clearly and perceptibly. Flashes of knowing went through me. Knowing that I had done so little with what had been given to me lovingly. And at that very moment I decided to change all that and asked for help from the Light. I knew I could do it differently. I saw the tears of my parents and wished I could be close to them again.

Peter had completely collapsed; his tears were gone. He thought of what 'could have been' and I realized how much he had loved me, even if I turned my anger against him. I saw my dear friend with her husband. There was no judgment anywhere. She is a very spiritual woman and her strong thoughts reached me. She forgave me for my behaviour; she was full of compassion. She thought of the nice things we'd been through and sent them to me as a message. She visualized a beautiful bunch of flowers: peonies, we both loved them. Carefully she created the image, flower by flower, and asked the spiritual world to send me those flowers together with her love.

On my return there was that huge bunch of peonies. And because spiritual flowers do not perish I always take them with me. I was allowed to go to a healing chamber where I was surrounded with love and there stood my peonies. They were a great support. The heartfelt love of my friend accompanied me on my new path. I was later allowed to meet her in Summerland. It was an emotional reunion, but very valuable. It gave us both a certain peace. Many people who end their own lives want to do absolutely nothing for a long time and are therefore in a kind of spiritual vacuum until they are ready to accept help. For me that was at the moment of my cremation, that's when I became conscious and immediately got help. It is extremely important that you want that yourself. I prayed for help and help came. From that moment on I went to places where I was surrounded with a lot of love and attention.

I recognized the nurse I once was, in the nurses who helped me: people who specialize in the shelter and further guidance of someone who has killed himself. Certain moments of my life kept appearing in my mind's eye. Again and again I saw the moment when I ended my life. I became aware of what I had done in the family, how I had manipulated these sweet people and how I had interfered in every aspect of my illness. Not once had I tried to adapt and I had been totally unwilling to turn the new situation around. I saw how Peter had found all those solutions, from his heart, for me to make life as pleasant as possible. And while reading my book of life I now myself felt the pain I had caused my daughters and husband. Those are really hours of truth when you go through parts of your life like that. It's a hologram in which you feel what you've done to others and so I was confronted with my actions, like every human being after his transition.

Now I contemplate the next life for which my dearest wish is to balance my enormous 'urge for complete control'. The signs are encouraging. On a soul level I have contact with Peter when he is out of his body at night. We meet at a special place in Summerland. He has met a new lady friend and they want to get married. She is ten years younger than Peter and still has a child wish. The Council of Karma is now considering if I can incarnate as a boy with them. Such a thing is well prepared and never happens against your will. In a male incarnation there are certain possibilities to balance that old energy. The propositions that have been made to me are very encouraging. I long with all my being to experience the intended purification. Close to the people I have caused so much pain as Ellen, there are many possibilities to balance that.

Leviahnarah: When I visited Ellen at a later time, she had made her decision. She was preparing for her new incarnation, training with the best teachers in this field. She now knows better why she had such a need to manipulate and how that arose in multiple lives. She was in a vicious circle for several lifetimes and could not escape. In her life as Ellen she learned the necessary lessons, especially about the negative aspects of manipulation. She is fully aware that suicide is not a solution, but also that she was not condemned for it, as certain religions would like people to believe. It just doesn't solve anything. The lessons the soul wishes to learn are only postponed by it. In her new incarnation there are wonderful possibilities to balance the energy in a relatively short period of time: she will be surrounded by exactly the same people as in her life as Ellen.

The laws now in force during this process of transformation of the Earth and its inhabitants allow her to go through certain processes in an accelerated way. This is important to know because there are so many misunderstandings about euthanasia and suicide. In this time of great change of consciousness, new insights will gradually emerge and those issues that are now taboo will be looked at differently, i.e. in a lighter and less judgmental way.

30. Fjodor

Fjodor and the artists

Margaret: Together with Ohan I was with a group of people, in a place of extraordinary beauty. The landscape reminded me of a moor in late summer. The trees had many different colours, from warm red to yellow and green. The first impression was one of peace, of a certain kind of serene beauty. I was given all the time I wanted to quietly take in all the beauty. The landscape was undulating slightly and was bathed in a range of purple hues, incomparable to any moor I had ever seen on Earth. I am especially aware of the intensity of the colours. To stand here is a pleasure for my entire being. In the distance I can hear music, the sound pass me by like mist before it is silent again.

Ohan brings me to a glass building of the same colour as the surrounding landscape. It could best be described as 'tinted glass'. It is one with its surroundings, as if it grew. The building is huge with wings everywhere. There are wooden chairs everywhere: low, wide, wooden chairs as we used to see in the countryside. They have the same colours as the trees. They look comfortable and inviting.

At first I wondered if it was some kind of hospital, because it reminded me very much of the healing chambers I had seen. We entered a large hall, an immense, square space, high and transparent everywhere. Once inside, the view is as clear as when you stand outside, while from the outside you can't look inside. I have the same with my own house and saw that in many places here. A wonderful experience. In the corner next to the entrance there was an inner garden with succulents and rocks. There was a somewhat tropical ambience. In the middle was a pond with organic shapes: bowls in the form of petals; at the top large and bowl-shaped, with underneath the petals in a fan shape. Water flowed from the large bowl to the flower bowls underneath. I held my hand in the water, but it wasn't moist, a strange sensation. I tried it again a few times, but my hand remained dry.

A man walked towards us and welcomed us. It was a long slender figure who walked like a gazelle, smooth with every step. He introduced himself as Fjodor. He led us to a courtyard garden where a group of people sat together. Immediately I noticed the gracefulness of their movements. The way they held their drinks, their way they were sitting down, the posture of their heads. I became very curious. Fjodor explained that this wonderful place is a place for artists.

Fjodor: Here people come who want to be among artists. We created an environment in which we feel in balance. Just like the scientists and the doctors, people in this profession also attract each other in the spheres. Here we can be together as dancers, but there are also places where people from other art forms find each other.

In my last life I was a ballet dancer in Russia. Despite all the limitations of the regime at the time, I was given every opportunity to develop my talent. I enjoyed my life as a dancer and teacher. As a little boy I was already accepted into a special school, where I received a high school education, but also a very strict ballet training. I felt an inner calling to bring the vibrations of great beauty to the people of Russia.

My whole being was subservient to bringing art at a high level. I could see how people enjoyed our performances. The Russian people greatly appreciate the art of dancing. Art, in all its forms, has provided the necessary light energy in very difficult times. When we danced we attracted many Light Beings and through our movement and music that light was spread among those present. Those who were open to it allowed this light energy to penetrate them. Attending a concert or ballet gave people new energy, strength to continue in everyday life. I witnessed the disappearance of the Berlin Wall and a short period after that in which great changes occurred. The average Russian had difficulty coping with his new freedoms and you have to admit, from whom should they have learned about freedom? They did not have the experience of people in the West.

As Fjodor I had never been to the West, but my heart was open to more artistic and personal exchange. Later I became a teacher. Here I am a teacher again, and as we sit here together, we are all teachers. We work with souls who are going to incarnate and who in their blueprint for that new life plan to devote themselves to the art of dancing. Such a destination has often been a thread that runs through different lives for a very long time. In this place people can freely search for the form of expression they want. It is here that forms are created that are later brought to expression in material life. It is a kind of breeding ground of creativity in which expressions are sought for the innermost needs of someone's being. This is done by experimenting and exchanging experiences with others. Here the best people for their training can be found. We don't have any competition here, not among the students and not among the teachers. That is not necessary at all. I know that the world of ballet on Earth does have a lot of competition. That will change in the New Age. Heaven comes to Earth and vice versa.

We dancers will be drawn to each other like magnets. Over there, past the trees, you'll find a department of indigenous arts. Sometimes it's quite noisy there. The rooms are completely soundproofed, otherwise their percussion and singing could be heard everywhere. We sometimes hear something when the rooms are open and that's wonderful. The feeling that we are all busy with what we really want to do. Piano music always makes me happy, it belongs here and it makes me feel like I'm at my old dance academy again. For me that was a very good and nourishing time. This is a place in which we can thrive.

Not so long ago we had a mutual exchange. That was really great. There's a dance theatre between the trees down here: a wonderful place where every imaginable kind of dance can be performed. It would become a top performance for all of us in this dimension and at the same time a dress rehearsal for performances we will be giving in the different spheres. Our main goal now is to integrate various forms of expression. You could say 'as above, so below'. What actually happened was a splendid example of integration. All kinds of dance expressions were presented, from classical to modern, from the Western tradition to the African, Asian and South American, in countless variations. The whole should culminate in a kind of jam session. Spontaneously letting what is allowed to happen, happen. At a certain point classical dancers joined in a Papuan dance and the effect was magnificent. Everything merged into a beautiful spectacle. Another time I saw Javanese dances that were combined with dances from Africa: a game of motion and grace on a high level. We also laughed a lot with each other. I danced with a group of female dancers from Indonesia. What these women can do with their hands is amazing and I let my body be inspired by their beautiful hand and arm movements. I am now working with them to create a choreography that we will dance for a large audience.

The dancers here are happy to work with so many different cultures; they enjoy it. Experimenting with every imaginable dance form inspires some to want to incarnate in a certain dance culture. Of course I haven't always been a Russian dancer. Even though I was in Russia in my last life, I have lived in different countries of ancient Europe, in ancient America before the Europeans came, but also in Asia, Egypt and Palestine. In ancient America I have lived in Indian tribes several times and I am looking back on that with a lot of affection. These incarnations taught me to move gracefully in a very natural way, also for example as a hunter. Dancing was always important to me. I lived on Bali a long time ago and was a court dancer there. A life as a woman, so I have regularly alternated lives as a man with lives as a woman. That desire came from my Higher Self, to give expression to what I wanted to learn or express.

In Egypt I was a female dancer several times. I danced the Sacred Geometry in the temple. I was there in the new city of the Sun, El-Amarna during the magnificent period of Akhnaton and Nefertiti. How awful that this beautiful city was virtually destroyed by the black priest's, who ruled in the period before Akhnaton. I have seen the beautiful buildings and squares, and saw the library go up in flames. Beauty and simplicity went hand in hand in this beautiful city. Every inhabitant had a clean, comfortable home. There was care for mother and child, there were very good schools that every child could attend. Quite the opposite of Thebes, which I had fled because of its artistic unfreedom; the dictatorship of the black priests - I abhorred their black magic and all their dark practices to dominate and oppress the populace. They didn't like the new city where there was a worthy existence for every human being; where the healers with love and attention, free of charge, treated sicknesses. In Thebes the priests sold false amulets and asked a lot of money for them. The rich were extremely rich and the poor extremely poor. The same thing is happening on Earth right now.

I was very happy when I acquired a position as a dancer and teacher in the new city. I taught Sacred Geometry in the dance. I learned a lot there and enjoyed working together. I felt love and respect for Akhnaton and his family. I too was treated with respect. He was demanding, that is, he knew how to motivate people to get the best out of themselves. Artists were encouraged to do even better. The architects showed that it was possible to build a spacious, clean and light city. The wide avenues were a relief after the narrow and dirty streets of Thebes. Everybody got his share; every craftsman had a comfortable house, a spacious, light square home. Their work was highly valued and craftsmen formed guilds again, as in older Egypt. Their self-esteem grew, and rightly so. Every profession had its value and that's what made this society so special. There were communal vegetable gardens, but there were also many people who created a small place to grow food next to their house. Akhnaton asked people to take responsibility for themselves, their home, their street, family and work. These were golden years in which there was no place for poverty and hunger. All the people who lived there received a great treasure, because such an experience is carried along in your whole soul being. It was a city as you might expect in the Spheres of Light. In the spiritual world, El-Amarna still exists.

After the massacres, the stealthy poison murders, the mean gossip and backbiting, it seemed that evil had triumphed. The infiltrators of the black priests did everything they could to regain their power. There were even relatives of the Pharaoh who acted as spies. They had come from Thebes after hearing about the beautiful new city. They really wanted to prey of it, afraid of missing out on something. By the way, they did not like the new city and the new palace. They were used to a decadent lifestyle. In the old palace the furnishings, just like the buffets and the entertainment were of an overwhelming abundance. I know because I had danced there before I went to El-Amarna.

In the period after Akhnaton we were treated badly. We often had to dance for far too long, were poorly fed and our sleeping places looked more like a dog shed. Our managers were decadent people who were constantly bored. We also had to prostitute ourselves, both men and women. I was young and very beautiful, but fortunately not naive. My parents had told me a lot about life. I refused to let them use my body. Few however would dare to resist the priests and their powerful families. So I was locked up without food or drink. Knowing the fate that awaited us, I prayed to be allowed to die, because they were animals and their sexual perversions had nothing to do with love or respect. They were sadists. As an artist, my body was sacred to me. My prayer for help was answered. I did not die, fortunately, but was kidnapped. On the way to the priests' playroom we were ambushed, taken away and smuggled out of the palace. That's how I ended up in an underground resistance movement. They took care of me until I regained my strength. I got to know people I met over and over again in the course of my lives: in my Essene life in Palestine; in an underground Gnostic community in Italy; at a school in Alexandria where I taught the Sacred Geometry of Dance. El-Amara has been a breeding ground for souls who would later spread across the globe and all carried with them the inner treasure of the city of the Sun.

Here in the spheres I know that Akhnaton is a brother of Jesus and of Buddha. Here he is called Ahnahtah, Lord of the Ninth Light Area. All the souls who were allowed to live and work in the City of Light are all thus far connected with his work and mission. We met him as part of a project related to the transition of the Earth, holding a certain vibration. Many artists are connected to crystal chambers where together they maintain a certain vibration of light. That is one of my duties and at this moment in times even the most important one. It is a pleasure to be with Ahnahtah: he lifts us up and brings out the most beautiful in us; his light feeds us.

The High Masters are very active in this period of great change, together with the souls that are closely connected to them. The pleasure of being together cannot be expressed in words. It seems as if I am putting them on a pedestal, but that is not necessary. We are very aware that these High Masters are standing beside us as our brothers. They don't feel superior to us. Their great simplicity is exemplary. It still saddens me that the people at that time were so blind and ignorant and let themselves be deceived by the black priests who sabotaged the development of El-Amarna. There was much jealousy and people were not prepared to abandon their decadent lives in Thebes to devote themselves to the new. Akhnaton taught us about one Creator and one Creation, what was totally new in the Egypt of that time. We focused on the Solar Logos, the same universal energy that would later influence the world through Ahnahtah's brother Jesus as Christ energy.

Here, Ahnahtah teaches us not to be concerned with the pain of that time. In the end he was a pathfinder for his brother and that work was completed, although, seen through material eyes, it didn't look like that. Nevertheless, all kinds of things are happening on Earth right now, which has brought Akhnaton and his 'City of the Sun' back into the limelight. It is a pity that history judges this man so incorrectly and heartlessly. In the history books he is portrayed as a horrible ruler, a sick man and a weakling. I have seen with my own eyes how cartoons were made, some of which have even been preserved. Archaeologists, in particular, like to cling to the tangible evidence they can literally hold in their hands, and that's understandable.

In any case, the new rulers after his son, the child king Tutankhamun, have done everything in their power to completely erase the time of El-Amarna. They have largely succeeded in doing so. Nevertheless, many people have an inner knowing that, as so often happens, it went differently than the historians claim. Many carry that knowledge in their hearts.

After the murder of the child king I fled and wandered around for a while, hunted by servants of the renewed reign of the black priests. That was a terrible time. I was old by now. People were afraid and let themselves be manipulated by the new dictatorial regime. For the tomb of Tutankhamun we had to hand in all our gold. I think there was hardly a piece of gold left in all of Thebes after all those raids. The little I owned, which was nothing more than a memento of my family, I had to hand in. My house was ruthlessly searched and when they found a small object, my grandmother's pillbox, I was severely beaten. The soldiers of the black priests and the new pharaoh were extremely violent. And no one did anything. They grumbled in silence, like they always do, everywhere. But even that was dangerous. You could report someone who was opposed to the regime. People like me, the old teachers from El-Amarna, were being watched. I then fled the regime. I spent my last four years in a secret brotherhood, precursors of the Essenes, where the teachings of Akhnaton and his people were preserved and taught. I had not danced for a long time, I was tired of all the misery I had seen when the city was destroyed. I was cooking for the group, together with the other women.

I think that people, who feel deeply moved by the few artistic expressions that still originate from El-Amarna, lived there at that time. The three-dimensional art was developed at that time and beautiful things were made there. I have always cherished art from that period, even if they were only images in the books I owned. Unfortunately I never saw this art in real life during my last life. As an artist I have always been deeply touched when art is deliberately destroyed. Of course matter is logically subject to decay, but deliberate destruction hurts all the way down to the soul.

With the group you now see here in our courtyard garden, we regularly perform Sacred Geometry dances together with others. We pass it on to our students. These forms, adapted to the New Age, will return to Earth as high level art. There are students here who are so deeply touched by their inner experience in these dances, that they will dedicate themselves to this high art form. Here we see and feel the energy we create. The human of the New Age will also be able to do so. Impulses are given to an art that is again 'for everyone', because now on Earth this is often reserved for the privileged.

One of my students is a girl who hasn't been here that long. She was in a wheelchair on Earth, with a muscle disease that severely hampered her freedom of movement. She dreamed of moving, of dancing as if she could fly through the sky. When she told me her story, I felt great compassion for her. The soul lessons she had to learn in her last life she quickly and fully worked out and thus she fulfilled her karma. Her Higher Self wanted her to develop the art of dancing: a new experience for this soul, which will soon enter her first life as a professional dancer. I am amazed at what she has achieved here, of her strength and perseverance.

Sometimes she is too fanatic and I have to slow her down a bit. Her life in a wheelchair has something to do with that of course. Her interest is wide-ranging; almost every dance form has her sincere interest. I take her everywhere there is dancing, so she can observe and find inspiration. In her blueprint of life there are two possible dance lines. One is that of a performing ballet artist, the other is her wish to transfer the art in her own dance school. Of course there are many more options and life on a free will planet can be quite erratic. I help her to make the most of it. It gives me great satisfaction to see how she now uses the freedom of her body in dance expression. I think she will be in a ballet costume already early on in her new incarnation. The woman who becomes her mother is a dance teacher; she trains people for the world of entertainment. I know her soul. She's living in America now, dreaming of a baby. If there's anyone who can help my dear pupil, it's her.

It's fascinating to know about this plan. I meet the mother-to-be regularly in Summerland, where her guide brings her in the spirit. Know that every soul incarnates with a consciously created plan and is well prepared for it. Very often the work one wants to do in the material world has already been created in the spheres. This is common among artists and scientists, for example. They will also remain connected with their spiritual brotherhood throughout their lives, as we dancers do. We always also keep connected with our pupils who incarnate in a life on Earth. We support them in periods when they are struggling. We give positive incentives to stay true to their intended life blueprint.

I had the great pleasure of choosing whether to stay here or reincarnate. I chose to stay here and that shouldn't surprise anyone. After all, we are all growing into a beautiful, golden age, and that offers wonderful experiences here as well. I am working in the crystal chamber of my attunement and I feel that that is where my task now lies. The freedom I experience here is a great miracle. With the power of thought I am in my home, or in a concert hall, in the blink of an eye. I visit all my friends and family, who are in different spheres. Just 'being' with my parents and brothers, it is a great pleasure. They are preparing for physical lives in this time of transition of the Earth. But even though I will miss our family meetings, or rather soul meetings, we will always see each other again; in Summerland, or later after their lives on Earth. They create a new family with other souls from our soul group. It is like a crystal with many facets, each time a different part comes into play. They have known each other for so many lives, for ages. Here it is normal for someone to prepare his new life with his 'new' family, which is part of life here.

One of my brothers in my life in Russia has been here for a long time. He died of an accident at the factory where he worked. He's going to incarnate soon; everything is prepared. He chooses to go back to a life in Russia. He has completed a study here on this side that you can best describe with 'economics', but it is much broader than that. He is enthusiastic about the idea of giving positive impulses to trade; to a fair distribution of material wealth.

In his previous life he had an experience in Russia that was then spoiled by the gigantic corruption. The old regime was guilty of that. My brother was in the spheres for a long time and travelled through many areas. I know his soul being and his many lives. He will be able to make positive innovations together with others. He will be a distinctly "New Age child," with a great aptitude for a "we" awareness and work and live from the heart. He belongs to a whole group of New Age children, all with similar tasks. They will meet each other in the course of that life, their life threads will become interwoven, and hopefully they will be able to 'dance their ballet'. In terms of energy, they fit in perfectly with the pulses of light that come to Earth in an ever-increasing flow. We throw a big party when he goes, for the whole group. There will be music and I will dance for him. We'll have great fun preparing it.

My parents, who haven't been here that long, feel differently about that. Their spiritual attunement lies in the second sphere of Light and they are still earthbound in a certain way. They experience his departure differently than people in the spheres above. They also do not have such an overview and understanding of the bigger picture. That is to what they are waking up now. But they are being helped to learn to accept to let go of their son. They were so happy they had found him again after they died on Earth. A lot of time and energy is being put into this now, because it wouldn't be right for him if they kept pulling on him during his new life. They see his enthusiasm, also that of their other sons, and are now growing towards the idea of the cycle of the soul. A concept they didn't understand during their last life on Earth. Their journey through the spheres goes fast and I see how they grow enormously. That's also because so much has changed here. The 'transitional laws' allow people to grow faster because they now have to read their book of life. You can no longer postpone reading your book of life for some other time; it's a reality that no one can ignore. And the great insight one acquires in this way, even if only from the last life, brings acceptance, processing and thus leaps in growth.

Both my parents had a hard life in 20th century Russia. Especially my mother was very bitter because of certain experiences in that society. She can understand that her son now chooses for change and improvement, now that the energy is right for it. My father was very happy to find his son here; his death was the great tragedy of our youth. At that time I found it terrible to see that my father never got over the death of my brother. Father was in the healing chamber for a long time and I visited him there as often as I could. My parents can stay longer in these spheres before going back to Earth as the children of their now incarnating son. That will happen when the time is right. We sometimes joke about that, but I see my father enjoying that thought. He and my brother are very connected souls and have shared a lot of love and suffering together in their different incarnations. Time will tell how it will work out. My brother suggested the idea at first, and the guides were delighted with his proposal. It is all a matter of one's own free will. People who have to work out heavy karma always have to deal with the Lords of Karma, but there decisions are never made without consent. The Higher Self, the totality of one's soul, chooses the best path that makes the lessons the soul wants to learn possible.

I love to guide people, like little Emily, to a joyful future. And I see that many people are now arriving in the spheres who have worked out their full Earthly karma. How wonderful to be able to continue your way and then choose things you want to do with heart and soul. The more people know how to clean up their energy field - and they are now working very hard on that on Earth - the more beautiful the Earth can become. I see a stream of people that are going to generate the energy of the heart. If such souls go to Earth, a lot can change there. If life is lived from the heart, society will become more beautiful and loving. After all, it's all about the light, the love we generate as beings. I have guided many New Age children and put my hope in them. They live from the heart energy and will therefore approach problems and life in general in a very different way. Many of these children are true examples of the High Masters; they carry the Christ energy within them and will spread this light wherever they live. They will help multiply this energy in others. It is a miracle how small babies can make big changes and then they are just lying in their crib. Let's be very careful of the children, they can teach the adults a lot about Light and Love.

Margaret: Fjodor sits down. During his long story he walked around, or stood still and made graceful gestures with his hands. When he talked about the New Age children, he seemed to glow. I noticed a beautiful blue look around him. This man spoke so inspired; it touched me deeply. His story about El-Amarna touched me too and it was no coincidence that I was able to meet someone who would tell me something about it. I lived there too then and I worked with Thea in the temple of the healers, we were colleagues. Caring for women and babies was one of our tasks. I've lived through all aspects of it and now I know it was of great importance for all my lives since then.

I was killed in a massacre. I was taken by surprise in my sleep. But it has never been as traumatic for me as it apparently was for Fjodor. In the meantime I also attended a few meetings with Ahnahtah, moments with a golden touch. It also gives me the courage to continue with even more dedication. I feel nourished after such a meeting.

Sitting in his energy we are like one beating heart, we all carry the same dream with us and we know that its realization is very close. Even though it is not yet visible on Earth.

Thea Terlouw

Thea Terlouw was aware of a world that others could not perceive since her early childhood. The burden of 'being different' kept her from developing these talents as a child and young woman. She initially studied visual arts. In addition, she trained to become a yoga teacher like the study of Jnana Yoga philosophy. Thea worked as an independent artist for some time as well as a yoga teacher. For years she worked with groups of people, in schools with children and gave pregnancy yoga for pregnant women.

During her life as a visual artist, however, her special talent began to develop again. When she had a near-death experience (n.d.e.) because of an accident, everything gained momentum for her, partly under the inspiring supervision of her guides. This resulted in close contact with and work for the Merkawah Foundation, co-founded by Pim van Lommel, physician-cardiologist and author of the bestseller 'Consciousness Beyond Life'.

The care and counselling of people with a near-death experience and the counselling of dying people were the logical consequence. In the many years that followed, she helped hundreds of people with examining their past lives and to identify the root causes of diseases in close cooperation with therapists, doctors, and psychologists.

Many then asked her to write down her experiences. Thea had doubts however, and it was mainly thanks to the encouragement of Joanne Klink and later Bram Vermeulen, that she wrote two books on the topic: '*De Cyclus van leven en dood*', (The Cycle of Life and Death) and '*Een Cirkel Doorbroken*' (Ending the Circle).

At the same time, Thea also worked a lot with children. The exchange with Henri de Vidal de St. Germain was in service of that work. Together with her work as a yoga teacher and pregnancy yoga, you might say that in this way Thea has become an expert in 'transitions': to be born well and to die well has become a true passion for her. After writing her first two books and giving a great number of lectures on the subject, she decided, in the context of her own development, to 'retreat from public life', as she herself put it, for several years.

She stayed there until the end of 2017, when she felt that in the light of the Great Awakening it became more necessary than ever to face and complete the greater reality of our countless Earth incarnations, both individually and collectively. This is not an easy process, neither individually nor collectively.

However, Thea knows that we do not go through life alone nor do we have to. She is very aware of this because of her telepathic contact with her spiritual guides and teachers. For most of us, that contact happens unconsciously. Preconditioned as we are, we experience life as if it were something on its own, completely denying that greater universal reality.

The main purpose of this book is to let go of the fear for death. Reincarnation lies at the heart of our lives on Earth. Dying is merely a transition to a greater reality, one in which we prepare ourselves for a next life. There is nothing to be afraid of; besides, we have done it so many times. This book also aims to encourage people to renew, engage and develop contact with the spiritual realms. An extremely important and necessary step in the spiritual development of all of humanity and our planet. Slowly moving forward in our processes. This is necessary, or at least helpful, to become as whole as possible. Help is available to achieve this. Moreover, the so-called 'Heelkamers' (Healing Chambers), which became the title of her third book, can and will heal our hard experiences, sometimes, as physical beings in countless incarnations on our planet.

As people wake up and become aware of the precarious state this beautiful planet Earth is in, it is time to 'come home'. At home on our planet, at home with each other and at home with our brothers and sisters from other realms in the universe. Places we also know as 'home' and that many of us long for after our wanderings on this free will planet.

The main message of Thea is that although we do not always realise who we are and where we come from, together we can create brilliant Fields of Light Consciousness over the many unloving aspects of global society on Earth. After all, we know - we feel - what we want to change and in many cases we even know how. It is blatantly clear to all of us, that much of what is not based on Love has recently become prominently visible in the incoming flow of cosmic Light. This allows us to change and say goodbye to what no longer serves us.

Literature

- Eben Alexander, *Proof of Heaven*. Little Brown UK 2012.
- Masaru Emoto, *Hidden Messages in Water*. Atria Books 2005.
- Masaru Emoto, *Secret Life of Water*. Simon & Schuster 2011.
- Masaru Emoto, *Messages from Water and the Universe*. Hay House Inc. 2010.
- Joan Grant, *Winged Pharaoh*. Abrams Press 2007.
- Joan Grant, *Eyes of Horus*. Ari'El Press 2010.
- Joan Grant, *So Moses was Born*. Dawn Chorus 2010.
- Hazrat Inayat Khan, *The Inner Life*. Shambhala 1997.
- Bruce Lipton, *Biology of Belief*. Sound True Inc 2006.
- Pim van Lommel, *Consciousness Beyond Life*. HarperCollins 2010.
- Joel Martin and Patricia Romanowski, *Love beyond Life*. HarperCollins 1997.
- Elisabeth Kübler-Ross, *On Death and Dying*. Prentice Hall 1997.
- Elisabeth Kübler-Ross, *Life Lessons*. Scribner 2014.
- Lynne McTaggart, *The Intention Experiment*. Simon & Schuster 2008.
- Lynne McTaggert, *The Field*. HarperCollins 2008.
- Raymond Moody, *The Light Beyond*. Ebury 2005.
- Raymond Moody, *Life after Life*. Ebury 2001.
- Raymond Moody and Paul Perry, *Glimpses of Eternity*. Ebury 2016.
- Melvin Morse, *Closer to the Light*. Random House USA 1992.
- Michael Newton, *Journey of Souls*. LLewellyn 1994.
- Ian Stevenson, *Where Reincarnation and Biology Intersect*, Abc-Clio 1997
- Colson Whitehead, *The Underground Railroad*. Little Brown UK 2017.
- Roeland van Wijk, *Light in shaping life, Biophotons in biology and medicine*. Meluma 2014.

Thea Terlouw also wrote *The Healing Chambers – Love beyond Life*

Our Earth has been flooded with suffering for many centuries. Each of us has been traumatized to a greater or lesser degree during this life or in one of our countless past lives. Now, in this End Times, it is very important that all our traumas are healed and dissolved. It is therefore very reassuring to know that now, after our physical transition, we can indeed be healed. This happens in the so-called healing chambers, which are available for all kinds of traumas. Many in our world live with strong beliefs about hell and damnation and the fear of 'what comes next' prevails. However, it is of 

untold importance that we can let go of this fear of 'death' and transform it. This book will take the reader into personal stories of those who preceded us in 'death' and who want to share their experiences with us. Experiences of people who died from a natural cause, but also from a self-chosen death or euthanasia, for example. No easy subjects. Yet questions that concern us all: what happens to us, and what happens to our loved ones? There are many valuable lessons to be learned from this book, but perhaps the most important lesson is that hell and damnation do not exist, nor judgement and condemnation.

Thea Terlouw's special talent is that she can communicate with this other world at any time. As a young child, she tried to get rid of this talent. It took her many years to learn to handle it and to be able to use it, not only for herself, but also for others. She shares it with us not as 'truth', but as experience - the essence of our earthly life. However, guidance is available for those who ask: there is Love after Life. We hope the book will inspire you, reassure you, help you to let go of your unfinished affairs and become whole physically, emotionally, and spiritually.

9 789493 071285